# LAUGHING ON THE OUTSIDE

*The Life of John Candy*

## MARTIN KNELMAN

VIKING

VIKING
Published by the Penguin Group
Penguin Books Canada Ltd, 10 Alcorn Avenue, Toronto, Ontario,
Canada M4V 3B2
Penguin Books Ltd, 27 Wrights Lane, London W8 5TZ, England
Viking Penguin, a division of Penguin Books USA Inc., 375 Hudson Street,
New York, New York 10014, U.S.A.
Penguin Books Australia Ltd, Ringwood, Victoria, Australia
Penguin Books (NZ) Ltd, 182–190 Wairau Road, Auckland 10,
New Zealand

Penguin Books Ltd, Registered Offices: Harmondsworth,
Middlesex, England

First published 1996
1 3 5 7 9 10 8 6 4 2

Printed and bound in Canada on acid free paper ⊗

**Canadian Cataloguing in Publication Data**

Knelman, Martin
Laughing on the outside: the life of John Candy

ISBN 0-670-87027-7

1. Candy, John. 2. Actors - Canada - Biography.
3. Comedians - Canada - Biography. I. Title.

PN2308.C3K54 1996     792'.028'092     C95-933390-8

Visit Penguin Canada's web site at **www.penguin.ca**

*For*
Bernie, Josh and Sara—my own private comedy group


*and*
for two people who took personal generosity
and professional loyalty to astounding extremes,

Christina McCall and Helga Stephenson

# Contents

# LAUGHING
## ON THE
## OUTSIDE

# THE GODS OF COMEDY

*W*hen they're really on, great comics light up the space around them. They emit sparks; they give off a glow; they break new ground. This is a form of artistry expressing ecstasy, like the achingly precise steps of a brilliant dancer or the impossibly extended riff of a virtuoso jazz saxophonist. There's an element of sheer intoxication.

Right from the start, John Candy had the stuff that separates the great ones from comedians who are merely talented and funny. Second City founder Bernard Sahlins spotted it the instant Candy was prodded into auditioning at a Toronto church in 1973. At the age of twenty-two, the already pudgy young performer was a budding Falstaff of the baby-boomer generation. His skills were raw and undeveloped, but it was clear the gods of comedy had smiled on him.

They had granted him exuberance, ebullience and crackerjack reactive timing—and enough pain to create his need to propel himself into an alternative universe. As well, the gods of comedy had conferred on Candy a likeable sweet shyness, giving his persona a contrapuntal courtliness. It was as if Candy's rowdy comic spirit was kept in a special case, and withheld by a delayed-release mechanism.

In small cabaret theatres in Chicago, Toronto and Pasadena in the mid-1970s, audiences took an immediate shine to John

Candy. Then from 1977 to 1983, he broke through on the innovative, high-spirited satiric TV series "SCTV." Surrounded by several of the most dazzling comedy performers around, Candy was the one audiences chose as their special favourite.

Candy appeared to be on the brink of even greater success in the movies, but Hollywood played a dirty trick on him. It bequeathed to him the wealth and fame he had always dreamed of, but except for a few occasions mostly deprived him of the chance to be as funny and creative as he had been on TV. Of the forty-plus movies he appeared in, only a handful could be recommended to civilized, intelligent adults.

Yet for Candy fans, even a few triumphant moments in an abominable movie could be cause for elation and hope—proof that he still had that spark, in spite of everything Hollywood was doing to squeeze it out of him.

Candy knew intuitively that to get into comedy heaven you have to let go—and speed beyond the bounds of conventional behaviour and good taste. He loved the particular state of comic grace that can be reached only by becoming wild and crazy—throwing out the restraints parents, teachers and other authorities have spent years instilling.

On the road to a successful career in comedy, it helps if you've never quite become a grown-up. It's even better if you have a talent for misbehaviour. In those respects, Candy aced the entrance exam.

At its highest level, comedy is a belief system that sustains its followers through endless days of petty woes. Buster Keaton gave thrillingly pure expression to that credo in *Steamboat Bill, Jr.* Charlie Chaplin had it in *The Gold Rush*. Before he faltered into strained seriousness, Woody Allen reinvented the form for modern urban neurotics. Richard Pryor broke through boisterously with his first concert film. Robin Williams occasionally takes us to that higher place. And most recently, Eddie Murphy in *The Nutty Professor* relieved the junky tedium of current movies with his gleeful portrayal of an entire crazed family at dinner.

Within the realm of Candy and his peers, a perfectly executed comedy routine is mood-elevating and orgasmic, as sure to induce light-headedness as champagne. It delivers us to that state of consciousness where the entire world can bliss out together on laughter. It offers a more natural high than dropping acid or snorting cocaine. Best of all, it fills us with the grandest of all illusions—the confidence there is nothing we can't overcome as long as we savour the humorous aspects of misery and misfortune.

This is an unauthorized biography, and in the course of researching and writing it, I have encountered some people who apparently believe that loyalty to John Candy's official memory entails a shroud of secrecy. It became obvious to me that just as Candy during his life was imprisoned by the myth of his own affability, so in death he was in danger of being imprisoned by the myth of Saint John.

Below the surface of these myths, I found that the real John Candy was infinitely more complex and fascinating. That is the one I have tried to portray. In my view, true loyalty to John Candy's memory should entail understanding and embracing the facts about his life, not covering them up.

And if we're honest with ourselves, I think we have to admit that it isn't testimonials to his virtue that feed our curiosity about John Candy as a performer and a person. Rather, it's the promise of raucous laughter, clamorous good times, and a hair-raising ride on the Hollywood roller-coaster. Candy's gift to the world was not saintliness but his talent for creating a disturbance—in the most hilarious, sweetly nervous way.

In the course of reading other biographies, I have occasionally sensed that special horror that occurs when the writer discovers things he would rather not have known about the subject. I am happy to say that I did not have this experience. Though I found many sad and dark elements in John Candy's life, I never stopped liking him.

Neither did Candy's friends, although sometimes their love for him resulted in tension and frustration as he ignored their need for him to take better care of himself.

The John Candy I came to know was a man of tremendous appetites, given to excess in every aspect of life. He was excessively talented, excessively funny, excessively nice and excessively generous. But when he ran into problems, he became excessively resentful, excessively depressed, excessively curmudgeonly and excessively unwilling to face painful truths. He ate too much, drank too much, smoked too much, stayed up late too much, partied too much, and rarely knew when to quit.

There were even periods when things got so bad that John Candy stopped being lovable. "John Candy was two people," says a Toronto TV producer who saw him at his worst. "There was the John Candy of myth that everyone wanted to believe in—warm, friendly, happy, generous, loved by all. Then there was his evil twin that nobody wants to talk about—insecure, paranoid, bitter and mean."

Few people who knew Candy well would make such a harsh judgment, but some would say that if only Candy had done this or that, or hadn't done something else, his life need not have been cut short at the age of forty-three. What I came to understand was that if he had been a person of moderation, he would not have been John Candy. Lack of moderation was an integral part of the Candy package.

At the heart of John Candy's comedy lies his fierce determination to rise above grim reality and find a way to have a roaring good time anyway. It is perhaps most memorably expressed in a TV sketch that gives him the role of a pitchman for dance lessons, with a Spanish costume and accent.

"Good evening," he says, getting cozy with the audience. "Have you read the newspapers lately or watched the news on TV? There are hostages, terrorists, hijackings and towering infernos everywhere. The world is in a mess. And there's sweet diddly you can do about it. My only advice is when everything gets you down [voice rising to ecstatic crescendo], you get up and MAMBO..."

Toronto
July, 1996

*Chapter 1*

# HOCKEY NIGHT
# IN CALIFORNIA

*J*ohn Candy was sitting in the stands at the Great Western Forum on that momentous night—the sixth of October, 1988. This was not just hockey night in Los Angeles, not just the opening home game of the season. It was the biggest night of hockey mania in the history of the L.A. franchise, and for the first time, the Kings had a sell-out crowd of 16,000. When Wayne Gretzky skated onto the ice at the L.A. Forum wearing a Kings uniform for the first time, the crowd exploded with excitement and anticipation.

No wonder: Gretzky was almost universally regarded as the greatest player in hockey, period. He was capable of transforming the previously lethargic Kings into stars on ice and dangerous contenders for the Stanley Cup, thereby banishing California's bemused coolness toward this odd, quintessentially Canadian game. (Jack Kent Cooke, the Canadian sports tycoon who established the franchise in 1967, once quipped: "There are 800,000 Canadians living in the L.A. area, and I've just discovered why they left Canada: They hate hockey.")

This wasn't just a hockey game; it was a coronation. In Edmonton, hockey fans were so shocked that they hanged Oilers owner Peter Pocklington in effigy for trading Gretzky. Now just before Gretzky's first game as one of the L.A. Kings, the lights were turned off for dramatic effect, and each player skated through the darkness into the spotlight at centre ice, where, sporting their flashy new silver and black uniforms, they were greeted in turn by the new owner of the Kings, Bruce McNall.

When Gretzky skated into the spotlight, wearing his celebrated number 99 uniform, the applause was thunderous. And when he scored a goal on his first shot-on-goal of the night, the crowd at the Forum went wild. By the end of the evening, Gretzky had added three assists, and the Kings had defeated the Detroit Red Wings by a score of eight to two.

No one in the stands that night was more thrilled than John Candy—a shy, sweet-faced guy from Toronto who within a few years of arriving in Hollywood had become one of the most popular comedy actors in town. Candy looked more like a garage mechanic or an appliance salesman than a movie star, but that's precisely what made audiences warm to him.

Candy had four season's tickets in section twenty. That night he was accompanied by two old friends from Toronto— writer/director Martyn Burke and actor/businessman Stephen Young (also known as Stephen Levy). It was an unspoken custom that there would be only three people occupying those four seats. Candy had about three hundred pounds on his six-foot-three frame and he needed the extra seat to be comfortable.

As usual, Burke and Candy had convened at Candy's house in Brentwood and been driven to the Forum in Inglenook (near L.A.'s international airport) by Candy in his big black Mercedes. (When he was working on a film, Candy would be chauffeured around by his devoted driver, Frankie Hernandez, but on his days off, Candy preferred to be his own driver.)

The man of the hour, on his way to becoming the most revered and popular promoter/entrepreneur in California, was Bruce McNall. And he knew how to make the most out of a dramatic occasion.

McNall was a pudgy, friendly character who had made a fabulous fortune trading antique coins and art and racing horses. After dabbling for several years in the movie business, McNall had bought out the Kings' previous owner, and electrified hockey followers everywhere by buying Gretzky and bringing him from Edmonton to L.A.

With a background in show business, McNall was well aware of celebrity power, and that night he was being taken through the Forum by the team's media director, Scott Carmichael, who introduced him to notables in the crowd—celebrities who also happened to be sports fans. One of them was John Candy. In contrast to McNall, who was dressed in a natty black suit, white shirt and tie, Candy looked like an unmade bed, wearing a big ski jacket and rumpled chinos.

If anyone should have recognized a con artist, it was John Candy. After all, even before the combination of his sweet vulnerability and impeccable comic timing made him a favourite of movie audiences in *Splash* and a full-blown movie star in *Planes, Trains and Automobiles*, the lovable overgrown kid from the East York section of Toronto was cherished by followers of the inspired comedy series "SCTV" for his gleeful, over-the-top send-ups of rogues, blowhards and hypocrites.

And as a comedy writer and performer, Candy was at the absolute top of his considerable form when he was lampooning egomaniacal charlatans. His greatest comic creation was Johnny LaRue—that hilariously self-indulgent mover and shaker in the fictitious small town of Melonville, who managed to be producer, performer, politician, restaurant critic and *bon vivant*.

Yet in 1988 when Candy met Bruce McNall—exposed six years later as a prodigious white-collar criminal who defrauded banks and other investors of $250 million—Candy was impressed to the point of awe. He felt honoured to be introduced to him.

Unlike the other movie stars who became members of McNall's inner circle, Candy was destined to be more than casually involved. Not only would McNall become Candy's business partner in the ownership of the Toronto Argonauts football team (along with Wayne Gretzky), he would also become a role model, setting the pattern for how Candy would henceforth shape his whole career.

Looking back with bitter-sweet insights, a few old friends of Candy could not help wondering if the night Candy met McNall was a turning point in his life.

Candy was susceptible to a charismatic confidence man like McNall. To Candy, imprisoned as he was by secret yearnings to be a big operator taken seriously by the whole world, McNall's promises must have had the ring of answered prayers.

In interviews Candy confessed to having trusted people in the movie business he should not have trusted. Yet perhaps his transparent vulnerability was one of his most appealing qualities; that was one reason audiences had been embracing him ever since he first stepped onto a stage.

What was the nature of his magnetism? Well, as the great critic Pauline Kael described him, Candy was "a mountainous lollipop of a man, and preposterously lovable." Given his size, one surprise in Candy's personality was how amiable and empathic he turned out to be. Far from being threatening and aggressive, he gave the impression there was a shy, frightened mouse inside that enormous frame. And there was another way he confounded the fat-boy stereotype: Candy was delightfully bouncy, energetic and fast on his feet.

Candy was big, all right, but there was nothing mean about him. He telegraphed softness; he came across as a genial giant whose feelings could easily be hurt, and who would go to extraordinary lengths to avoid inflicting pain on others.

Lack of pretence and staying true to the kind of unassuming people he grew up with—that was all part of the John Candy package his fans bought into. The essence of what they loved was expressed in *Planes, Trains and Automobiles* when the Candy character, after being put down by the Steve Martin character, says: "I'm the real article. What you see is what you get." To Candy's loyal followers, that wasn't just a line in a movie; it was a summing up of what John Candy was all about.

Candy's sense of comedy was sharp and accurate—gleeful without being malicious. He managed to embrace the targets of his satire even while skewering their follies. He picked up on every trace of hypocrisy and sham and turned them into a carnival of human foibles. Not perhaps since Preston Sturges, the great satiric Hollywood writer/director of the 1940s, had anyone made vice so damned entertaining. Candy had the special gift of revealing the self-indulgent child within every crazed monster he depicted. His antics suggested that giving in to the spoiled child within all of us was terrific fun—for those who could get away with it.

*H*aving moved a long way from home psychologically as well as geographically, Candy liked going to the Kings games because it made him feel in touch with his roots, cheering for his team with the simple, heartfelt ardour of the shy and awkward baby-faced kid who used to watch the Maple Leafs from the cheap seats at Maple Leaf Gardens.

Since landing in L.A., Candy had held season's tickets between the blue line and the goalpost. Ever since his own personal aspirations to athletic glory were cut short by injuries in high school, Candy had had to settle for being a dedicated fan.

He showed the same staunch loyalty to his sports heroes as he did to long-time personal friends. And his devotion could go to extraordinary lengths; according to his friend Bill Sussex (a sound technician from Toronto), Candy would feel personally betrayed if a friend happened to make a critical remark about, say, one-time Leafs goalie Johnny Bower.

Still, the Kings had been disappointing, and Candy had missed so many games he was thinking of giving up his season's tickets. But the news that Gretzky was joining the team had given Candy such a thrill that he called the Kings office almost immediately to make sure he could hang onto his old seats.

Now he was doing what any red-blooded Canadian sports fan would do if forced by circumstance to live in Los Angeles: going to hockey games.

It seemed to be at least as meaningful a religious ritual for Candy as his sporadic attendance with his wife and two children at a Catholic church in Brentwood.

Within the confines of a simple, dramatic struggle for supremacy on the hockey rink, Candy could for an hour or two quell his anxieties, calm his demons. For despite what might seem like a fairy-tale ascent to stardom, and despite his penchant for entertaining friends and colleagues with a steady stream of uproarious anecdotes and impersonations, John Candy was still a man who almost always seemed to be hurting.

The pain certainly didn't stem from lack of acclaim. Candy's brilliant work on the comedy series "SCTV" had given him a cult following. And after a few years of knocking around Hollywood appearing in movies of uneven quality, he had broken through with *Splash*.

In *Splash*, Candy endeared himself to audiences as Freddie, Tom Hanks' chain-smoking, squash-playing older brother. Then, less than a year before this night at the Forum, he had become a star in the role of the unwelcome companion—a knuckle-cracking compulsive talker—Steve Martin is unable to get rid of in *Planes, Trains and Automobiles*.

In a way, Candy was finally getting what he had been fighting for and dreaming of for two decades. But one thing didn't change. As always, John Candy found a lot to worry about. He had a tremendous need to be liked and approved of. And no amount of success seemed capable of quenching his need for validation, of filling the hole in his heart that had always been there, as far back as he could remember.

Born with a name that perfectly encapsulated his quality of high-calorie sweetness, John Candy was also a walking illustration of the familiar thesis that great comedy is almost always created by driven, tormented people who hope the jokes can relieve or at least mask their pain. Candy had legitimate cause for anxiety: the weight problem he battled his whole life, and a family history marred by heart disease and early death.

Along with those real problems went the ones that Candy either invented or embellished. Perhaps because he was extremely shy, he often imagined slights that were not intended. Out of his need to be liked and his sensitivity to pain in himself and others came Candy's phenomenal generosity, which was known to his friends as one of his most wonderful qualities. But that generosity also got Candy into difficulties, because he sometimes mistakenly directed it toward people who didn't deserve it, people who exploited him.

As Candy became more famous, hence more exposed to such risks, he became almost haunted by mounting paranoia about what he regarded as bad people who took advantage of him. Typically he found a way to blame himself for allowing it to happen.

The self-destructive syndrome included letting his weight get out of control, which made him feel more insecure. His success in movies failed to offset that insecurity.

As Martyn Burke observed, "John cared so deeply what people thought, it was a fire that could never be stoked. He had a need for recognition that could never be satisfied."

Candy used his own psychological problems in creating comic characters, almost as if he could exorcise his demons by making a mockery of them. Perhaps his greatest creation was SCTV's big operator Johnny LaRue—a cartoon of vanity, corruption and narcissism.

A lewd hustler and would-be *bon vivant*, LaRue would typically wear garish sequined robes and hobnob with minor celebrities. Whether delivering shameless bits of self-serving rhetoric or shrugging off endless scandals, Johnny LaRue always, above all, would find a way to keep the party going.

Los Angeles was a long way from Melonville, but there was more than a touch of Johnny LaRue in Bruce McNall—a chubby, gregarious reincarnation of Jay Gatsby from one of L.A.'s blandest strip-mall suburbs who for a few years in the late 1980s and early 1990s threw a spirited ongoing bash unlike anything the world capital of glitz had ever seen before.

It was an episode of sublime folly, southern California style. As Kevin Cook later wrote in *GQ* magazine, McNall threw a ten-year party with other people's money.

Hitherto known as a showman and sports promoter, McNall had teamed up with disgraced former Columbia Pictures executive David Begelman to produce such movies as *The Fabulous Baker Boys*.

But it wasn't until he became the owner of the Kings and created hockey hysteria by buying Gretzky that McNall became the toast of L.A.

The spell cast by McNall was almost frightening. He had that combination of affability and apparent business acumen that Hollywood loves. He was turning the Kings into a hot franchise, and it was said that everything he touched turned to gold.

Something about him seemed too good to be true, but everyone insisted it was true.

There could be no doubt he had a knack for creating excitement. Never before had hockey fever been as rampant in Los Angeles as it was that fall night in 1988 when Candy met McNall. As a gregarious promoter and all-around entrepreneur, McNall showed a special genius for merging the glamour of show business with the glamour of pro sports.

Not since that giddy interlude in the 1950s when Joe DiMaggio, the pride of the dominant New York Yankees baseball team, married Marilyn Monroe, the big screen's most attention-drawing object of male lust, had the high rollers of the sports world and the entertainment world been cross-pollinated to such spectacular effect.

No one could accuse McNall of failing to appreciate the value of a star. It was McNall's understanding of showbiz economics that made him decide eighteen million dollars was not too high a price to pay Edmonton Oilers owner Peter Pocklington for Wayne Gretzky. McNall was the new boy among NHL franchise owners, and he had a strikingly different attitude from the others, who privately thought he was out of his mind when he bought Gretzky.

Being in show business, McNall had a different way of looking at things. Certain film stars were paid as much as ten million dollars per picture. Some might balk, but in McNall's view, if an actor added five times that much to a movie's box office, he was worth it.

McNall doubled Gretzky's salary to $2.5 million. At first, McNall wanted to pay Gretzky three million dollars, which seemed excessive even to Gretzky. The superstar said he was sure two million would be enough, and the story of their reverse negotiation became a cherished anecdote in NHL lore. (By 1996, Gretzky's salary had climbed to eight million dollars, and the Kings could not afford to keep him. Gretzky was traded to the St. Louis Blues.)

Just as McNall anticipated, Gretzky's aura would turn the Kings from a losing proposition into the hottest property in pro sport. Thanks to Gretzky, the value of the franchise rocketed from twenty million dollars to more than one hundred million.

Movie stars were not incidental to McNall's strategy. He realized that if you could get movie stars turned on to hockey, the rest of the population would follow. Once Gretzky joined the team, an odd ritual became part of the Kings' routine. After every home game, for half an hour or more, the corridor outside the Kings' dressing room would be full of movie stars and other celebrities.

This was part of Bruce McNall's never-ending private party. In other cities players might think there was nothing to do after a game except take a shower, get dressed and give a quick quote to sports reporters before going home. But in the peculiar atmosphere that McNall created, shmoozing with stars was part of the scene. And as one pro sport executive puts it, "If you're an athlete who grew up in Sault Ste. Marie, it kind of turns your head to find yourself living in a Malibu beach house, earning a million dollars and hanging out with Clint."

McNall seemed an outgoing sort of guy who had overcome his own shyness, and was almost universally popular. Perhaps in retrospect it has become clear that the emperor had no clothes—let alone collateral. What seemed striking about the Kings' locker room in the McNall era was that in contrast to the athletes, who were often routinely naked, the emperor was one of the few who did have clothes. And what clothes! McNall favoured impeccably tailored Italian suits.

The night that McNall was introduced to Candy, he invited him to come down to the dressing room after the game. In the corridor outside the Kings' locker room, Candy was introduced to Wayne Gretzky, who had changed out of his uniform into a light grey houndstooth suit.

Gretzky was chatting about his differences with the general manager of his former team, the Edmonton Oilers. Candy and Gretzky seemed to be equally starstruck about meeting one another, and McNall suggested that the three of them ought to get together.

On the way back to the parking lot, Candy let Burke and Young know he was thrilled about the prospect of having McNall and Gretzky as friends. He also began talking about his own days of playing football, and spoke fondly about his beloved Toronto Argonauts football team. Burke and Young were getting a preview of things to come.

*Chapter 2*

# MELONVILLE DAYS

*W*hat caused the feeling of emptiness that drove John Candy to work so hard, play so hard and stay up most of the night? There may not have been a Rosebud that explains his drives the way the lost sleigh explains the psyche of the protagonist in *Citizen Kane*. But one event overshadows all else in his early life.

John Franklin Candy, the younger of two boys, was born in Newmarket, Ontario, on Halloween, 1950, and spent the first few years of his life in King City. When he was five years old, his father—a returned war veteran named Sidney Candy who worked as a car salesman—had a fatal heart attack at the age of thirty-five.

Sidney's widow, Evangeline, moved to East York, where she and her two boys—John and his brother, Jim, two years older—shared a small, humble brick bungalow with her parents and sister.

East York, a borough rather than a suburb, at that time had a distinctive identity, almost as if it had been sealed off from the rest of metropolitan Toronto.

Before the Second World War, the district had been mostly farmland. After the war, the fields were divided into small lots, each of which had a neat, tiny low-cost bungalow on it. Other sections of Toronto had modest neighbourhoods, but only in

East York did this modesty become the dominant, characteristic feature. The tiny house on Woodville Avenue where Candy grew up was typical of the area, with its façades of painted fences and tall flowers in front.

Candy's family, like most families in East York, was working-class rather than middle-class. Many of the people who lived there were the families of enlisted men who had returned to Canada after the war. Some had come from smaller, outlying towns, seeking work closer to the city but still preferring the atmosphere of a small town.

Most of the population had either English or Scottish roots; it was only decades later that the area would acquire a noticeable Greek and Chinese flavour. John Candy's family conformed to the norm except for an exotic touch: Evangeline's mother was Polish. There was always a lot of food in that tiny house, including a steady flow of cabbage rolls.

In those days East York had the kind of innocence associated with earlier times and other places—with elements of country towns in the British Isles before the war, of Mariposa, the Canadian town mythologized by Stephen Leacock, and even the kind of Americana for which Meredith Willson expressed nostalgia in *The Music Man*.

Like Willson's River City, Iowa, in 1912, East York in the 1950s evidently regarded pool rooms as the devil's playground. If you wanted to play pool, you had to take a streetcar to the more worldly Leaside section of Toronto.

Consumption of alcohol was frowned on in East York long after the rest of Toronto had begun to change its repressive, Methodist notions of public morality. Drinking in East York was mostly done at for-men-only taverns.

East York was not unlike Melonville, the typical town supposedly served by the bumpkins depicted on "SCTV." The borough's most familiar icon was its celebrated spinster mayor, True Davidson. The daughter of a Methodist minister, she was a champion of proud working people who carried lunch pails so they could save enough money for the down payment on one of those little bungalows.

*E*ven after he became famous, John Candy spoke very sparingly of his childhood years, but he gave the impression there was a lot of pain.

"The loss of my father left a great emptiness in my heart," he once remarked.

Sidney Candy, who was with the Forty-eighth Highlanders, fought in World War II in North Africa and Germany—and never entirely recovered from the experience.

"He had a lot of psychological scars," Candy remarked during an interview with *Parade* magazine in 1992. "He'd wake up in sweats. He bounced from job to job. He finally got his own used-car lot, Champion Motors. I still have some of the stamps and invoices."

Candy remembers being taken to the funeral. He was distraught and confused. "I didn't know why he died. I never understood it. Later when I had kids I realized how much I missed and needed him. I didn't have a role model."

Candy had something in common with the young hero of the marvellous Hungarian movie *Father*. The film's main character builds daydreams about his dead father, only dimly remembered; as he gets older, he invents a mythical father to suit his needs.

In a 1993 interview with Larry King on CNN to promote the movie *Cool Runnings*, in which he played the coach of a Jamaican bobsledding team at the winter Olympic Games, he was asked whether he had gone bobsledding as a child.

Candy replied that he did not participate in bobsledding, but instead watched other kids do it.

"I was very depressed and sad," he explained.

Perhaps, but for the most part he kept it to himself. Friends and teachers remember him as a quiet, seemingly content child, eager to please.

It is not surprising in a fatherless family that a child prematurely assumes the role of provider and caretaker, but it's usually the oldest sibling who takes on the father role.

In the Candy family, it was John rather than his older brother, Jim, who started playing Daddy at an early age.

John developed a compelling need to protect people close to him, and this was an enduring personality trait that made him a benevolent, fiercely loyal friend throughout his life. In a way, he was likely more comfortable with people who needed his help than those who didn't, because it gave him a continuing role he was confident he knew how to play.

"I probably took on the father role as children will," he acknowledged to an interviewer many years later. "I know I did."

John Candy is remembered by old childhood friends as steady and reliable. Evangeline and her sister, Frances Aker, both worked in the toy department at Eaton's department store downtown. (Colleagues knew them as Van and Fran.) John helped them make ends meet by working as a delivery boy for the local drug store, and later had a job at a local fish-and-chip shop.

Evangeline, a religious woman, enrolled her boys in the local Catholic school, Holy Cross, and took them to the adjacent Holy Cross church, where John was an altar boy.

One of the favourite escapes John Candy found from his somewhat dour, duty-bound childhood was the nearby Donlands theatre, just down the street, where he often bought his ticket with money earned by collecting and selling bottle-caps. At the Donlands, the future comedy star devoured Hollywood movies two or three times a week, and also encountered some British comic actors who made a big impression on him: Alec Guinness, Peter Sellers, Alastair Sim, Sidney James.

Looking back on his childhood years later, Candy would suggest that it was at the Donlands that he first caught the acting bug.

"I would come home and re-create every movie," he recalled. "Our backyard became a battleship, a war zone, a western town. There was a wardrobe department in every closet of our house."

Acting provided a welcome relief from Candy's daily reality. "I think I may have become an actor to hide from myself," he explained. "You can escape into a character. You can get lost and take up another life."

TV arrived in Canada when Candy was a toddler, and he was a first-generation TV watcher. Like many other baby boomers he found solace in watching hours of TV. Years later he even jokingly recalled being warned that he was in danger of turning into a TV.

Candy once told *Playboy*: "I loved watching Jack Benny, Jack Paar, the Honeymooners, Burns and Allen, George Gobel, the Munsters, Rocky and his Friends, Howdy Doody, Rin Tin Tin, and Lassie. I wasn't influenced by any one show. I was influenced by the medium."

On TV Candy encountered such cultural models as Jackie Gleason playing Ralph Kramden in "The Honeymooners"—the basis for one of Candy's most memorable sketches two decades later on "SCTV."

At the same time, the constant portrayal of the ideal middle-class family depicted in popular TV shows of that period must have added to Candy's feeling of alienation. Those TV shows didn't show boys growing up without fathers, or boys whose mothers worked in department stores. A sense of how he might have felt comes through in one of SCTV's most-talked-about skits, its parody of "Leave It to Beaver," with Candy playing the Beaver and saying in a mild-mannered way at the end, "Life stinks, Wally."

Candy not only watched network shows but also became an aficionado of such esoteric phenomena as the crime-and-disaster sleaziness of the local Buffalo news broadcasts. Fond lampoons of these shows later became a fixture of "SCTV." And the difference between the sober, restrained newscasts on the Toronto channels and the lurid style of their Buffalo counterparts gave Candy an early perception of the difference between the Canadian take on reality and the American one.

At school, John was no better than an average student. Though he was eager to please, he was admired more for his friendly, helpful personality than for his intellect. While Candy did show some aptitude as the class clown, he was also so painfully shy that appearing in school stage productions, which he did on occasion, made him extremely nervous. He was more at ease playing let's pretend games and putting on shows for other kids in someone's garage.

*A*t the end of grade eight at Holy Cross, John Candy was sent to Neil McNeil, a Catholic high school in the Beach area, which took almost an hour to reach by streetcar and bus. Assessed as a

less promising student than his older brother, he was placed in
the four-year diploma stream (rather than the five-year stream
for university-bound kids).

Candy achieved passing if undistinguished grades and chan-
nelled most of his energy into other pursuits.

By the time he reached high school, Candy already felt self-
conscious and awkward about his size. That was why—according to Gerry Boyle, a classmate and friend—when basketball
teams were formed by dividing a gym class into "shirts" and
"skins," Candy always wanted to be on the side of those who
kept their shirts on.

He played clarinet in the school band and was elected to the
student council, serving as treasurer—in which capacity he
became a minor impresario, booking bands for school dances.
But Candy is best remembered among his old classmates for
playing offensive tackle on the school's football team. With helmet and pads, young John Candy was a formidable, intimidating figure. Off the field he was known as a gentle giant, but
there was nothing gentle about his conduct in football uniform.
The game gave him a way of letting a more aggressive personality emerge. Even then, Candy was just so big that opponents
found it impossible to get past him.

Candy's days of gridiron glory didn't last long. After enjoying
the gratification of playing for the team in its championship season, Candy's on-field career came to an end because of a knee
injury.

From then on, he expressed his enthusiasm for football solely
as a fan of the Toronto Argonauts team in the Canadian Football
League, whose home games Candy frequently attended at
Exhibition Stadium. Candy and Gerry Boyle had season's tickets
near the twenty-five-yard line. According to Boyle, Candy was a
flamboyant fan who yelled and screamed a lot.

Despite his cherubic face and eagerness to please, John
Candy was no angel. His penchant for smoking cigarettes,
strictly forbidden on school property, sometimes landed him in
trouble.

He also experimented with marijuana while in high school,
and made occasional trips to Buffalo, because the state of New

York had a lower drinking age at that time than the province of Ontario.

Candy held a variety of part-time jobs and in his final year of high school, when he was working nights and weekends at Towers, a department store chain, he was one of the only students at Neil McNeil who had a car—a big old Chevrolet which he dubbed the White Knight. That gave him a special role within his family.

"I was the sixteen-year-old driving everyone to bingo and shopping," he recalled later. "It was quite a responsibility. It made me the man in charge of a lot of things. That's one reason why, when I eventually left home, it was quite traumatic for everyone."

It was while at Neil McNeil that Candy took his first drama class. According to the drama teacher, Ernest Brown, when Candy signed up for the course it was only because the typing class was full. Among the student productions Candy appeared in was a modern-dress version of Shakespeare's *Julius Caesar* and *Burning Effigy*, a play written by Brad Reid, one of Candy's classmates. The play was intended as a serious piece of counterculture social commentary. Reid played the lead, but in the role of a dog, Candy drew laughs by growling and barking.

The sound of that laughter must have had tremendous resonance for John Candy. And he loved to entertain friends with impressions in the manner of Jonathan Winters, a giant in the field of American comedy who was one of Candy's favourite performers.

One of Candy's closest friends in high school was Jonathan O'Mara, who later became a schoolteacher. Though O'Mara had a more studious, intellectual bent than Candy—he was studying Greek and working for the school newspaper—they hit it off to the point of becoming confidantes. Once they went on a fishing trip together, drinking generous amounts of Irish whiskey during the expedition.

"We cried on each other's shoulders," O'Mara recalls. "He was a big eater, he liked to party, and he was garrulous. He was a classic clown, but he could get quite morose. At first he would just strike you as a fun guy to be around, very jolly, but he also had a side to him that a lot of people didn't see. He was very sensitive, and eager to be liked. A lot of the guys had girlfriends, and he didn't. That really bothered him. Girls found him entertaining, but they never seemed to stick around long. Romantically he could never get to first base with them."

According to O'Mara, Candy felt he didn't have a lot going for him. He was much heavier than most of the other boys, and that troubled him. By their final year of high school, Candy had decided he wanted to join the U.S. Marines. He had the idea this would be a way to get himself into shape. At the time, the Vietnam War was at its peak and the population of Canada was inflated by thousands of young American men who crossed the border to avoid being drafted. One of the very few who tried to reverse the flow, Candy was fatalistic about the risk he could wind up in a body bag in a rice paddy.

"Everyone tried to talk him out of it," recalls Gerry Boyle.

Jonathan O'Mara went along for the ride when Candy drove to Buffalo planning to enlist. O'Mara was hoping to dissuade Candy from going through with it, but he failed to do so. When they found a motel, Candy registered as a single, to save money. Consequently he and O'Mara had to share a bed—and spent a night that was like a preview of *Planes, Trains and Automobiles*. To O'Mara's relief, when Candy went to the recruiting centre the next day, he was rejected because of his old football injury. Candy was disappointed about being turned down, but to take his mind off this letdown, he and O'Mara went to a movie. It was *Bullitt*, starring Steve McQueen and the steep streets of San Francisco.

Back in Toronto that summer, shortly after they both graduated from Neil McNeil, O'Mara and Candy went to another movie together. It was *Midnight Cowboy*, with Dustin Hoffman and Jon Voight as a pair of low-life drifters who bond amid the squalor of New York City. Candy was so taken by the movie that he and O'Mara saw it three times. Years later, Candy and Eugene Levy would concoct their own fondly mocking version of *Midnight Cowboy* for "SCTV."

After finishing high school, Candy had no clear career path in mind. The next year he enrolled in the journalism program at Centennial College in Scarborough but showed little aptitude or enthusiasm for it, and rarely attended class.

"I was a confused young man," he admitted, looking back on this period. "I didn't know what I wanted to be. Football was out because I'd hurt my knee. I had a series of odd jobs—selling sporting goods, mixing paint, you name it. One of my jobs was working with an ice show. I drove a small portable rink around. I made the ice. It was one of my first tastes of show business."

By his second year at Centennial, Candy had switched out of journalism and was concentrating on theatre courses. He would drop out of school before the year was over, but by then he had committed himself to becoming an actor.

# THE JOLLY JESTER

*W*hen Catherine McCartney met John Candy in 1970, he was a shy, baby-faced nineteen-year-old working part-time while taking courses at Centennial College and looking for a way to break into show business. McCartney, one of Toronto's most prominent talent agents then (and later a manager of artists), shared an office with her partner at the time near Fran's restaurant on College Street. Candy was employed across from McCartney's office as a salesman at Eaton's (the same department store his mother and aunt worked for).

Whenever McCartney bumped into Candy at Eaton's or on the street, he was friendly, and they developed a rapport. After he mentioned his acting aspirations, McCartney told Candy she was looking for someone to play a high-school football player in a TV commercial. Did he want to audition?

Definitely yes, said Candy, who hardly needed acting technique to play a high-school football player. Only a couple of years earlier he actually had been a high-school football player.

This was a toothpaste commercial, and Candy got the part. He found himself playing opposite radio and TV game-show host Art Linkletter, who had achieved celebrity status as the ringmaster of "People Are Funny" and the author of *Kids Say the Darndest Things.*

Candy drew a rebuke when he lit up a cigarette on the set.

Linkletter sternly told him he shouldn't smoke. The crew broke up when Candy—who was already a large fellow and seemed even bigger in football gear—delivered a deadpan reply with perfect comic timing: "Yeah, it might stunt my growth."

Linkletter was not amused.

Candy soon landed another commercial—for Molson's Golden Ale, which established him as something of a hero with some of his old school friends. But Candy was hardly well established in show business.

For a while, he was a regular visitor to McCartney's office, where he would sit on the floor talking about his life and ambition.

"John had a quality of vulnerability," McCartney recalls. "He was young and awfully cute. He was really eager to be an actor, so we kept trying to line up auditions for him."

McCartney hardly realized that the kid she was trying to help was destined to become as major a star as anyone she had ever worked with, and a friend for life as well.

But she knew from the start there was some kind of special bond between them. "John had a tremendous heart," she remarks, "and a helping-hand quality."

Moreover, they had something meaningful in common. Both had gone through the painful childhood experience of having their fathers die; in both cases, the father was under the age of forty. (McCartney grew up in Glasgow; her father died of war wounds ten years after being wounded.) Candy reminded McCartney of her older brother. He had a protective instinct, and always wanted to take care of people.

"John had the ability to make people feel special even if he had only known them a short time. Once he became your friend, he was always there for you, to listen and provide a shoulder to cry on."

While he was working at Eaton's, Candy met an aspiring writer/actor named Lorne Frohman.

"We were just desperate to break into the entertainment business," recalls Frohman, now a comedy writer/producer for commercial television. But in Toronto at that time there hardly was any entertainment business. There was very little TV production and no place for comedians to perform.

Frohman had just graduated from York University, where he had written and performed in a variety show.

"John and I liked one another," Frohman recalls. "We shared the same sense of comedy, so we decided to write a TV show together."

Candy and Frohman took an office over a strip club on Yonge Street. Their office was on the third floor, and Frohman recalls it would take them a long time to get to and from the office because they spent a lot of time staring at the young, beautiful girls who worked for the strip club downstairs.

The TV show they were developing was called "I Spy News." It was a take-off on a Buffalo channel's local "Eyewitness News" show which had intrigued Candy as a boy.

"John brought in a group of weird people to work on it; we would all sit around trying to get people to contribute their ideas."

Finally Frohman and Candy made an appointment with Gerald Rochon, a producer at CFTO, the Toronto station affiliated with the CTV network. After making the long drive to the CFTO headquarters in Agincourt, they arrived with a thirty-page treatment.

Almost as soon as the meeting began, Rochon began to ask questions to which they could not supply answers.

"What's the budget?" Rochon asked.

Frohman and Candy looked at one another. They had no idea what a budget was.

"What's it going to cost?" Rochon persisted. "Haven't you costed it out?"

Frohman and Candy were dumbfounded.

"We thought that's what you do," one of them said.

"Well who's going to star in it? And who's going to direct it?"

Frohman and Candy were totally unprepared. They felt like bumbling idiots.

"He basically told us to come back when we had our act together," says Frohman.

The two novices got into their car feeling humiliated, embarrassed and depressed. That was the end of "I Spy News."

Years later, the incident became a running gag. Whenever Candy ran into Rochon at industry gatherings, he would feign anger and jokingly assail Rochon for having thrown two budding young geniuses out of his office.

*L*ate in 1971, Candy earned a small part in a new Canadian play that was to become something of a legend. It was *Creeps*, David Freeman's memorable exploration of cerebral palsy, told from the inside.

Bill Glassco, a University of Toronto English professor who wanted to make a full-time career of directing plays, had commissioned Freeman to write *Creeps* after reading a personal essay by Freeman in *Maclean's* magazine. The play got rave notices when it opened at the Factory Theatre Lab in February 1971 on a double bill with a shorter play called *Snails*. That fall Glassco decided to remount *Creeps* for the inaugural season of the Tarragon Theatre, which Glassco had just established as a showcase for original Canadian work.

Many of the actors from the first production reprised their roles in the second production, but Glassco had to replace two guys who played members of the Shriners.

Kay Griffin, a talent agent, had recently had a meeting with Candy, who was looking for work, and he made a good impression on her. She thought he had a flair for comedy. Griffin also did some acting, and she had appeared in the earlier version of *Creeps*. She suggested to Glassco that Candy would be suitable to play one of the Shriners in the second production.

The other Shriner was played by Charles Northcote, who later became an agent. Northcote and Candy were both large young men. Northcote got a bit more attention, because he appeared on roller skates. Candy didn't have much chance to make an impact, but he developed an amusing Jack Benny stare.

Candy and Northcote, who were being paid $40 a week each, were absolutely thrilled to be appearing in a professional theatre production, and they developed a bond that endured for two decades. In later years when Northcote would hear from Candy, it often made him feel that Candy looked back on this period as his happiest days.

After rehearsals or a performance, Candy and Northcote would sometimes pile into Candy's big car and go to the Clinton Tavern, where draft beer was priced at five for a dollar. On other nights, Rosemary Hobor, who was then studying at the Ontario College of Art and had begun dating Candy, would prepare a big thermos of coffee or hot chocolate, and the three of them would drive over to a public skating rink near Eglinton and Avenue Road so that John—who still had athletic inclinations despite his high-school injuries—could participate in a late pickup game of hockey. Northcote and Hobor would sit in the stands, watching and keeping warm with the help of their thermos, while Candy played hockey.

It was during this period that Candy began working as a door-to-door salesman for Perkins Paper, hawking face tissue, paper napkins and candles.

*I*n the spring of 1972, Candy signed on with a children's touring troupe, the Caravan Theatre, which had a small LIP (local initiatives projects) grant from the federal government. The Caravan was presenting two plays. Some days the shows were presented at the Poor Alex Theatre on Brunswick Avenue in Toronto; on other days the plays were also put on at outdoor venues, often in city parks.

Most of the cast of six had already been chosen before Candy was hired. One member of the company, Valri Bromfield, wanted her friend Dan Aykroyd—who was also her partner in a comedy act—to take the parts Candy eventually played. But Aykroyd regarded himself as a comic, not an actor, and certainly not an actor in children's plays. He turned down the gig. To fill the void, the director, Stephen Katz, suggested someone who was unknown but in Katz's view very talented. This is how John Candy came to spend the summer of 1972 playing toadstools and blocks of wood.

One of the producers was Bill House (later an executive with the government film agency Telefilm), who recalls: "John was only twenty-one but already big and destined to get bigger. He was shy and very concerned about his appearance. He felt he wasn't attractive. He gave the impression of being one of those guys who had not had much success with girls as a teenager."

In one play, the story of a dark-eyed princess, Candy played a villain with one of those meant-to-be-twirled bankers' moustaches. In the other, Candy and Gale Garnett played toadstools in matching outfits—with purple and blue polka-dots—designed by the award-winning Mary Kerr.

"John and I were tethered to each other," recalls Garnett. The outfits were cylinders that went all the way up to their necks and around their faces, with headgear and hats. It was part of the comedy routine of the show that everything the big toadstool (Candy) did, the little toadstool (Garnett) aped.

"It was John's idea that we be tied to one another by the ankles, so that neither of us could get far away from the other. As a result, he was literally jerking me around."

According to Garnett, the members of the company all got along with one another, but Candy was the person everyone adored.

"He had what appeared to be bottomless even-temperedness," remarks Garnett. "We were doing children's theatre outside in the rain, which led to a certain amount of grumbling. John was the only one who never complained."

Other people assumed John was a happy-go-lucky guy, but Garnett took a different view of Candy's non-stop ebullience and jocularity.

"I sensed that he had an ancient anger that he was keeping under control. His weight wasn't what it later became but he was already somewhere between pudgy and fat. And I saw something in his eyes that we never talked about. It signalled that if he let go of his equanimity he would go berserk and be consumed by terrible rage. I recognized that syndrome because I had known other unflappable guys who had to cling to that middle ground; they knew if they ever left it they would be in serious trouble."

That perception never became an issue because it was never acknowledged by either Candy or Garnett. Their relationship was friendly, playful and superficial.

Garnett remembers that Candy had a special talent for doing impersonations of producers; he did a provocative impression of John Sime, who owned the Poor Alex.

"It was wicked but never crossed the line into being malicious," Garnett says.

"John had a quintessentially Canadian sort of cunning—a way of being funny and lovable so the person he was lampooning couldn't feel he had grounds to sue."

Garnett took the view that comedy was often a way of dealing with deep anger—a socially acceptable alternative form of expression when you feel like attacking someone. "In a way," quips Garnett, "every stinging joke can be viewed as a murder averted."

Candy was an utterly delightful companion but by the end of their summer being tethered to one another's ankles, Garnett felt she didn't understand him any better than she had at the beginning of the summer.

"I felt he was a totally professional, supportive and wonderfully generous guy whom I didn't know at all."

It was Valri Bromfield who introduced John Candy to Dan Aykroyd. Bromfield and Aykroyd had both recently moved to Toronto from Ottawa. Bromfield told Aykroyd she wanted him to meet this big, funny new friend of hers because, as she put it, "he's just like you."

Aykroyd was a rebellious child of relative privilege. He grew up in Ottawa, where his father was a deputy minister in the Canadian government. But perhaps in reaction to the burden of family respectability, Aykroyd developed a combative, subversive wit and a rowdy lifestyle. And unlike the essentially shy, insecure Candy, Aykroyd was full of self-confidence.

Aykroyd (who was working for the post office as well as performing comedy) was walking along Yonge Street past Bromfield's apartment one day when Bromfield leaned out of a window and called him. She wanted him to come up, because John Candy was visiting her, and this was her chance to introduce them.

Taking a break from his job going door-to-door for Perkins Paper, Candy had dropped in to chat with Bromfield. He was wearing a brown suit and had a brown Pontiac outside.

Candy didn't find selling paper nearly as much fun as acting.

"I was terrible at it," Candy confided to an interviewer years later. "Out of forty salesmen, I was number forty. I was having so much fun doing theatre my heart just wasn't in flogging napkins. Finally the boss called me in.

"'Candy, you're fired,' he said. 'I should never have hired a damned actor.'"

To Candy, it was a revelation that anyone regarded him as an actor.

"I'm thinking, actor? Somebody's recognized me as an actor? I like that."

He returned to his acting gig with renewed dedication, cherishing the camaraderie actors had with one another.

"It was then that I decided not to take any other jobs except what came my way as an actor."

And he never found himself out of work.

Aykroyd and Candy—destined to be lifelong friends—hit it off because they had similar senses of humour. They drove around town and hung out at parties together. Aykroyd introduced Candy to his friend Marcus O'Hara (brother of Candy's future Second City colleague Catherine O'Hara). O'Hara lived with his girlfriend, Gilda Radner, a performer from Detroit who had landed a major role in the Toronto production of *Godspell* that summer. O'Hara and Aykroyd jointly ran a sleazy but hip after-hours club on a down-and-out stretch of Queen Street East. The premises also doubled as living quarters for a few people, including Aykroyd.

*I*n the fall of 1972, Candy found a steady a job in one of the less glamorous branches of showbiz: low-rent touring children's theatre.

The Jolly Jesters was a shoestring company created by a man named James Iwasik who had more theatrical ambition than talent but managed to persuade an affluent friend to invest in his venture—which involved hiring a small band of actors to visit schools and perform, for a small fee, sketchy versions of well-known stories such as *Robin Hood* and *Treasure Island*.

According to Elaine Waisglass, who worked at Iwasik's office for a few months, Iwasik—who liked to think of himself as a playwright—would scrawl his rough, rambling scripts on yellow legal pads and then get someone to type them up unedited. They would then be passed on to the young actors, who would make as much sense as they could out of them for audiences of school children often sitting on the floor of school gymnasiums. Waisglass had the task of phoning school principals and getting them to agree to pay a fee of, say, one hundred dollars for a performance.

Candy worked not merely as an actor but as the stage manager or road manager of the company. That meant he drove a rented van with scenic canvases and props stored in the rear. His salary was sixty-five dollars a week.

Bryon White, then a young aspiring actor who wanted to prove to his father there was an alternative to enrolling in medical school, auditioned for a role in a play called *Rats*, which was to be produced at the Global Village Theatre in midtown Toronto. He lost the part to an actor who had been playing Long John Silver in *Treasure Island* for the Jolly Jesters. Shortly afterward White received a call from the Jesters asking whether he would be available to step into the void created by the defection of the actor who got the part in *Rats*. White said yes, and was immediately introduced to John Candy.

"John was living at home in East York. In the morning he would drive the van to pick me up in the north-west part of the city, and he would also pick up the other two actors. We'd turn the radio on real loud and we'd all be singing and smoking cigarettes."

White was very nervous because he was stepping into the part with no rehearsal time. After arriving at a school for a show, the four actors would set up the lights and change into their costumes. Candy, who had the role of Captain Handy, would be dressed in a bandanna, chunky knickers and funny shoes. He also assumed the task of entertaining the other actors with improvised comedy routines along the way—creating sketch variations in which Captain Handy would become gay, or Swedish, or a construction worker. His colleagues became like an audience at a comedy club, responding with a steady stream of laughter.

It took White several days to learn his lines, and Candy was gracious about it. He assured White the kindergarten kids would assume it was just part of the show when White had to be prompted for every line by Candy in a loud whisper.

White on occasion visited Candy at his family's bungalow, where John would entertain friends in his big basement room. White observed that John treated his mother as if he had become a substitute for his deceased father. That was one reason it seemed to White that making it in show business was so important to John.

But that didn't prevent him from having fun. "John warmed to people, and they warmed to him," recalls White. And White was also captivated by Candy's girlfriend, Rosemary Hobor, who was quiet and petite. White asked himself: "Why can't I find a girl like that?"

Sometimes Candy and White would go out to lunch and have serious talks. On one of these occasions, White asked what his ultimate dream was, and Candy replied that it was to play the kind of major role in a serious drama that would allow him to make a real impact on people's lives. He imagined himself playing Willie Loman in *Death of a Salesman*.

In the fall of 1972, Stephen Katz, who had directed Candy at the Poor Alex, cast him in a show at the Tarragon. Adapted by Sheldon Rosen from an eighteenth-century Italian comedy, and designed by Mary Kerr (who had become a friend of Candy), *The Stag King* was a spectacular baroque fairy tale for adults, full of oriental splendour as well as mystery and enchantment. There was a cast of ten—all wearing masks.

The story featured magical animals, scheming courtiers and thwarted lovers wandering about palace and forest. The king is trapped in the body of a stag while his sinister prime minister attempts to steal the throne and the fair maiden. Among the actors were George Sperdakos, Ron Ulrich, Francine Volker and Monica Parker.

Parker, who was Gilda Radner's best friend, had already crossed paths with Candy. She remembers Candy as someone who "made people crazy" because he was always late.

But, according to Parker—who, like Candy, was fighting a weight problem and would remain a friend of Candy's for twenty years—Candy was such a cheerful, amusing guy that nobody could get mad at him.

"When John was around, you always knew you were going to have a good time because it was important to him to entertain everyone and make other people feel good. It wasn't until you got to know him that you'd realize there was another side to him—that he carried these scary demons inside him."

Mary Kerr also struck up a friendship with Candy, who volunteered to help work with students in a theatre class she was teaching. She remembers that Candy revered Charles Laughton (he aspired to play the title role in *The Hunchback of Notre Dame*, as Laughton had), and that when Candy brought Rosemary Hobor over to spend an evening with Kerr and her boyfriend of that time in their High Park apartment, Candy joked about his hopes of becoming rich and famous. Candy's fantasy house of the future would include an applause machine that would give him a deafening ovation every time he arrived home.

Early in 1973 Dan Aykroyd and Valri Bromfield got word that Second City, the legendary Chicago revue comedy troupe, was planning to open a Toronto branch. Searching for local talent, Second City brass were coming to Toronto to hold auditions. The rules of the game: each aspiring performer had to present five different comedy characters to the adjudicators.

"We were all kind of scared of the audition," Aykroyd recalls. Knowing that Candy would be more terrified than anyone, Aykroyd took drastic action. Candy was invited to have lunch with Bromfield and Aykroyd, then accompany them to the audition.

"Unbeknownst to me," Candy claimed in an interview years later, "Dan and Valri put my name down on the list. My name was called. They pushed me into a room. Sweat was all over me."

According to Aykroyd, it wasn't so much Candy's material that astonished the judges as his presence and personality.

"As soon as they saw him on stage, they were thrilled," Aykroyd recalls, "more thrilled, in truth, than they were with Valri and me."

Aykroyd and Bromfield earned places in the new Toronto Second City company but Candy was destined for a higher calling. Two days after the audition, he got a phone call offering him a temporary spot with the main troupe in Chicago's funky Old Town district.

In the spring of 1973, Candy left for Chicago, not knowing how long he would be gone. He wound up staying the rest of the year.

*Chapter 4*

# MY KIND OF TOWN

*W*hen John Candy flew to Chicago to join the Second City company, he was instantly adopted into the most fruitful comedy family in the world. Founded in 1959, Second City was an outgrowth of the Compass Players and other experimental theatre groups of Chicago in the 1950s. By the time Candy arrived, Second City had already been transformed from a collection of unknowns doing material unlike anything the audience had ever seen before into an established academy of social satire with an impressive list of distinguished graduates—including Alan Arkin, Joan Rivers, Paul Mazursky, David Steinberg and Valerie Harper.

Much of Second City's sensibility was inherited from the Compass Players, which lasted for only a few years in the mid-1950s. Compass was based on a concept producer David Shepherd borrowed from the *commedia dell'arte* (a form of theatre popular in Renaissance Europe, mainly Italy).

*Commedia dell'arte* troupes of actors would travel from town to town, giving shows without having a formal written script. Instead the actors worked from notes and ideas, as well as the inspiration of the moment, emphasizing such farcical devices as slapstick, mistaken identity, disguises, deceptions and swindles. The actors would operate within certain broad frameworks (which included exits and entrances and basic plot) but had a great deal of freedom within that framework to improvise, extend dialogue, and shape the work according to the mood and response of the audience at the moment.

The essence of *commedia dell'arte* was to connect with the audience. Shepherd aimed to create a contemporary version of this popular theatre, with an emphasis on local comment, social criticism and topical humour. For a while, Shepherd meant to do shows for blue-collar workers to be performed in factories and steel mills, but once it became clear the intended proletariat audience was mostly indifferent to theatre, he settled on re-creating the sort of environment in which Kurt Weill and Bertolt Brecht had developed political cabaret in Weimar Germany.

Shepherd collaborated with a number of students at the University of Chicago who were trying to create innovative, socially relevant forms of theatre, including Paul Sills and Elaine May. The mandate was to create new material, often in shorter form than conventional plays. The hip comedy was an escape from the America of General Eisenhower, McCarthyism, Ozzie and Harriet, and "The Ed Sullivan Show." It was also influenced by the outrageous, taboo-busting work of that bad boy of 1950s comedy, Lenny Bruce.

When the Compass Players set up in the back room of a Chicago bar in 1955, several talented young performers took to improvising satiric scenes of contemporary life. Among them were Mike Nichols, Elaine May, Barbara Harris and Shelley Berman. By the end of the decade, Nichols and May (who left the group to do their own show) were the toast of Broadway but the Compass group was defunct.

Then in 1959 Sills, along with several survivors of the Compass troupe, joined forces with another adventurous producer, Bernie Sahlins, to open a nightclub featuring satiric, improvisational theatre sketches.

They chose as their venue a former Chinese laundry on North Wells Street, which they turned into a 120-seat theatre. Sahlins decided to call the place The Second City—a sarcastic reference to the condescending way New York views Chicago. (The phrase was taken from an article by A.J. Liebling in *The New Yorker*.)

The opening show included sketches about Eisenhower, a strike-breaking businessman, the cultural pretensions of FM radio and the sins of the medical profession. At the end of each performance, the cast would ask the audience for suggestions, and do improvised sketches inspired by those suggestions—the best of which were then used to work up set pieces for future shows.

The Broadway breakthrough of Nichols and May was already demonstrating that there was an audience ready to embrace smart topical social satire, and Second City was successful right from the moment the doors opened. Acclaimed by national newspapers and magazines, it began making visits to other cities. Regular workshops became part of a system that helped it keep flourishing and reinventing itself.

Candy could hardly have dreamed of a better training ground. The fact that the presiding gurus of Second City came to his home town looking for new talent was a stroke of luck and a turning point in his career.

According to Joe Flaherty, Bernie Sahlins was sure Toronto was the town of the future. It had been transformed by postwar immigration, plus a building boom and a spree of government spending on the arts. In the wake of the Vietnam War, it had also become a lively city-in-exile for American war dissenters, within a day's drive of New York, Chicago, Washington and Boston. And it had plenty of talent waiting to be discovered.

"We had visited Toronto and performed successfully at the Royal Alexandra Theatre," recalls Sahlins, who remained in Chicago as a kind of elder statesman after selling his stake in Second City in 1985. "We got an excellent review from Nathan Cohen [of the *Toronto Star*], and there were some local people including Sam Shopsowitz [founder of Shopsy's deli restaurant] who were so sure we would do well there they were willing to invest. Toronto struck me as a younger Chicago—more innocent, sweeter, safer."

Sahlins was not wrong about that, but in its early days, Second City in Toronto ran into some discouraging problems.

The audition that Candy was taken to by Dan Aykroyd and Valri Bromfield was essentially designed to scout local talent for the Toronto branch of Second City.

In that endeavour, Sahlins & co. were almost unbelievably successful. Among the performers they recruited were Gilda Radner and Gerry Salsberg (both then appearing in *Godspell*) and Jayne Eastwood (who had been in the Toronto-made film *Goin' Down the Road* two years earlier) as well as Aykroyd, Bromfield and Candy. Among the hundreds who did not get chosen were Eugene Levy (also in the cast of *Godspell*) and Martin Short. (Levy was offered a spot a few months later; Short had to wait four years before he could become a member of the Second City clan.)

The presiding adjudicators at the auditions were Sahlins, director Del Close and Flaherty—who was being sent to Toronto to work with the new company. Recruiting performers for Chicago was not part of the plan, and Candy was the only discovery to be sent directly to Chicago. He was so green it seemed like a good idea to let him develop in the company of more seasoned performers, and a temporary replacement was needed in the Chicago company while Brian Doyle Murray came to work with the new Toronto group.

Joyce Sloane, a producer destined to spend twenty years with Second City, went to pick up Candy at O'Hare airport.

"I was watching for this young actor I had never met when I saw coming through customs this big fellow with about twelve suitcases. I couldn't hear what was being said, but he kept talking and talking to the customs officer.

"Of course he had no work permit, and he was trying to give the impression he was only staying for the weekend, but then he had to explain what he was doing with all those suitcases. Somehow he managed to convince him."

Years later during a TV interview Candy told Brian Linehan: "I had to cross the border without a visa, and the U.S. immigration guy thought I was a draft dodger sneaking back after moving to Canada."

Candy was a twenty-two-year-old kid with little travelling experience, and he was frightened. But after he had been detained for forty-five minutes, the atmosphere lightened when the conversation turned to hockey.

"Who do you like in the play-offs?" asked the interrogator. After hearing Candy's enthusiastic and well-informed answer, he waved his arm and said: "Go on through."

Looking back on his Chicago days, Candy later remarked: "I'd never really been away from Toronto before, and I had all these weird images of Chicago. I guess it went back to my infatuation with "The Untouchables" on TV. Once I got there I realized Al Capone and Frank Nitti weren't around any more."

Candy started out as very much an apprentice who would need a lot of seasoning.

"At first he was very raw," recalls Sahlins, "but even then it was obvious he had a kind of stage magic."

"I'll never forget when I first went down to Chicago, how in awe I was," Candy recalled years later. "The company I joined had Bill Murray, Betty Thomas, Jim Staahl and Ann Ryerson. I remember watching them perform one night and I thought, I'll never be able to fit in. I can never do this. Then Del Close (the director) leaned over to me as I was watching and said, 'You'll be doing this Wednesday night...'

"I was so nervous that on my first night while the stage was dark between sketches, I ran smack into one of the guys and hit him so hard I split my lip. And I had to introduce the next sketch—our VD sketch. Blood was running down the side of my mouth as I talked. Everyone started laughing. I guess they just thought it was part of the act."

Before long, Candy's warmth, sweetness and eagerness to please made him a favourite of both the audience and colleagues—especially toward the end of his Chicago period, when he was part of a hugely popular Second City cast with so many large actors, not one of whom was Jewish, that it became known as the Seven Giant Goyim.

Bill Murray took the young Canadian under his wing. "He took me all over the city, showed me every landmark," Candy marvelled. "We'd have a hamburger at the original McDonald's, a pancake at the first International House of Pancakes. We went to every weird, seedy area imaginable. He'd always say 'This is my town and this can be your town too.' When we'd go to Wrigley Field he knew every Cubs player that had ever lived. In fact I had my first case of sunstroke seeing a Cubs game."

According to Joyce Sloane, Candy was fondly nicknamed Johnny Toronto. "John was a lot of fun to be around," she recalls. "There always seemed to be a party. We teased him about being the ultimate consumer. He thought if you were buying tickets it was better to get them from scalpers because they cost more. Even in those days, when he didn't have much money, he was very generous, bringing gifts and flowers for every occasion."

Facetiously, Candy used to say that in Chicago he learned "how to stay up real late and spell d-r-u-g-s."

Candy's girlfriend from Toronto, Rosemary Hobor, came down to join him, and Candy furnished his Chicago apartment entirely with rented furniture. According to Sahlins, Candy wanted to stay in Chicago, but by the end of 1973 he was needed in Toronto.

"We forced him to go back to Toronto," says Sahlins. "He was having such a good time in Chicago he really didn't want to go home. But once he got there, he fell in with an excellent cast and found himself in a company that was just right for him."

The Toronto branch of Second City, which had opened on Adelaide Street under the management of Sahlins in the summer of 1973, started out in disastrous circumstances. There was no publicity, no air-conditioning, no liquor licence, and much of the time, almost no audience.

Five months after it opened, the place went bankrupt. No one told Gerry Salsberg, who returned to work after being sick and found a sign on the door: THEATRE CLOSED.

Sahlins was upset because Toronto was the key to his plans for expanding the empire, and he knew the company was full of sensational young talent.

In the fall of 1973, Andrew Alexander—an aspiring young Toronto showbiz magnate—heard about the Adelaide Street blues from theatre friends. Alexander was a budding impresario in search of a project. This was a big chance.

Up to this point, Alexander's track record was not exactly dazzling. After studying business at the Ryerson Institute of Technology in Toronto, Alexander sold ads for a suburban weekly newspaper. Then he published a ski magazine for a while, and in 1970 negotiated the publishing rights for the aborted John Lennon Peace Festival in Toronto.

Other odd jobs included masterminding a promotion campaign for Toronto Arts Productions and raising money from doctors and lawyers for the musical *Justine* at Toronto's Global Village Theatre. Finally, Alexander hammered the last nail into the coffin of that once venerable revue *Spring Thaw*, buying the rights from the show's creator, Mavor Moore, and then putting on a dreadful show that Alexander recalls with a shudder as "eight weeks of total misery."

Several other investors helped keep Second City afloat, but it was Alexander who took control, despite being flat broke. In early 1974, Alexander bought the rights to Second City in Toronto from Sahlins for one dollar. If ever there was a project suited to a budding impresario with no money, this was it. Given his unimpressive track record, Toronto's Second City branch may have seemed like another losing venture waiting to deliver a blow to a star-struck young masochist, but Alexander fooled a lot of people by turning it into a thriving empire that would eventually gross more than a million dollars a year. Within less than three years, he would control Toronto's top cabaret show, the theatre/restaurant where it was housed, and a weekly TV program with fans all over North America.

Five months after the Adelaide Street theatre was padlocked, Second City reopened around the corner at the Old Firehall—a floundering beer hall on Lombard Street that Alexander took over with $7,000 of other people's money and turned into a theatre/restaurant.

It was part of the deal that Sahlins would still be responsible for the creative side of Second City, and that a portion of any profits from Alexander's operation would go toward paying off debts that remained after the Adelaide Street debacle.

Alexander had trouble persuading some of the old cast members to return, partly because they had been discouraged by their experience the previous year and partly because in the interim some of them had found other work.

But the operation was on the brink of turning into a major

success. The resurrected group included Radner, Candy, Levy, Flaherty and Rosemary Radcliffe. The troupe—which was soon to include Catherine O'Hara, Andrea Martin and Dave Thomas—would become legendary for the range of its talent. Already it was attracting positive notice in the media.

However, attendance was still discouraging, and sometimes on a Monday, the slowest night of the week, Candy would fill out the house by recruiting audience members from the line-up outside a singles disco around the corner. Candy was living nearby in an apartment building on Alexander Street. He and Rosemary would occasionally have the members of the cast over for dinner or drinks.

Some Toronto critics complained that Second City was just recycling Chicago sketches and had no Canadian content. After reopening at the Firehall, the company worked to change that perception by developing new material with local references. At the time, Canadian theatre was dominated by naturalistic plays about troubled families by writers including David French and David Freeman. A parody of these plays, entitled "You're Going To Be All Right, You Creep, Leaving Home and All, Eh?" became a classic.

The three problem kids were Levy as the gay son, Radner as the retarded daughter and Candy as the ordinary boy who just wanted to be a hockey player. Flaherty played their tyrannical father, Radcliffe played the mother, who was just trying to keep the peace. This sketch—which was later adapted for television on "SCTV"—helped establish Second City as a genuinely Canadian institution, firmly entrenched in contemporary Toronto.

What made Second City take off was the rapport the performers had with one another. Talking about this period a few years later, Gilda Radner remarked: "There would be nights when this magical, chemical, extrasensory thing would happen between you and the others.

"Something incredible would happen onstage… Later, you'd be so excited about what had happened, you couldn't sleep all night. You'd be trying to remember exactly what made it click so well and made it come together like a piece of art, with rising action and a climax and an end."

In this environment, Candy improved his skills as a comedian and an actor, developing a boyish persona and dead-on timing.

For a while, Candy was the overgrown kid of the group, especially compared to Flaherty, who was definitely the grown-up. But given the rapid turnover of talent, within a couple of years, Candy would make the transition from everyone's favourite rookie to one of Second City's seasoned veterans—so much the *éminence grise* that he would be chosen to work with the raw recruits who were being sent out to the hinterlands with Second City's young touring company.

# Chapter 5

# KID STUFF

*T*revor Evans—a senior TV producer for the Canadian Broadcasting Corporation in Toronto—was given a surprising challenge in the spring of 1974. The CBC wanted to create a new after-school show for kids that would be less earnest and "educational" than its traditional children's programs. This was supposed to be the beginning of a new era in which CBC children's programs would break out of the bounds set by such reliable and predictably wholesome programs as "Razzle Dazzle," "Mr. Dressup" and "The Friendly Giant."

The idea was to develop a funny, entertaining program that would win the loyalty of kids who might otherwise be watching commercial sitcoms on U.S. stations. That's why the call went out to Evans, who was then at the helm of the CBC's most prestigious adult comedy program, "Wayne & Shuster." Determined to break new ground, Evans began searching for fresh young performers to help him deliver what the CBC wanted—kid fare with a sophisticated flair—on a limited budget.

It was inevitable that he would be drawn to the Old Firehall, because the new Second City show there had already started to create a buzz around town. Evans was dazzled by the Second City cast, but following democratic procedures, rather than hire any of them immediately, he invited them to audition at an open casting call for a new half-hour children's comedy show which would eventually make its debut on the CBC schedule in a twice weekly after-school slot the following fall under the title "Dr. Zonk and the Zunkins."

Scores of performers turned up for the auditions, and Evans brought various potentially humorous accoutrements (such as a stuffed pig) to the studio from the CBC props department. Each performer had fifteen minutes to improvise a comedy scene.

Three of the regulars Evans hired for "Dr. Zonk" were from the cast at the Firehall: Gilda Radner, Rosemary Radcliffe and John Candy. Another, Fiona Reid, had been in the cast the year before at Second City's ill-fated first Toronto venue. The other regulars on "Dr. Zonk" came from outside the Second City family: Dan Hennessey and John Stocker, Bob McKenna, Robin Eveson, and the Zunkin puppets worked by Nina Keough.

Almost instantly, Evans recognized that Candy had the goofy overgrown-kid quality he was looking for. To Candy, Evans was a man he could trust; as a teenager, Candy had been a viewer of "Kiddo," which Evans produced for the CTV network in the 1960s. The adoration of audiences at the Firehall was gratifying to Candy, but he yearned to reach a wider public. "Dr. Zonk" may have carried "not ready for prime time" overtones, but it was the kind of opportunity Candy was hungry for. He wanted to reach a much larger audience, and he was eager to make more money than Second City was paying.

"Dr. Zonk" was offering the performers no more than CBC scale, but that was still around $200 for each day of work, whereas Andrew Alexander was paying only $160 for a whole week of work at the Firehall. Of course the CBC gig was seasonal; an entire year's batch of episodes would be produced in about ten weeks, working perhaps three days a week.

"Dr. Zonk" consisted of comedy sketches. Though Evans handed the cast a script, it was understood that the actors were expected to improve on it by improvising bits of comic business. In one enjoyably silly routine, Gilda Radner played the host of a kids' help-line, and Candy played a slow-witted, long-haired teenager who has trouble eating spaghetti. She gets him using scissors to make the noodles shorter, which works fine until he accidentally cuts the telephone cord and disconnects them.

Like Candy, Gilda Radner was the kind of performer adored by audiences from the moment they encountered her. She was a sweet, ditsy girl from Detroit who, thanks to *Godspell*, had earned a following in Toronto even before she joined Second City.

Radner and Candy had great performing rapport, but their collaboration was relatively brief—less than a year. The two members of the Second City company with whom Candy would form more enduring bonds were Joe Flaherty and Eugene Levy. Flaherty was rarely embraced by the public the way Candy was, but being nine years older than Candy and more of a veteran than the other performers, he had a godfather role. Candy respected Flaherty and regarded him as a kind of mentor.

Levy was more of an equal, and they had contrasting personalities which they were always playing off one another. Candy liked to say that he and Levy were like Ralph Kramden, the bus driver played by Jackie Gleason on "The Honeymooners," and Ed Norton, the sidekick played by Art Carney.

"I'm wild and impulsive," Candy would explain. "Eugene is slow and incredibly meticulous. He can drive you crazy just by the way he orders food. You can eat an entire meal, have dessert and get the bill and Gene's still studying the menu."

But the member of the Dr. Zonk troupe who soon became Candy's closest friend for a time was neither a member of the Second City family nor destined for stardom.

"We were inseparable for a few years," recalls John Stocker, who was known as a voice performer and had worked with Evans on "Wayne and Shuster." Since Stocker was a head shorter than Candy, a Woody Allenish figure in horn-rimmed glasses, there was a Mutt and Jeff quality to the pair.

"We were just sympatico," says Stocker. "We had the same sense of humour, and we laughed hard at one another's jokes."

Candy and Stocker—who each called the other "Johnny"— began hanging out together whenever they both had time off. Though Stocker was married and Candy had a girlfriend, they mostly spent their time without women, two high-spirited guys on the lam. The women in their lives regarded each of them as a bad influence on the other. Stocker and Candy would go out drinking in the afternoon, before a performance at the Firehall, or stay up most of the night—talking and drinking—after a Second City show. Candy was such a heavy cigarette smoker that his index finger was already the colour of an amber traffic signal.

"John always seemed bubbly and effusive, always up," says Stocker. "At a bar, he insisted on picking up the tab for whoever was at the table. He partied hard, but he was a big guy, and he appeared to have the kind of metabolism that made it possible for his body to absorb a lot of punishment. After a while I began to realize that nobody could be that happy, that bouncy and that giving all the time. John did have a down side, but he didn't like to let anyone see it. We would laugh and get loaded, and there were times when he would get sad, but he would never explain why.

"He was the opposite of me in that regard. If I got upset, I would tell complete strangers exactly how and why I was upset. The most John would ever say was: 'It's nothing. I'm just having a down moment.'"

Rosemary Radcliffe, who worked with Candy both at Second City and on "Dr. Zonk," found Candy completely amenable and very generous as a performing colleague, but was still aware of his tremendous hunger for stardom.

"I swear he got up in the morning thinking about fame and went to bed at night thinking about fame," says Radcliffe. "When you're that driven, you may not know how you're going to get there, so you try all the avenues."

One of the most obvious avenues leading to fame was the movies. Candy had made his debut as an extra in a 1971 film called *Faceoff* (about a hockey player's romance with a pop singer). And he landed a small part in *Class of '44*, a sequel to the Hollywood hit *Summer of '42*. It was shot in Toronto and used Canadians in minor roles. Candy played Paulie, the class dummy in the high-school graduating class of Hermie, the protagonist. While Hermie and his friends go on to college, poor Paulie goes off to fight in World War II.

But Canada was in the early stages of developing its own film industry, and in the summer of 1974, Candy got a chance to perform in a home-made movie. *It Seemed Like a Good Idea at the Time*, directed by John Trent and produced by David Perlmutter, was a forgettable sex comedy with imported stars— Anthony Newley and Stephanie Powers. The script also featured a pair of bumbling detectives. In these roles Candy was paired with Lawrence Dane, an experienced actor who was older than Candy and had a tough, lean look. The chemistry between them was good, and they stole the picture—to the extent that the next year, their two characters were reincarnated in another Perlmutter/Trent trifle, *Find the Lady*, which had only a brief theatrical release before landing on TV.

Like many of the people who worked with Candy, Dane struck up a friendship with him. "I went to see him at Second City. He came across as a humble, gentle soul who really cared about how people perceived him and truly wanted to do the right thing. He was always gracious and deferential."

This was the basis for the rapport between Candy and Dane, who perceived himself as shy and insecure. Dane, fourteen years older than Candy and not part of the wisecracking Second City crowd, noticed a side of Candy that gave him some concern. Even at that early stage, at the age of twenty-three, Candy's weight was starting to balloon. And though he was good at taking care of others, Candy did not seem capable of taking care of himself.

"He celebrated too hard," remembers Dane. "He opened up the faucet and it all came out. It was as if he said to himself, 'My mortality is on a string, so I might as well throw caution to the wind.' Unfortunately he attracted people who wanted to take advantage of him. And it seemed to me he was just terribly hard on himself."

Later on, almost everyone associated with those early days of Second City would look back on them as some sort of golden age, when everyone was flourishing creatively and having a great time. But the kids in the show were under tremendous pressure to come up with funny new material. The improvisational sessions at the end of the show were crucial to the format of Second City, because it was the way new material was created. And some members of the cast found it hard to cope.

"I lived in terror of improvisation," recalls Rosemary Radcliffe. "The more the crowds started to come, the higher people's expectations became. I drank a lot—we all drank a lot—and it was hard on everybody."

There was a feeling that the Second City players were a family. But at times they seemed like the hilariously dysfunctional family depicted in their brilliant satiric sketch "You're Going To Be All Right, You Creep, Leaving Home and All, Eh?"

In an effort to make the group more cohesive, Andrew Alexander would arrange such activities as baseball games in which the performers would form a team and take on the employees of some radio station. This had the effect of making Radcliffe, who felt incompetent at all sports, feel more acutely than ever that she didn't fit in. After a year of high stress, Radcliffe quit.

Second City was a voracious machine that devoured performers, so there was a constant need for new talent. After a while, Gilda Radner (who had financial freedom thanks to a wealthy father) decided she'd had enough and moved on. Catherine O'Hara, an aspiring funny girl from Etobicoke who had worked at the Firehall checking coats while doubling as an understudy for Radner and Radcliffe, honed her comic skills in the touring company, and then earned a chance to replace Gilda Radner in the main company. O'Hara soon became the perfect performing partner for Candy—a point that was perhaps most sublimely demonstrated when she played Katharine Hepburn to his Orson Welles.

When Radcliffe left, she was replaced by Andrea Martin—who had moved to Toronto in 1970 after growing up in Maine and landed a role in *Godspell* along with Levy and Radner. Another recruit was Dave Thomas, a witty kid from Hamilton who wrote radio scripts and spent several months in the replacement cast of *Godspell.* Thomas had decided to quit showbiz and was doing very well as a copy writer for a large advertising agency before he gave it up to join Second City.

In the spring of 1975, Candy was part of a splinter group that went to California to open a spinoff Second City show at a shopping mall in Pasadena. Sahlins had made the deal, but he persuaded Alexander to get involved in the venture. Most of the cast came from Chicago, but Sahlins needed a couple of reinforcements from Toronto.

Second City's Pasadena show, presented at a shopping mall, was called *Alterations While U Wait*. It was a sign of how ill-fated the venture was that passersby, seeing the sign, thought they were at a tailor shop rather than a cabaret theatre. The cast included Joe Flaherty, Betty Thomas, Eugene Levy, Doug Steckler and Deborah Harmon.

Candy made several trips between Pasadena and Toronto in 1975. On one occasion he drove across the continent with Dan Aykroyd on a four-day odyssey. Years later Aykroyd would recall: "We played old music, sang and talked and focused on what we'd do when we got older. It was one of those great drives."

As soon as they arrived in California, Aykroyd got a call from New York asking him to work for NBC's new late-night show "Saturday Night Live," which was preparing for its premiere that fall.

Candy had hoped that his chance to work in California would give him a chance to be discovered by Hollywood. He didn't get the break he had hoped for, despite going to L.A. armed with a list of contact names and numbers. But he did appear in a zany, low-budget movie comedy that was one of the early attempts to transfer the new cabaret humour of the period to the big screen. The movie, called *Tunnelvision*, was written and directed by Neal Israel. Since it was scraped together with little money, the cast worked for hardly more than a handshake and a free lunch.

In a way, *Tunnelvision* anticipated "SCTV" by using TV itself as its satiric target. Israel, who had a job as director of on-air promotion for CBS, said the film was prompted by his anger at the industry's emphasis on success at any cost, without regard to integrity.

In an interview with Harlan Jacobson published in *Variety*, Israel charged that he had been fired by CBS because of *Tunnelvision*. CBS claimed he was fired for other reasons.

Many of the comedy ideas in *Tunnelvision* fizzle, and in retrospect the film is most notable for featuring a number of performers who would later become well known—including Chevy

Chase and Bill Murray. One of the few genuinely funny bits in *Tunnelvision* is a parody of a game show with Joe Flaherty and Betty Thomas (a graduate of the Chicago Second City company who went on to fame in the TV series "Hill Street Blues"). Candy appears only for a minute or two as a crime-fighter whose partner happens to be a disembodied head.

$\mathcal{B}$y the fall of 1975, the Pasadena club was forced to close for lack of customers, and Candy returned to Toronto. Trevor Evans, who had employed Candy in "Dr. Zonk," was doing a follow-up show called "Coming Up Rosie," which made its debut in the CBC schedule that fall. Unlike "Dr. Zonk," it had a continuing story, about a group of low-life characters reminiscent of the Bowery Boys. The regular cast included several holdovers from "Dr. Zonk"—Rosemary Radcliffe, Fiona Reid, Dan Hennessey and John Stocker.

Candy would have had an ongoing role, but because he was going to Pasadena, Evans replaced him with Aykroyd. Barry Baldero was added to the cast. When Candy returned to Toronto, he did some guest appearances on "Coming Up Rosie." And he became a regular in the show's second and final season in 1976. He was also appearing in another show for kids, TV Ontario's "Cucumber."

Candy took a serious role in *The Clown Murders*, a drama about a caper that turned into kidnapping, written and directed by Martyn Burke, a young novelist and CBC documentary film-maker. The story was inspired by a sensational true crime in rural Ontario that earned headlines in 1969.

What began as a prank at a Halloween costume party turned into kidnapping and murder when a wealthy young woman named Mary Nelles was abducted from the converted school-house where she lived with her husband by six men dressed as clowns who held her at a hideaway while demanding ransom. (In the end, Mary Nelles came home unharmed, the ransom money was recovered, and the kidnappers were jailed.)

In the somewhat modified version of the tale devised by Burke, the part of the ringleader—the victim's ex-boyfriend—

was played by Stephen Young, a handsome actor who had been on the TV shows "Seaway" and "Judd for the Defence," and was known as a globetrotting playboy. Lawrence Dane was cast as the unpopular husband.

For the role of Ollie, the sweet sadsack of the gang who is required to have a breakdown on camera, Burke was looking for a young unknown. Al Waxman, who was playing the sheriff, suggested Burke drop down to the Firehall to have a look at John Candy.

Afterward, Burke was introduced to Candy and told him about the role. "I told him this was not a comedy part," Burke remembers, "and he seemed eager to try something different. I had the feeling he wanted to go beyond getting laughs and be taken seriously."

Candy was the youngest actor in the film, and according to Burke, "John was the puppy dog on the set. He was an overgrown kid, and everyone loved him. He seemed very hungry for approval. Some actors go out of their way to gain the approval of the producer or the director in a professional way, but John seemed to want it on a personal level as well. He struck up a friendship with Stephen Young; you could sense he had tremendous respect for Stephen and looked up to him."

As a movie, *The Clown Murders* was at best an honourable failure and a curiosity item. But it was the beginning of a three-way friendship among Candy, Burke and Young which extended into the late 1980s, when all three lived in Los Angeles and would go to hockey games together at the Great Western Forum.

In the fall of 1975, the Canadian producer Lorne Michaels scored a breakthrough with the debut on NBC of his weekly ninety-minute show "Saturday Night Live," providing a vast new audience for some of the sharpest young talent coming out of comedy clubs in North America. It was through "Saturday Night Live" that Bill Murray, Eddie Murphy, John Belushi and Chevy Chase began their ascent to movie stardom.

Among the Saturday Night players making their mark that first season were two of Candy's recent cohorts at the Old Firehall—Danny Aykroyd and Gilda Radner. Excited as he was for them, this development inevitably raised a troubling issue for Candy. Some people from the Toronto Second City group were making it big, and John Candy wasn't yet among them. In the next few years he would refer with increasing resentment to the lack of recognition he was experiencing.

In 1976, however, there was no lack of work—especially on television. Almost unbelievably, Candy made regular appearances that year on four TV shows and became a familiar face on all three of Canada's English-language television networks.

When he joined Radcliffe, Stocker and the others on "Coming Up Rosie," Candy created one of his most memorable characters—a security guard by the name of Wally Wipazipachuck who would turn up in slightly different form in the 1983 movie *National Lampoon's Vacation.*

Candy also made a number of appearances on the CBC's ambitious but ill-fated late-night talk show "90 Minutes Live," with host Peter Gzowski, which was taped five nights a week before a studio audience. On one of the earliest episodes, Candy and fellow performer Jayne Eastwood flew to Vancouver while the show was doing a kind of try-out road tour. After performing a couple of comedy sketches, they chatted with Gzowski. Candy never seemed comfortable in this setting, and in fact after he became a movie star he still had an aversion to appearing on talk shows, even to plug his movies.

Candy also became the ringleader of a regular spoofy feature of "90 Minutes Live"—the Bargain Basement Talent Search. Candy's role was to introduce bizarre novelty acts. It turned out to be less than a triumphant gig. The show's staff enjoyed having Candy around but, owing to tight budgets and the pressures of doing a daily show, they were rarely able to take advantage of the ideas Candy came up with for creating episodes.

Perry Rosemond, a successful TV producer who had worked in Los Angeles before returning to Canada to create "King of Kensington" for CBC, left his new hit show after one year to develop "The David Steinberg Show" for CTV's 1976-77 season. Steinberg and Rosemond had both grown up Jewish in Winnipeg and were roughly the same age. The format of the program was similar to that of the old Jack Benny show (which moved from

CBS radio to CBS television in the 1950s), with Steinberg playing more or less himself and surrounded by a group of regular comic sidekicks involved in each week's storyline.

Steinberg was a graduate of Chicago's Second City. Both he and Rosemond were attuned to the young talent coming out of the Old Firehall. Among those chosen to be regulars on the CTV show were Candy and Martin Short. Short played an obnoxious lounge lizard named Johnny Del Bravo.

On the first few episodes Candy played Sven the cook at the Hello Deli restaurant, but he didn't have much to do except yell "Coming up!" often. Recognizing Candy's potential, Rosemond promoted him to the part of Spider the band leader. Spider was the sort of fellow who always did everything wrong but was so well-meaning that nobody had the heart to confront him with the error of his ways.

"The David Steinberg Show" was lively and entertaining, and consistently funny, but CTV dropped it after one season.

Candy's big TV chance would turn out to be another show making its debut that same season. It was the one Andrew Alexander was developing around his performers from the Old Firehall.

One night John Stocker got a call from Candy at 1:30 a.m. He sounded loaded.

"Johnny, it's Johnny. What are you doing right now?"

"Johnny, it's the middle of the night. What do you think I'm doing? I'm sleeping."

"Well, listen, we're down at this sound studio in Yorkville doing some work on our new show, and we realized after a while we need an outside performer to do some voice work. I suggested you. Can you do it?"

"When would you need me?" asked Stocker.

"We need you right now. Can you come down?"

Stocker staggered into some clothes and drove to the recording studio. There he recorded a line which became a standing introduction for the series: "There were six people who loved to watch television but they didn't like what they saw, so they decided to do something about it. They started their own network..."

"SCTV" was almost on the air.

*Chapter 6*

# "SCTV Is On The Air!"

*J*ohn Candy finally got a chance to reach a large audience with his best work when "SCTV" made its debut on the Global television network in the fall of 1976. By then, Andrew Alexander had his back against the wall. The Second City stage shows were a magnet for fresh young talent, but with its low budgets and small audiences, Second City was an institution writer-performers were happy to graduate from as soon as they sniffed the opportunity for bigger audiences and larger paycheques.

Alexander's company would soon be grossing more than one million dollars a year at the Old Firehall but he knew he wouldn't be able to hang onto his gifted young performers unless he could make a breakthrough into television. This was especially true now that Lorne Michaels had developed the equivalent of a Second City troupe on network U.S. television, thus giving his performers the advantage of exposure to a huge weekly late-night viewing audience.

Alexander was being pressed by Bernard Sahlins, the Chicago Second City founder from whom Alexander had purchased Toronto's branch plant. Sahlins thought the time was right to get onto TV. Alexander had hardly any TV experience, but he agreed to give it a try with Sahlins as his partner. Sahlins came to Toronto to help develop the TV show, bringing two of his most trusted Chicago associates, Sheldon Patinkin and Harold Ramis, with him.

The obvious home for "SCTV" would have been the Canadian Broadcasting Corporation. The publicly owned CBC dominated production of Canadian shows. But Alexander had run into endless frustration trying to interest the CBC, which during that period was obsessed with current affairs programming (including "90 Minutes Live"), and somewhat committed to drama (especially while the prominent stage director John Hirsch was head of drama) but weaker in the comedy and variety area.

Jack Crane, then director of programming for the public network, says with regret: "I wish the CBC had embraced 'SCTV' from day one, but we had not yet gone through the change that led us to seek independent production."

In those days, given its restrictive union contracts, the CBC was prepared to handle only shows it produced on its own. Andrew Alexander was proposing something else—that the CBC provide its facilities for outside producers in exchange for rights to broadcast the show in Canada. The CBC did not find a way to accommodate that request.

Global was hardly even a real network. It was licensed to broadcast only in Ontario, and operated on a shoestring. It made its money by simulcasting U.S. shows. It produced little original programming, and did so on the cheap, doing the bare minimum to meet the Canadian-content rules of government regulations.

For Alexander, going to Global was a desperation measure. He knew he couldn't hold onto his rising comedy stars with only a small stage show. Two of the most popular members of the Toronto Second City cast, Radner and Aykroyd, had already moved to NBC's "Saturday Night Live."

Unable to negotiate a good television deal, Alexander decided that a cut-rate deal was better than no deal. The shows were taped at Global's Toronto studio on a ludicrously small budget—initially $35,000 per half-hour episode. Alexander needed Global to get the shows produced, but once they were in the can he knew he would be able to sell them to independent stations in U.S. markets—and if it was any good, the show would eventually catch on, find an audience, and pay big dividends.

There would be thirteen half-hour shows for the initial season in 1976-77 and then another thirteen episodes for the 1977-78 season.

Six of the performers chosen for the TV show had worked on Second City stage shows at the Old Firehall: John Candy, Joe Flaherty, Eugene Levy, Andrea Martin, Catherine O'Hara and Dave Thomas. The seventh, Harold Ramis, was brought in from Chicago and functioned at the beginning as the show's head writer. (Ramis would be the first cast member to leave the show and move to Hollywood.)

At first production values were ragged. "I guess they thought we were going to walk out there with a few lights and bentwood chairs and improvise for half an hour," Candy recalled sarcastically. But the performers turned the show's cheapness to their advantage, making it into a comment on the sleaziness of TV in general.

"Our producers found the cheapest studio and made the cheapest deal possible," Candy explained in an interview some years later. "Being the simpletons that we were at the time, we accepted their offer."

The genius of Second City on television was that instead of merely putting some of the more successful cabaret sketches in front of a camera, the show took as its landscape the self-contained world of TV itself. It was during a meeting in Alexander's office at the Firehall—attended by Sahlins, Patinkin, Ramis, Flaherty and Del Close—that the idea emerged of presenting the broadcasting day of a small TV station.

The concept was to satirize TV itself for baby-boom audiences. But the breakthrough, freewheeling format of the show emerged almost by accident.

According to Patinkin, who worked on the show as an associate producer and writer, "'SCTV' originally was intended to be a little show in which all the pieces were tied together with a running plotline, as they would be in a conventional sitcom. The first episode was about the crack-up of Johnny LaRue, and featured a backstage rampage. But we were really pressed for time and short of money, and we had to shoot the material one segment at a time. After a while we realized that the bits spoofing TV could work on their own and we didn't really need the plot connection stuff."

The original notion, Sahlins explains, was to develop a parody of television with a continuing story set in a small-town TV station. "We had written a script which was connected and characterized," recalls Sahlins. "John played a has-been star returning to his home town. Gene Levy was the station's security guard. Harold played the owner of the station. But when we got through shooting the first show, we could tell it wasn't working. After three days in the editing room we tried taking out all the story elements. Suddenly, it worked great."

The sensibility of the program came almost intuitively from the age of the multichannel TV converter. Viewers got samples of various lunacies flourishing all over the TV schedule, but they were delivered as punchy, fragmented flashes, just the way they would be if we happened to be sitting impatiently in front of our TV sets with trigger-happy fingers always jumping from one channel to another.

Structurally the show was laid out with brilliant intricacy, bombarding the audience with a whole range of promos, previews, commercials and commentaries—which all seemed to be interrupting one another and played off against one another. The sense of a continuous schedule was achieved by the repetition of certain features and characters—including such regulars as Joe Flaherty's Sammy Maudlin (the self-congratulatory talk-show host), Eugene Levy's Bobby Bittman (the world's most obnoxious stand-up comic), Catherine O'Hara as Hollywood gossip columnist "Rhoda" Barrett and airhead starlet Lola Heatherton, and Dave Thomas as Bob Hope and Art ("Women Say the Darndest Things") Linkletter.

When "SCTV" did a movie parody like *Grapes of Mud, Lust for Paint* or *Murder on the Sandwich Express*, it wasn't only the movie that was parodied. It was also the local yokel at your station who introduced the movies, and the banal plugs that always seem to break into a film just when you get hooked.

All the performers were supposed to be involved in writing material, but some were more prolific than others. Flaherty was a workhorse and an ideas man. Candy did not like to write, and would do anything to put off writing. Yet he was the one who came up with the idea (used in the opening montage) of heaving TV sets out an apartment window. And some observers could tell very early on that Candy was destined to become an audience favourite and was the best bet to break through to stardom.

"Joe was a better actor," says Sahlins, "but he hid behind his characters. John Candy took the limelight, as did Andrea Martin, because his vulnerability was right out there, and no matter what character he was playing, he was always John Candy. The audience knew who he was and loved him and responded to that vulnerability."

Candy made a specialty of spoofing hefty male celebrities including Orson Welles, Jackie Gleason, Babe Ruth and Luciano Pavarotti. In one episode, Candy played a role that was deliciously right for him—Elvis Presley in his obese Las Vegas phase. But the sketch had to be dropped when Elvis suddenly died before it could be aired.

Candy also created certain regular characters, such as Melonville's pipe-smoking Mayor Tommy Shanks, the near-sighted, formally attired Peter Lorre lookalike Dr. Tongue and a sleazy huckster by the name of Harry who would paint snakes on his face or wear a satellite dish on his head to promote his products. But none was as cherished by viewers as Candy's Johnny LaRue—who could always be counted on to let his nasty habits and bad temper come out.

George Bloomfield, who was brought in as director after the first season, says that Candy was the "grand master" of the group. "He had an instinct that everyone in the group trusted. He wasn't the most prolific writer, and there were others who brought more brain power and analysis to the material. His special talent was for what he could do in lifting something off the page. He could take something that didn't seem that funny when you read it and turn it into something hilarious. He was the most predictably unpredictable member of the cast.

"John would always extend a sketch beyond what you

anticipated, and I got into the habit of telling the cameramen not to stop when I called 'cut' because so often John would do something brilliant after he thought the scene was over. My credo was that if I laughed it was funny, and if I didn't laugh it wasn't funny. Sometimes John made me laugh so hard I would go home in pain. Once I fell off a chair backward because of what he did when he was playing the Incredible Hulk."

Wearing a deliciously tacky slime green monster suit, this Hulk grunts while Andrea Martin, playing a shrink named Cheryl Kinsey, says:

"I'm not going to be able to help you unless you tell me a bit about yourself."

In a ferocious rampage, the Hulk throws her paintings, plants and filing cabinet out the window. After she gives an interpretation of his hostile behaviour, the Hulk throws Cheryl out the window, too.

Historically, the Chicago Second City had a reputation for cerebral, literary humour, but it was only occasionally that "SCTV"—influenced by Flaherty—slipped in a Chekhov skit on Masterpiece Theatre or a vaudeville version of Molly Bloom from *Ulysses*. More typically the show zeroed in on the low-brow vulgarity of TV itself. Certainly that was the turf on which Candy, who was sharp-witted but not intellectual, felt most comfortable.

Watching the show, you got the sense that the performers were not playing down to the audience but felt a natural affinity for the medium in which they were working. Mind you, the SCTV gang weren't accepting, uncritical boob-victims; they were genuinely steeped in TV's hype, its images, its rhythms, its vocabulary, its idioms. Their jokes naturally assumed a pop frame of reference, encompassing old B-movies, used-car hucksters and self-promoting celebrities. This was not the kind of satire intended to improve the world; rather, it was a celebration, mocking and loving at the same time, of the most insane excesses in a media-stoned world. At its highest level, "SCTV" achieved a wacky surrealism.

The satire was so good-natured it was hard to get offended on behalf of any of its targets, but several early sketches caused trouble. The B'Nai B'rith's Anti-Defamation League was not amused by "Match Unto My Feet," a spoof of a Sunday-afternoon series on Jewish topics. There were also complaints about a "Sunrise Semester" episode on which Andrea Martin delivered a guideline for women on how to fake orgasms. And a skit about vasectomy was dropped from the U.S. version.

The show included itself on its list of fair-game satiric targets. In one of the standing film clips that introduced the show every week, the show's regular performers were seen taking their hot idea for a TV series to top programmers at NBC, CBS and ABC—and, in escalating slapstick episodes, they get the boot at each of the big networks. As a last resort, they start their own network—SCTV.

This was not so far from the truth. Though "SCTV" in its early years had a small and devoted following, it was inevitably compared to "Saturday Night Live." Connoisseurs might recognize "SCTV" as the superior show—one of the greatest achievements in the history of television comedy, on a par with "Your Show of Shows" in its salad days. Yet "SNL" was a hot show and "SCTV" was not. It remained that little underground show from Canada that hadn't been given a tumble by any of the major networks. When Freddie Silverman, a celebrated U.S. network programming czar, dismissed it as "far too intelligent," the backhanded compliment sounded to some ears like a death knell.

$\mathcal{P}$rior to the arrival of Bloomfield, "SCTV" was directed by Milad Besada, who was on the Global staff. There were some major accomplishments that first season, but in bringing on Bloomfield the idea was to improve the show by involving someone who had a track record in weekly television drama and comedy shows. Bloomfield had worked with Jim Henson of the Muppets, and had been a guest director on "King of Kensington." He had also done many CBC dramas, and had worked with some of the SCTV performers on other projects.

The members of the cast were comfortable with Bloomfield and they didn't even seem to mind that he was getting paid much better than they were. In making his deal with Andrew Alexander, Bloomfield set stiff conditions and basically put

Alexander in a take-it-or-leave-it situation.

During the period Bloomfield was directing the show, it was routine to tape three half-hour shows a week. The shows were taped at the Global studio outside Toronto after rehearsals in a hall near the Firehall. During the writing phase, the troupe would be closeted with one another, and Bloomfield would be marginally involved. Often he would see sketches on paper and find them not so funny—only to discover later that in execution, the material became hilarious.

Bloomfield's ambition was to develop a career as a movie director, and he regarded "SCTV" as a temporary diversion. But when the SCTV group began to do parodies of movies such as *Grapes of Wrath* it provided a delicious challenge for Bloomfield. It gave him a chance to be a stylist instead of a technician and traffic cop.

At the end of Bloomfield's first thirteen-episode season, both Harold Ramis and Sheldon Patinkin left "SCTV." According to Patinkin, the tension within the show was oppressive. "There was friction between everybody and everybody. It was more conflict than I cared to deal with. There was a lot of anger and competition. Not that we didn't like each other, but it just got too competitive. Gruelling fifteen- or sixteen-hour days were routine, and it wore people down."

Ramis got a head start in the inevitable defection of SCTV members to Hollywood. Ramis—the guy with the sweet smile and the Harold Lloyd glasses who played the owner of the SCTV station—got an offer he couldn't refuse from Ivan Reitman, the toothy hustler from Hamilton who was on the verge of becoming one of Hollywood's most successful producers. Ramis was one of the screen writers for *Animal House*, which turned into the runaway hit of the 1978 movie crop. Though he continued to work as a part-time writer and occasional guest star for "SCTV," his move to Hollywood was permanent. There he would became a kind of godfather for his old SCTV colleagues, getting them involved in such movies as *Stripes*, *National Lampoon's Vacation* and *Club Paradise*.

While George Bloomfield was working on "SCTV," he began what became an ongoing friendship with John Candy.

Early on, Bloomfield became aware that in Candy, he was deal-ing with someone who had opened himself in a trusting way.

"He wanted to improve," recalls Bloomfield. "Because I had come from the world of drama and his focus was comedy, he welcomed the coming together. His approach to comedy was character. I could see he was very inventive. That came out of something in his nature. On a personal level, John's generosity was striking. When he threw a party it was not just hot dogs. There would be some people from work there, and then there would be a whole pile of other people who had nothing do with show business."

Bloomfield soon met Rosemary Hobor and came to the con-clusion that she was exactly the right woman for Candy. "He was drawn to real people rather than the showbiz crowd. That's where he would get his ideas and characters...people walking through the malls. Rose was an earth mother. She was a potter, and he was proud of the work she did. For him it was a plus that she had nothing to do with the entertainment business."

Candy took a childlike joy in spending his money. For a while Candy fixed up old Mustangs. Then as soon as he could afford it, he bought an eight-year-old Jaguar which he proudly showed off to his colleagues.

"Whatever John earned he would spend. He was like Johnny LaRue with a cocktail. It never occurred to him to worry about the next job or to think that he might need some of his money for later. On the surface he was a happy-go-lucky guy but he struck me as extremely complicated—someone who felt every-thing very deeply. I could see he was vulnerable, and there was a lot of pain there."

John Candy's pain and anger became most visible in his rela-tionship with Andrew Alexander, and George Bloomfield got a close-up view of it.

"What went on between John and Andrew was sort of a run-ning gag," Bloomfield recalls. "It had to do with the fact that Andrew was making piles of money and these performers weren't. That's the bottom line. They started as kids who had been playing at the Firehall for less than $200 a week. All of a sudden they were in TV where they were making what seemed like a lot. Then after six months they realized they were hardly making scale for TV actors. As the show became bigger and more successful, they wanted something more akin to what they felt they were worth to the show. That didn't happen."

One source of continuing friction was John Candy's discovery that his pay-cheque was smaller than the one Dave Thomas was getting. Someone had told Alexander that Candy, O'Hara and Martin were not writing sketches, and on that basis he paid them slightly less than Ramis, Flaherty and Thomas. Candy took it as evidence that he had been betrayed and was being treated unfairly. This became a grudge that lasted for years and resulted in a lawsuit that Candy eventually launched against Alexander and his partners.

Bloomfield used to hear the cracks the performers would make about Alexander in the hall where the rehearsals were held. Alexander had the only walled office; the rest of the space was open. The SCTV gang used to shout barbed comments that were meant to be heard on the other side of Alexander's office wall.

"The remarks were not subtle. The kids knew they were a hit, and they felt they had some clout. These remarks were humorous but they weren't only humorous."

Candy's comments went further than those of his colleagues, and he became a ringleader in the fight with Alexander. Because he had more movie offers, he seemed to be in a stronger position, and there was a sense that he was fighting on behalf of others as well as himself. When Alexander asked the performers to sign away future royalties for what seemed like a very modest sum, the others complied but Candy balked. This drama was incorporated into an episode of the show when Guy Caballero, the bullying president of the station played by Joe Flaherty, tries to force Johnny LaRue to sign some documents and a tearful LaRue resists the pressure.

According to Bloomfield, it was possible to see Candy's behaviour as self-destructive, given that Alexander was his employer. And the breach was about to become public. At the end of the third season, Global abruptly pulled the plug on "SCTV." Alexander made another deal which involved producing the show in Edmonton. Candy bowed out.

He was spending more time in Hollywood where he seemed on the brink of a movie career. Candy was so eager for work he had even gone to Edmonton to appear in a TV movie about a boy and his dog, produced by Jon Slan for NBC. Candy had only a small role in *Kavic the Wolf Dog*, as Pinky the gas station attendant, but audiences began to laugh as soon as they saw him. For years afterward, Slan would tease Candy by asking him why *Kavic the Wolf Dog* never appeared on Candy's résumé.

When Candy returned to weekly TV comedy, more than a year after defecting from "SCTV," it would be to front a show that was in direct competition with his former colleagues.

# Chapter 7

# AT LARGE

*B*y the spring of 1979, "SCTV" had earned enough of a following that John Candy and the other performers were in a strong position to demand much higher fees than they had been getting. At the same time, more money was needed to enhance the production values of the show. But Andrew Alexander was unable to negotiate an acceptable budget increase with the Global network, and in one of the most questionable decisions in the history of Canadian TV, Global decided not to pick up "SCTV" for the 1979-80 season. Many people in the broadcasting industry and the media believed this turn of events spelled the end of "SCTV," though Alexander was working hard to find a new partner and get the show back on the air.

To some members of the cast, the apparent demise of "SCTV" must have seemed like a catastrophe, but for Candy—who was already looking forward to a film career in Hollywood—it presented an opportunity to try his wings. More than any of his cohorts Candy was regarded by insiders as a movie star of the future, and if his big-screen breakthrough was imminent, then perhaps putting "SCTV" behind him wouldn't be a bad idea.

Although "SCTV" would eventually have a reincarnation and Candy would return to the show within two years, in 1979 both those developments seemed highly unlikely. In the meantime,

Candy would discover that landing roles in high-profile movies was one thing, but getting the chance to make any impact in them was quite another.

In 1978 Candy appeared in one of the rare Canadian-produced movies to reach an audience outside Canada. *The Silent Partner*, directed by the gifted Vancouver film-maker Daryl Duke, was a nifty thriller starring Christopher Plummer as a flamboyant crook with a taste for dressing up as Santa Claus, and Elliott Gould as a bank executive who gets drawn into his scheme. (Candy's friend Stephen Levy, who under the name Stephen Young had acted alongside him in *The Clown Murders*, was one of the producers of *The Silent Partner*.)

Toronto's Eaton Centre—a kind of contemporary clone of Milan's Galleria—provided a sleek setting. And the movie earned good reviews and several Canadian Film Awards. But Candy was stuck in the minor role of a polite, reliable bank clerk. The movie offered no chance at all for Candy to show off his penchant for creative wackiness; he played his part conscientiously, as if vying for a good citizenship award.

The next year Candy appeared in *Lost and Found*, a Hollywood comedy directed by veteran writer-director Melvin Frank and filmed mostly in Canada. It wasn't as good a film as *The Silent Partner*, but it made better use of Candy. Toronto had become a favourite location for U.S. producers seeking lower costs along with good crews and technical facilities. Usually the stars of the movie would be American but for minor roles, local actors would be cast.

There were reasons for Toronto actors to be ambivalent about the opportunity this development afforded. On the one hand, it was possible to make more money doing an easy job for a few days than you might earn for playing a hugely demanding role on a Toronto stage for two months. On the other hand, there was something demeaning about an environment in which the greatest of all possible rewards went to whoever was chosen to play, say, Mary Tyler Moore's best friend.

*Lost and Found*—a wisecracking romantic comedy that reteamed Glenda Jackson and George Segal after their success with *A Touch of Class*—provided work for a number of Toronto actors including Barbara Hamilton, Hollis McLaren and Sandy Webster. For most of them, this brush with Hollywood was merely a passing windfall. But for John Candy it was more like a rite of passage along the way to the eventual Hollywood stardom that he and his fans felt certain was his due.

Candy's role in *Lost and Found* is small, but it does demonstrate his gift for comedy. Though Candy was still in his twenties, Melvin Frank cast him as a fifty-five-year-old French used-car salesman. As Candy recalled a decade later in a TV interview with Brian Linehan, at their first meeting Frank leapt across the room, grabbed Candy's cheek and said: "I love this baby fat. How do we age this baby fat?"

Candy had to grow a beard and dye his hair black. (To his embarrassment, before returning to its natural colour his hair turned purple.) The plot has Segal and Jackson meeting in hospital after almost killing each other on the highway in the French Alps. Candy is obliged to inform Segal that the letter Jackson has written in French—supposedly admitting her culpability in the mishap—actually says quite the opposite.

It's just a tiny scene, but Candy's witty sensibility peeks out of it. Years later, he would joke about how unconvincing he was as a middle-aged Frenchman, but unlike most of the other movies Candy had appeared in, *Lost and Found* offered a glimmer of his comic talent.

The word was getting out that John Candy was someone to watch. The SCTV group spent some time in Los Angeles in the spring of 1978 in order to work on scripts with Harold Ramis for what turned out to be the show's third and final year on Global. When they finished writing shows for their next season, the group gave a huge celebration party. Hundreds of guests turned up—including Steven Spielberg.

*Jaws* and *Close Encounters of the Third Kind* had already made Spielberg the hottest young director in town. His next picture, *1941*, was to be a partly satiric look at the hysteria that engulfed L.A. after the Japanese bombing of Pearl Harbor, and he was in the process of casting it.

The party was full of aspiring actors who would have given

anything for a chance to work with Spielberg, but Candy was the one Spielberg approached with the suggestion there might be a role for him. Candy didn't take the offer seriously.

"I was under the influence of a lot of rum and coke," Candy explained afterward. "I said, 'I appreciate your interest but I know this is a party, and we've all been drinking.'"

Then Candy looked around the room, full of fawning wannabes, and advised Spielberg: "Anyway, there are any number of leeches around here who want the job more than I do."

To Candy's surprise, when he returned to Toronto, there was a follow-up call from Columbia Pictures officially offering him a role in *1941*. It made a strong impression on Candy's SCTV cohorts that he was being courted by Hollywood's reigning new genius.

In his chat with Candy, Spielberg described the project—a period comedy written by Robert Zemeckis and Bob Gale and conceived on an epic scale—as a cross between Stanley Kramer's *It's a Mad Mad Mad Mad World* and Robert Altman's *A Wedding*. Given Candy's strengths, the comic ambition of the film must have been tantalizing. So was the prospect that, playing one of the frantic young men in uniform, he would be in the company of such rising stars as Dan Aykroyd, John Belushi and Tim Matheson.

Watching the film that finally arrived on the big screen, it's hard to believe Candy spent every day for more than half a year turning up for work on *1941*. The film has too many stories intertwined, and Spielberg's method was to film much more material than he could use and then hope to impose a shape on it in the editing room. Most of what Candy did wound up on the cutting-room floor, and what's left (less than ten minutes of screen time) is not especially funny. The most Candy gets to do is deliver such lines as: "You see the mess in the streets? Well, I'm not taking the rap for that."

The film's release was delayed by re-editing, and there was so much gossip about *1941*'s problems that by the time it opened, the media were gunning for it. The reaction could be summed up as "You see the mess on the screen? Well, Steven Spielberg is going to have to take the rap for that."

And so *1941* turned out to be the first big slip on a banana peel in Spielberg's career—though it was far more imaginative and engaging a film than that suggests. Spielberg's miniature re-creation of Hollywood Boulevard at night was truly memorable, and there was a great buzz of energy to the USO jitterbug number he staged (with Candy's buddy Joe Flaherty used effectively as the bandleader).

But the movie was accused of being obscenely overproduced (the costs climbed steadily to the then astronomical figure of $40 million) on the one hand and racist on the other. It became that rarity, a Spielberg film that failed commercially. And for Candy, who had hoped this movie was going to be his ticket to stardom, *1941* turned out to be a long, aimless ride to nowhere in particular.

He had a good experience making it, meeting a lot of stimulating people and learning a lot about Hollywood, but later he decided something had gone awry in the editing, and what reached the screen was not the movie Candy thought they had been making. Yet even if he was critical, he resented the way the movie was being dismissed.

"I think people reviewed the price tag," he observed. "The underlying attitude seemed to be, 'You wasteful kids, look at what you're spending!'"

When the picture opened in the fall of 1979, Candy was so depressed by its hostile reception that, he later revealed, he didn't go out for a week.

*O*n a personal level, 1979 had been a good year. In April, after a courtship that had lasted most of the decade, John Candy married Rosemary Margaret Hobor at St. Basil's Roman Catholic Church in midtown Toronto.

The woman he called Rosie and everyone else called Rose was regarded by many of their friends as a stabilizing influence and an anchor—quiet, sane, patient. And she was undazzled by showbiz glitter.

As recalled by Second City founder Bernie Sahlins, the wedding had certain resemblances to a Second City sketch.

"When John lived in Chicago he'd met a hippie designer lady," recalls Sahlins. "He decided she should make his wedding suit. I don't think she had ever made a suit before."

Sahlins and his wife, Jane, who were about to travel from Chicago to Toronto for the wedding, got a call from the groom asking if they would bring his suit.

Sahlins asked: "John, you mean you haven't tried it on?"

"Oh no," said Candy. "Don't worry. It will be fine."

On the morning of the wedding, Bernie and Jane Sahlins dropped by Candy's house on Avenue Road just north of Eglinton. (John and Rose had lived there since 1976, and the house had a long Second City association; Eugene Levy and Martin Short were among its former tenants.) Sahlins rang the bell but nobody answered. The door was open, so he and his wife walked in and left the suit.

"John came to the wedding in this thing," giggles Sahlins. "It looked as if it had been made out of sacking. We were sitting in the church next to Sheldon Patinkin, who used to live in the same house as John and Rose. As Rose was coming down the aisle, she said to Sheldon, 'Any mail for us?' During the ceremony when Rose was asked 'Do you take this man?' there was a long pause. It was very funny."

Despite the disappointment of *1941*, Candy was more determined than ever to take Hollywood by storm. It was clear he was going to need some expert help. Candy discussed strategy with Catherine McCartney, who was one of his closest friends as well as his agent and then his manager. They came to the conclusion that Candy needed a manager in Los Angeles, and she recommended Bernie Brillstein.

Candy had a meeting with Brillstein, but he was afraid of getting lost in the shuffle because Brillstein had so many other clients. Shortly after that, Garry Blye got a call from McCartney. Blye was a Canadian in Hollywood who had worked with Brillstein and had also known McCartney and Candy for years. He had been involved on the production side of "The David Steinberg Show," on which Candy had played a continuing role. Although Blye had worked in the past as an agent and manager, by this time he had moved into production. But McCartney persuaded Blye to take on managing Candy, because he needed special handling.

"John Candy was like a man on a train that was clearly going somewhere," Blye recalls. "At the end of every project, he always had the sense that there was something better just around the corner, and he was in a rush to get to it. He wouldn't spend more than a week without work of some kind."

During the making of *1941*, Candy made plans with Spielberg to develop other projects together, but after the film's disappointing reception, those plans were dropped, and they never worked together again. (However, at the time of Candy's death, he had agreed to appear in a Spielberg film.)

Candy was offered a major role in the next film by *1941*'s writers, Zemeckis and Gale. *Used Cars*, a screwball comedy about mendacity and crookedness in middle America, was directed by Zemeckis and produced by Gale, and it's one of the more entertaining studio movies of its period. But Candy felt it wasn't right for him. (Years later Zemeckis would make the Oscar-winning hit *Forrest Gump*.)

Instead Candy accepted a role backing up Aykroyd and Belushi in *The Blues Brothers*, conceived as a new style of musical combined with slapstick comedy based on sketch material that Aykroyd and Belushi used to do on "Saturday Night Live." The sketches, which evolved from Belushi's fond fascination with old-time blues musicians, featured Belushi as Jake Blues and Aykroyd as his brother, Elwood. Both looked like mobsters, in sunglasses and black suits, and worked hard at being hip.

As directed by John Landis, *The Blues Brothers* has a lot in common with *1941*, being a hugely expensive, overproduced demolition derby hurtling along with cartoonish frenzy. The story has this super-cool rhythm-and-blues duo chasing all over Chicago to round up their band so they can raise money to pay the taxes and save the orphanage where they were raised. Along the way they run into Aretha Franklin, Ray Charles, Cab Calloway, James Brown and John Lee Hooker—who get a chance to show why they are legendary performers.

Yet the film-makers wind up treating all these great musicians as if they were strictly also-rans compared to Belushi and Aykroyd. The audience might well wonder why, considering how little musical aptitude these two dudes demonstrate. Cast as a hash-house waitress, the great Aretha just about blows everyone else off the screen when she sings "Think." But afterward she simply disappears from the movie without explanation—as if the producers had no idea how electrifying her presence was.

As had happened the previous year on *1941*, Candy wound up spending months working on a movie in which he barely seemed to exist, apart from kicking in a door and running into a truck. Candy plays a parole officer who pursues the heroes all over the state of Illinois. Once again Candy's scenes ended up on the cutting-room floor. Still, there was one major difference between *1941* and this movie. Despite less than glowing reviews, *The Blues Brothers* turned out to be a huge hit. For a change, Candy was associated with a box-office winner, which was bound to boost his career even if the movie wasted his talent.

*C*andy had been spending so much time in L.A. that he had rented a house in Sherman Oaks. While he was in Chicago doing *The Blues Brothers*, he sublet it to Blye. When Candy returned to L.A. after finishing the film, "SCTV" was still in limbo. But whether or not the show would ever go back into production, there was still a struggle about royalty payments to the writer/performers for reruns.

Blye had attended a meeting at which Candy—who was more aggressive than his colleagues about pressing Andrew Alexander for money he thought was owed him—appealed to the other performers to take a united stand so they could all get a fair deal.

Candy had been set to star in a Canadian movie in the fall of 1979. *At Large*, which was to have been directed by Rex Bromfield (brother of Candy's friend Valri) was a comedy about a society in which being overweight is against the law. Candy was cast as the rebel hero who is sent to a fat farm, and escapes. The Toronto producer Peter O'Brian (who later made *The Grey Fox* and *My American Cousin*) had the support of Telefilm Canada, and—this being the era of tax-shelter incentives in the Canadian film industry—had lined up private investors. O'Brian had paid Candy a fee to guarantee his availability.

Both Candy and O'Brian had married that spring, and they happened to be neighbours, so the two couples even got together for a barbecue in O'Brian's backyard during which both men enthused about their impending project. But in September, O'Brian learned that a crucial piece of the financing had been withdrawn, and he was unable to replace it. As a result, when Candy finished filming *The Blues Brothers*, he was truly at large.

However, Candy was full of ideas for a new TV comedy project. He and Joe Flaherty (who was listed as Joseph P. Flaherty in the credits of *1941* and *Used Cars*) had cooked up the idea of doing a satiric show from the floor of the U.S. political conventions in the summer of 1980. Blye got involved in negotiations with Viacom, but according to Blye, the idea had a bit too much edge for the Viacom executives, and they backed away from it.

Instead Candy was drafted to star in a new comedy show involving his former Second City mentor, Bernie Sahlins. Sahlins was in partnership on this venture with NBC and a producing company owned by the family of Donny and Marie Osmond, which had a vast TV production facility in Utah, of all places, and not a whole lot to produce in it.

According to Toby Roberts, who was then president of the Osmond organization, there was an opportunity to provide a half-hour comedy show to be shown on NBC's five owned-and-operated stations in an early-evening time slot before network prime time. (In other markets, the show would be sold to independent stations.) Several performers from the Chicago Second City company had been lined up, including Ann Ryerson, Tino Insana, Tim Kazurinsky and Audrie Neenan. But the show needed a host. It was Sahlins who suggested Candy.

Perry Rosemond, who had hired Candy for "The David Steinberg Show" a few years earlier, got a call from Carolyn Raskin, an NBC executive he had worked with, inviting him to go to Utah to direct the pilot.

"Carolyn and Bernie recognized the success of 'SCTV,'" recalls Rosemond, "and they thought they could develop another hit show using some of the Chicago-based performers. I remember there was a bit of a rift between the Toronto branch of Second City and the Chicago branch. The producers of 'SCTV' took the position that when John left the show, he couldn't take the characters he created for 'SCTV' with him; those remained the property of 'SCTV.' So for the new show he had to come up with different characters."

That's why a clone of Johnny LaRue was named Johnny Toronto (the nickname Candy had been given by his Second City friends in Chicago in 1973).

For some performers, according to Rosemond, there are inherent problems in making the transition from the stage, because they can't stylize on TV, and they can't improvise on TV. "John had the rare gift of lifting material off the page. He had progressed from being a sketch comedian to developing real acting skills."

The group assembled in Provo, Utah, in late 1979, and Rosemond recalls that while the pilot was in pre-production the mandate changed. Instead of doing a single one-hour show, he produced three half-hours.

By early 1980, the quarrel between Candy and Alexander—over royalty payments—was becoming more public. Alexander was working on plans to get "SCTV" back on the air, but Candy told Sid Adilman of the *Toronto Star* that he had no intention of being part of it.

On the contrary, he was looking forward to being the host of the new comedy series, which would be called "Big City Comedy," thus avoiding any battle with Alexander over use of the Second City name. NBC executives had committed to a series of thirteen half-hours of "Big City Comedy" to go on the air in the fall of 1980.

Candy was afraid the competition between Alexander's show and "Big City" could be destructive. "It certainly hurts friendships," he told Adilman. "Everyone could suffer."

Candy had not enjoyed being marooned in Utah, where there was nothing to do but look at the mountains, and he would not have been pleased if the whole "Big City" series had been taped there. At one point there was talk of doing the show at the NBC studios in Burbank. But in the end the Osmonds made a deal with CTV, and the shows were produced during the summer of 1980 at CFTO, the network's flagship station, just outside Toronto.

That same summer, "SCTV" got back into production after Andrew Alexander accepted an offer from the Allards, whose family broadcasting business, ITV, was based in Edmonton. The Allards became the show's principal investor, and "SCTV" was produced in their studios in Edmonton. In the absence of Candy and Catherine O'Hara (who also left the show and later returned) the performing ranks were temporarily shored up by Tony Rosato and Robin Duke. During the 1980/81 TV season, "SCTV" and "Big City Comedy" were competing half-hour shows in the syndication market.

On "Big City Comedy," Candy was being paid better than he ever had been on "SCTV," and he was being showcased as the star/host rather than being just one of an ensemble group. But brilliant as he was, his name was not yet big enough to draw a mass audience. That was one reason each week's show had a guest star. Among them were Rita Moreno, Jimmy Walker, McLean Stevenson, Conrad Bain, Betty White and Billy Crystal.

According to Carolyn Raskin, there was never enough money to do the show the way it should have been done. Candy was often frustrated because he would come up with great creative ideas—and then be given the reason why the show couldn't afford to do them.

The quality of the sketches was uneven, and none of the other regular performers made much impact. But Candy was at the top of his form and did some of his best work. He exuded energy and confidence. He also looked great. And the week that Betty White was the guest star, there was a glimpse of why the summer of 1980 might have been an unusually happy time in Candy's life.

Jennifer Candy, who was only a few months old, made her TV debut in the arms of her father and under the gaze of Betty White. The premise of her appearance was that Rose Candy had some errands to do and had asked John to look after Jennifer for a while. Probably Candy was so full of paternal pride he couldn't resist introducing the audience to his wonder child.

Unlike "SCTV," which has been in perpetual rerun for

years, the tapes of "Big City Comedy" sit unwatched in the archives. That's a shame, because the show boasts some classic Candy sketches.

In one of the most hilarious, Candy impersonates Orson Welles in a black suit and grey beard, regally dining alone at a formal restaurant until he is joined by an unwelcome guest— Billy Crystal as an insufferable autograph hound known only as Willie.

Later in his career, Candy would become extremely touchy about fat jokes, but here he seems to relish it when Crystal/ Willie tells Candy/Welles he looks even fatter in person than he does on TV, and compares him to Shamu the Killer Whale.

"Willie, you are the most ignorant man I have ever encountered," sniffs the autocratic Orson. "Be gone. You're taking up my valuable air."

But when Willie asks for his autograph, Orson is only too happy to comply. Willie is perplexed when he examines it. It seems he thought he was talking to Raymond Burr.

On one episode the guest star is not an American entertainer but Margaret Trudeau, estranged wife of Canada's prime minister at that time. Ms. Trudeau had begun working as an interviewer on a daytime Ottawa TV show, and in one of her sketches with Candy, she demonstrates her killer journalistic techniques.

We see her being perfectly sweet to her guest before they go on the air. Candy says he feels vulnerable and uncomfortable; she tells him not to worry, they're friends. Then they go on the air and she turns into an assassin. When he gets out of answering a question by saying he's forgotten because he had a couple of martinis, she zeroes in for the kill: "How often do you have these alcoholic blackouts, Mr. Candy?"

As he whimpers and recoils into a fetal position, she keeps up the abuse, alluding to his "wild night life" and "druggy friends."

"You promised me this would be off the record," he squeals, by now reduced to a quivering wreck.

If you watch this sketch years later, what's striking is how dangerously close to home Candy was willing to go for the sake of good material.

Unfortunately, these memorable satiric high points weren't enough to keep "Big City Comedy" on the air. The public was hardly aware of the show's existence and barely had time to discover it before it had run its thirteen weeks and expired. "Big City Comedy" had too many strikes against it—including the fact that its material was more suited to late-night than to the early-evening time slot it actually had in most markets.

Candy was rattled by "Big City's" demise. He remarked ruefully that a lot of promises had been made to him, and few of them had been kept. "It was the old story with the old excuses," he said wearily. "I learned a few things—don't go near certain people, and never pay attention to verbal agreements."

Once again, fame and success had seemed tantalizingly close, only to be snatched away at the crucial moment.

# Chapter 8

# IT CAME FROM EDMONTON

*I*n *Stripes*, a 1981 Hollywood comedy about U.S. Army dunderheads who accidentally turn into great national heroes, John Candy landed the best role of his movie career up to that time. As an oversize recruit named Dewey Oxberger, known as Ox to his buddies, Candy drew laughs just by waddling across the screen.

There's a bit of autobiographical truth to Candy's lines when Ox tells the other recruits why he decided to enlist.

"You might have noticed," he remarks sarcastically, "I have a bit of a weight problem."

Then he gets a determined look on his face and vows: "I'm going to walk out of here a lean, mean fighting machine."

Candy couldn't help remembering his own experience when at age eighteen he had been rejected by the U.S. Marines.

*Stripes* gave Candy a chance to play out on celluloid his own old chubby teen fantasy of macho redemption, and at the same time to be reunited with an old Chicago Second City friend, Bill Murray, and a former SCTV cohort, Harold Ramis.

Murray and Ramis were co-starring in this comedy concocted by Canadian expatriate Ivan Reitman, the scrawny boy mogul from Hamilton's McMaster University who had already become one of Hollywood's wealthiest producers thanks to *Animal House*, and still had his biggest success, *Ghostbusters*, ahead of him. The same summer *Stripes* was playing, another film produced by Reitman went into release.

*Heavy Metal,* a Canadian production directed by National Film Board veteran Gerald Potterton, was a full-length animation feature based on the monthly magazine. It featured an anthology of hip sci-fi stories, rock music and the speaking voices of well-known actors. The episodes are of highly variable quality, but John Candy was involved in two of the funniest. First he plays a deprived suburban teenager who finds sexual opportunity on another planet. And then he's hilarious as a squeaky-voiced robot having a wild affair with a voluptuous human, female and Jewish, who resists his proposal on the grounds that mixed marriages never work.

Reitman took on the job of directing *Stripes* as well as producing it, with a script by Reitman's long-time collaborator, Dan Goldberg, and Goldberg's partner, Len Blum. Shrewdly, Reitman gave the film the feeling of a Second City escapade not only by casting Bill Murray, Harold Ramis and John Candy but also by including entertaining cameo turns by Dave Thomas and Joe Flaherty.

Thomas plays the ringmaster of a porn mud-wrestling attraction, and Flaherty is one of the thick-headed Russian guards outsmarted by Murray and Ramis.

At the beginning of the film, there's a scene about a basic-English class for immigrants that has the stamp of a Second City sketch. Though it lasts for less than a minute, it helps set the tone of the movie—which is wittier than previous Reitman movies like *Meatballs.* The Second City touches save Reitman's comedy from seeming mindlessly boorish.

Bill Murray's droopy eyes, vacant expression and delayed reactions add up to an out-of-it quality that helped make *Meatballs* a hit. In *Stripes,* the role of John Winger is tailored to Murray's narcoleptic manner. Winger is a drifter whose life is such a shambles that he joins the army out of panic and for lack of anything better to do. Murray plays the part with the kind of charm that is so laid back it almost lapses into a coma.

With glasses that seem too old and wise for his baby face and a mild, good-boy demeanour that is played off against the hidden streak of lunacy in his personality, Harold Ramis has more than a fleeting resemblance to that earlier Harold, legendary silent comedian Harold Lloyd. But silence would not become Ramis; verbal stings are his secret weapon. In *Stripes* Ramis does for Bill Murray what Bob Hope used to do for Bing Crosby in *Road to Zanzibar* and the other *Road* movies in an earlier movie era; he provides the crackle that saves lazy charm from becoming limp.

Candy's role is secondary to those of the two stars, but nobody who saw *Stripes* could forget he was in it. It would prove to be a valuable advertisement of his potential for big screen comedy. Yet the making of *Stripes* was an agonizing experience for Candy. In fact, when he first read the script he was reluctant to do it—as was Bill Murray.

"The original character didn't look like much," Candy explained to the *Toronto Star*'s Ron Base. "But Ivan said we could change it and I could do some writing. Everything fell together and we realized it could be a lot of fun."

However, filming sequences in which Ox kept falling into mud—both in the field and in a bar where he competes against six women in a wrestling match—were anything but fun for Candy. He found the experience so painful that some of Candy's Toronto friends received late-night calls from him.

"He was very worried about the character he was playing, and questioned what he was doing," recalls George Bloomfield. "He wondered whether he was doing the right thing by participating in the mud-wrestling scene. He was afraid it might make him come across as a pig in mud. He felt degraded."

Indeed, from the time he first read the script until the week the scene was filmed, Candy campaigned hard to have it changed.

"I was fighting right up to the end to get out of it," he told Ron Base. "It was so painful, and we spent three days doing it. If you're going to mud-wrestle with six women, you want to do it in private. It's somewhat inhibiting when there are three hundred people watching."

Even when *Stripes* was about to be released, and was clearly going to be a hit, Candy felt wounded when he was described as "the elephant" in an unflattering review.

"Jerks like that are obvious," Candy grumbled to a reporter from *People* magazine, referring to the reviewer. "I'm sensitive about my weight. I'm the one who has to look in the mirror, and after a while it begins to eat at you."

Encouraged by his friend John Belushi, who had recently lost forty pounds, Candy said he was hiring an exercise coach to help him do the same. Like Ox, he was determined to turn himself into a lean, mean machine.

Just before *Stripes* opened in hundreds of theatres all across North America, John Candy became the most sought-after free agent in television comedy. He was up for grabs in the spring of 1981, after the failure of "Big City Comedy."

Andrew Alexander was negotiating with NBC to get a spot for "SCTV" in the elusive promised land of network U.S. TV. Meanwhile Candy was getting overtures from "Saturday Night Live"—the show that had made stars of Dan Aykroyd, Gilda Radner, Bill Murray, John Belushi, Chevy Chase and Eddie Murphy.

By this time Candy had parted company with Garry Blye and hired Claire Burrill—a Sunset Boulevard lawyer with a special interest in show business—to sort out his messy business affairs. One of Burrill's mandates was to get rid of people who had previously been involved in managing Candy.

This was to become an oft-repeated motif in Candy's career. He would typically bring in new people to dispose of other people he had formerly put his trust in. Since Candy hated confrontations, he was never the person giving the bad news to those about to be fired. More likely they would learn the axe was about to fall when they heard from third parties that Candy was making stinging comments about them behind their backs.

Burrill became one of the most prominent examples of Candy's capacity for turning against those once trusted, and also of Candy's capacity for seeking reconciliations with those he had cut off. The higher Candy's star rose, the more pronounced this pattern became. In the mid-eighties, Burrill would become one of those Candy decided to purge. But in late 1988, there would be a reconciliation, and Burrill would be brought back to run

Candy's production company—only to be dumped a second time a year later. This sort of reversal became a familiar occurrence in Candy's business life.

In the spring of 1981, Candy counted on Burrill to help him reach a larger audience on TV than he had managed so far. That agenda placed Candy at the centre of a bewildering internal war within NBC.

At one point, NBC was seriously thinking of cancelling "Saturday Night Live" and replacing it with "SCTV." Instead a decision was made to try to resuscitate "Saturday Night," and the show was given a new executive producer—Dick Ebersol. Even before accepting the job, Ebersol had mentioned to Brandon Tartikoff, who was then running NBC, that he was thinking of bringing in some of the performers from "SCTV." Unbeknownst to Ebersol, another NBC executive, Irv Wilson, was about to sign a deal with Andrew Alexander to have "SCTV" fill a late-night Friday spot (following "The Tonight Show" at 12:30 a.m.) which had opened up with the cancellation of "The Midnight Special."

Ebersol was enraged, and tried to enlist the support of Tartikoff to stop Wilson from foiling his plans to raid "SCTV." When word of this battle leaked to the press, reporters began calling Candy to ask whether he was planning to join "Saturday Night" or return to the SCTV fold.

Candy was embarrassed about being in the middle of a controversy, and there was nothing he wanted to do less than face an interrogation by journalists. Media questions made Candy nervous; he brooded about critical comments in the press or cracks about his weight, and in interviews he was nervous lest he say the wrong thing and be made to look like a fool.

The way Candy handled the media curiosity about his discussions with "Saturday Night Live" was to go into seclusion at his family farm near Newmarket, north of Toronto, and refuse to answer the phone.

Candy had heard, along with a lot of other people, that "Saturday Night Live" was a viper's nest compared to which the tensions at "SCTV" seemed as benign as a Sunday picnic in the country. Moreover, the cast of "SNL" was so large that it was harder for any one performer to make a mark. Besides, Candy had a strong sentimental streak, and after the stresses caused by his defection to "Big City," he was eager to be reconciled with his former SCTV colleagues and heal any wounds.

In the end, Candy opted to sort out his differences with Andrew Alexander—which involved royalty payments for previous SCTV shows—and return to "SCTV" now that it was going to be seen on NBC. Alexander found himself in the role of the bad daddy who had been defied and repudiated but was now being offered a chance to acknowledge the true worth of his prodigal son and woo him back.

Contract negotiations were especially tricky because the SCTV stars were writers as well as performers, and the deal was being made while the Writers Guild of America was on strike. Burrill played a key role in sorting out the glitches.

Ebersol settled for signing two other performers—Robin Duke and Tony Rosato—who had been appearing with "SCTV" during the first year of its production in Edmonton.

*P*art of the price of returning to "SCTV" was that Candy, along with his colleagues, would have to spend four months of the year in the showbiz wasteland of central Alberta. But Edmonton proved to be surprisingly conducive to creativity, perhaps because there were few distractions. Everyone was living away from home, occupying a hotel room or a rented house (as in the case of John and Rose Candy) and so there was a stronger need for bonding.

The playing field had changed drastically from the one Candy had known during SCTV's days at Global's Toronto studio three years earlier. Because of the NBC deal the show had a budget (about $475,000 per episode) that would once have been beyond anyone's wildest expectations. But there was also more pressure than there had been previously.

NBC needed a ninety-minute show, which meant sixty-five minutes of sketch material every week. The network preferred certain kinds of material, and parachuted in its own producers to promote its viewpoint. NBC wanted musical groups to appear on "SCTV" (for a while, they did), and also had some strong opinions about the order in which sketches would be scheduled. In NBC's view, skits with drug themes could be counted on to improve ratings, especially if they were placed at the beginning of the program.

"SCTV" had more stars than before—seven. Catherine O'Hara returned to the fold at the same time as Candy, and Rick Moranis, who had been recruited during the absence of Candy and O'Hara, stayed on when they returned. This inevitably led to more rivalry over who was getting the best material and the best time slots.

Facilities and equipment in Edmonton had certain limitations. "SCTV" could never tape on Wednesdays and Saturdays—because those were the nights of televised Edmonton Oilers hockey games. And in this part of the universe, nothing generated more excitement than Wayne Gretzky and the Stanley Cup. This charming bit of inside detail about working conditions in the hinterlands was always good for a chuckle when one of the cast appeared on a talk show in New York or L.A.

In fact, though, production values were better than ever, and the new, more expensive version of "SCTV" set higher standards in such areas as costumes, hair-styling and make-up—giving the performers greater opportunities to go further with their creation of characters.

"The sophistication of the make-up team opened doors for the performers and allowed them to do whatever they wanted to do," explains Jason Shubb, an associate producer brought in by NBC. "People like Beverley Schectman and Judy Cooper Sealy were geniuses in their field. The process was very labour intensive. One of the performers might have to spend four hours a day in the make-up chair, and it was exhausting. But everyone on the show was young and creative, and willing to work extremely hard. We all felt we were breaking new ground."

One of the most triumphant combinations of make-up and costume wizardry with performing brilliance occurred when Candy appeared in drag as Divine. And when Candy played Luciano Pavarotti, he looked as if Pavarotti's face has been super-imposed on his own. There was a gleefully wicked perfectionism to this impersonation—confirming how shameless Pavarotti could be in his rabble-rousing pyrotechnics.

As Candy portrays him, Luciano is in the wings at the Metropolitan Opera, talking to the TV audience while the opera audience is wildly cheering his latest triumph. And what is he doing on TV? A commercial for chewing gum.

"It lights up my mouth," explains this inflated tenor. "The only thing I like in my mouth besides a beautiful aria is a beautiful piece of gum."

Candy's most popular character, Johnny LaRue, returned to the air in better form than ever. In one of the most memorable LaRue sketches, the great publisher, producer and all-around *bon vivant* holds court in pink lounging pyjamas at a Hugh Hefner-style party.

"He's a big man getting bigger all the time," comments Geraldo, played by Joe Flaherty.

As that most obnoxious of all Vegas-style entertainers Bobby Bittman (Eugene Levy) puts it: "This is the side of Johnny everybody loves—the parties, the broads, the booze."

Meanwhile Johnny sits surrounded by bunnies, boasting about his wine cellar, looking down from his penthouse at the common folk and telling Geraldo: "You see all those people down there, Geraldo? They look like bugs. I could squash them if I wanted to."

The CBC, which was carrying a one-hour version of "SCTV" on Fridays (and airing it almost an hour earlier than NBC), had its own requirements, and to that end Thomas and Moranis created those one hundred per cent Canadian dummies, the McKenzie Brothers. The McKenzies were originally intended to fulfil a Canadian-content requirement, but ironically this send-up of thickheadedness in the Great White North became phenomenally popular among U.S. viewers. Mocking the notion that the show wasn't Canadian enough, these parka-wearing, beer-guzzling bumpkins would use their imaginary talk show to discuss such pressing issues as the shortage of parking spaces at doughnut shops. And their ultimate putdown, "Take off, eh?" became a codeword greeting craze among fans of the show.

Thomas and Moranis became almost a separate wing, and

their partnership provoked a rift with others in the group. Moranis was an upstart and the only member of the team who had not come up through the Old Firehall stage show. There was so much friction that at one point Joe Flaherty remarked that if Thomas and Moranis were returning to the show, he wasn't. In fact, Thomas and Moranis left at the end of the 1981-82 season—they made a McKenzie Brothers movie, *Strange Brew*—and so did Catherine O'Hara.

"The problem was Rick and Dave became a team within the show," Flaherty explained at the time. "They wanted more control, they wanted to produce the show, and when they found out they couldn't, they wanted out. Rick was very high strung, and things could get antagonistic. They probably just needed to get away for a while."

If Thomas and Moranis had the McKenzies, John Candy and Eugene Levy developed their own hilarious brothers act. It was while they were in Edmonton that Candy and Levy happened to catch a polka show on a local TV station, out of which came one of their most successful collaborations—the Shmenge Brothers.

Candy remembered that his Yiddish-speaking friend Stephen Young was fond of the word "shmenge," as in his frequent admonition: "Don't be such a shmenge." Candy didn't know what it meant, and he was afraid to ask.

Therein came the name for Yosh and Stan—two irresistibly square immigrant Leutonians who both have monotone speaking voices, prominent facial moles, and a reverence for cabbage rolls. The Shmenge Brothers would prove to be so enduring that Candy (the clarinet-playing Yosh) and Levy (accordion-playing Stan) would bring them back for one farewell hour-long special ("The Last Polka") a couple of years after "SCTV" had ceased productions and gone into reruns.

Even after their reconciliation, Candy continued to regard Andrew Alexander with a suspicious eye. In Candy's view, Alexander did not show enough respect for the many people who were giving everything they had to the show. Throughout his life Candy felt it was his obligation to protect those who were less powerful than himself, and defend them from exploiters.

This ongoing drama reached a crescendo of sorts one night in Edmonton when the crew, after working punishing hours, were offered a meal that was, in Candy's view, not up to the demands of the occasion. Candy expressed this view by hurling a container of Swiss Chalet chicken into a wall.

Candy was by no means alone in his attitude to Alexander, who had a continuing battle with the cast over the slowness of royalty payments. Alexander claimed he had a cash-flow problem even when large sums of money began coming in from NBC. The show's $475,000 budget exceeded the combined fees coming from NBC and the CBC, and Alexander had to pick up the deficit. Of course he knew his big payoff would come later, when the show went into daily syndication—it would make him a multi-millionaire—but in the meantime he was crying poor.

Waiting for cheques to arrive and often hiring lawyers to protect them, the performers enjoyed one big advantage over Alexander. They could score points against him on the air on his own program. Needling Alexander with private jokes that few of their viewers would fully comprehend, they turned him into an ongoing satiric target—specifically in the person of the slippery, blatantly self-serving Guy Caballero, the station president portrayed with gleeful malice by Joe Flaherty.

"There's no question Guy Caballero is an Andrew Alexander figure," says Jason Shubb.

Caballero—a curmudgeon who zips around in a wheelchair—is forever cutting budgets, bullying writers, cancelling shows and stabbing SCTV employees in the back. And in a lengthy sketch that has to be considered startlingly vicious even by SCTV standards, Caballero became a stand-in for the disgraced Hollywood mogul David Begelman, whose cheque-forging was exposed in the book *Indecent Exposure* (and who would later become, like John Candy, a business partner of Bruce McNall).

In the SCTV version, Caballero's cheque-forging goes to hilarious extremes, but the board of SCTV gives him a vote of confidence, and Caballero goes on the air to beg forgiveness from viewers—without offering to give back any of the money.

Of course everyone knew Alexander was no criminal, but because they felt he was using his control of the purse-strings to take unfair advantage of them, the performers took pleasure in trashing him. They didn't expend a lot of energy worrying about whether they were being unfair to him. They were playing a kind of game in which Alexander was the guest of honour at a never-ending celebrity roast. And if his transgressions were outrageously exaggerated for comic effect, the barbs were not entirely without affection.

According to Shubb, the negative feelings some members of the cast had about Alexander were balanced by their recognition that he was a man who made things happen, and who was responsible for giving them the great opportunity they were now enjoying.

"When they were upset with him," says Shubb, "it was in the way you might be upset with a parent."

Because he had been consumed with "SCTV," 1982 was the only year in which Candy did not have a movie coming out, except for *It Came From Hollywood*—a forgettable anthology of clips from amusingly dreadful movies about aliens. Candy was one of the narrators, along with Cheech and Chong, Gilda Radner and Dan Aykroyd. Candy's main contribution was to make jokes putting down that prodigious director of cheap, amateurish movies, Ed Wood. But the jokes seemed every bit as tacky as Wood's movies.

In March, 1982, about a month after production of "SCTV" moved from Edmonton back to Toronto, John Candy got some shocking news from Los Angeles. His friend John Belushi had been found dead of a drug overdose at the Chateau Marmont on Sunset Boulevard in West Hollywood.

As an overweight comedian who had served his apprenticeship at Chicago's Second City club and then graduated from television to movie stardom, Belushi had been a kind of role model for Candy. They were both close friends of Dan Aykroyd. When Belushi visited Toronto in the mid-1970s, performing with the National Lampoon touring show at the El Mocambo club, Candy took Belushi out on the town. Later Candy joined the supporting cast of two movies Belushi and Aykroyd were starring in, *1941* and *The Blues Brothers*.

Beyond that there was a special bond between these two guys who were not only both fat and both funny but were also known and loved for their excesses. Suddenly Belushi's death became a warning sign of the price that might have to be paid for excess.

John Stocker, Candy's friend from the days of CBC children's shows, remembers that Candy was so devastated by Belushi's death that he sank into a black depression, refusing to go out or even talk to anyone on the phone.

Dan Hennessey, another old colleague from "Coming Up Rosie," recalls that when Candy did emerge from seclusion, it was clear what kind of impact Belushi's death had on him.

"It was like a bad Woody Allen joke, and he saw it as a kind of message," says Hennessey. "John knew it was time to go home, clean up and get his career in order."

A few years later, Candy let friends know he was proud of himself for kicking his cocaine habit.

TOP: East York house where John Candy grew up. BOTTOM: 1063 Avenue Road, where John and Rose lived 1976 to 1980.

From the collection of Lawrence Dane

Arnaud Maggs

ABOVE: Cast of "SCTV" in 1979. From left: Eugene Levy, Catherine O'Hara, Andrea Martin, Dave Thomas, John Candy and Joe Flaherty.

OPPOSITE PAGE, TOP: Second City cast, Old Firehall, Toronto, 1974: Eugene Levy, Dan Aykroyd, Gilda Radner, Rosemary Radcliffe and John Candy. BOTTOM: Caricature of John Candy and Lawrence Dane in *Find the Lady*, 1975.

Courtesy of Baton Broadcasting System

Canada Wide

TOP: Cast of "Big City Comedy," 1980: Don Lamont, Patti Oatman, Audrie Neenan, John Candy, Tino Insana.
BOTTOM: Candy and Levy in *Midnight Cowboy* spoof, 1982.

John and Rose Candy, 1982.

T. Szlvkovenyi / The Globe and Mail

Lee Lamonthe / Canada Wide

By permission of Paramount Pictures

By permission of Paramount Pictures

TOP: John Candy in *Summer Rental* (1985). BOTTOM: Candy and Steve Martin in *Planes, Trains and Automobiles* (1987).

OPPOSITE PAGE, TOP: Candy with Andrea Martin, Catherine O'Hara and Eugene Levy at the Firehall, Toronto, 1983. BOTTOM: The Shmenge Brothers, 1984.

ABOVE: Candy with Macaulay Culkin, Jean Kelly and Gaby Hoffman in *Uncle Buck* (1989).

OPPOSITE PAGE, TOP: Toronto Argo owners McNall, Candy and Gretzky, 1991.
BOTTOM: Candy at the Horsehoe Tavern with Blues Brothers Jeff Healey, Larry Thurston, Eddie Floyd, Dan Aykroyd.

Mark O'Neill / Canada Wide

Canada Wide

ABOVE: Candy promotes Genie awards, 1992.

OPPOSITE PAGE, TOP: Candy at CPI show, Skydome, with Dusty Cohl, Bill Ballard and Michael Cohl.
BOTTOM: Candy with Banff Television Festival director Pat Ferns.

Tom Sandler

Joe Bonner / Banff Television Festival

Michael Peake / Canada Wide

John Candy's mother and brother arrive at Toronto church
memorial service, 1994.

# Chapter 9

# GOING BERSERK

*D*uring a hiatus from "SCTV" in the summer of 1982, John Candy returned to Los Angeles to shoot the first Hollywood movie to give him the starring role. It had begun as a script called *Drums Over Malta,* written by several SCTV people. But the movie that was actually released by Universal in the fall of 1983 under the title *Going Berserk* had few traces of *Drums Over Malta,* and it turned out to be one of the most disillusioning experiences of Candy's career.

Candy, Levy and Flaherty were brought to Universal by Montreal producer Pierre David. With fellow SCTV writers Paul Flaherty (Joe's brother) and Paul Belucci, they wrote a spoof roughly patterned after Alfred Hitchcock's *North by Northwest.*

At first executives at Universal waxed enthusiastic about the script for *Drums Over Malta,* but they dragged their feet about proceeding with it, partly because Gene Wilder had made a similar movie called *Hanky Panky.* The next thing Candy and colleagues knew, David Steinberg had been assigned to direct the project, and outside writers had been hired to do a second draft—which, as it turned out, retained almost nothing of their material.

Steinberg was no stranger to the SCTV gang. A fast-talking, ambitious operator from Winnipeg's North End (where he was known as Duddy), Steinberg had studied at the University of Chicago, going through an eclectic series of apprenticeships—

first a young rabbinical student, then a literary scholar sitting at the feet of Philip Roth, then a budding Second City satirist picking up pointers from Elaine May, Barbara Harris and Alan Arkin.

Several members of the SCTV group had worked with Steinberg during his short-lived CTV series. By the late 1970s Steinberg had landed in Hollywood doing stand-up comedy on the one-night touring circuit and then becoming a favoured substitute for Johnny Carson on "The Tonight Show." Now he was determined to build yet another career as a director of Hollywood comedies.

Steinberg liked to think of himself as a kind of godfather, and of the SCTV kids as his Canadian farm team. Candy sometimes stayed at Steinberg's guest house during his California sojourns. And one night in 1979 Steinberg had a kind of family reunion on the CBC's ill-fated late-night talk show, then called "Canada After Dark." Appearing as guest host, he welcomed Catherine O'Hara, Martin Short and Dave Thomas to the show.

What got Andrew Alexander into a flap were press references to *Going Berserk* as an SCTV movie. He thought he had the problem straightened out after he ran into Steinberg at the NBC studio in Burbank and asked him not to encourage such misconceptions. A couple of weeks later Alexander turned on his TV and found Steinberg guest-hosting "The Tonight Show." Asked what he had been doing lately, Steinberg said he'd just finished "a movie with SCTV." Alexander lost his temper.

Steinberg wanted to use other SCTV performers besides the three who appeared in the movie, but several turned him down. Levy wanted to get out of the project but was advised not to break his contract. Steinberg kept promising there would be changes but Flaherty, for one, became more and more disenchanted as shooting progressed.

"David is very smart, and he loves the idea of being a director," said Flaherty. "He keeps talking about the shot and the location. We kept saying, 'Yeah, but what about the content?'"

*Going Berserk* was an especially painful experience for Candy because he had by far the largest role. Afterward he described it as a learning experience, because it taught him what not to do when making a movie.

For all his talk about the shot and the location, Steinberg would seem to be, judging by the movie that reached the screen, somewhat lacking in the instincts that Sergei Eisenstein called "the film sense." The craftsmanship of *Going Berserk* is poor; the film is so ineptly shot that Candy, Flaherty and Levy hardly have a chance to get any comedy rhythms going; they are done in by choppy editing. The problem is so fundamental that in any given scene, the camera never seems to be in the right place.

As for the script, it's a bewildering shambles. Candy plays a part-time limousine driver engaged to marry the daughter of a notorious U.S. congressman. Alley Mills plays the bride-to-be and Pat Hingle plays her father, who is trying to destroy a religious aerobics cult (whose leader is played by Richard Libertini). Flaherty plays Candy's partner.

Eugene Levy somehow manages to be entertaining as a sleazy film-maker who also runs a celebrity look-alike service on the side. He shows a few amusing clips from his biggest success, *Kung Fu U*, and he carries around a picture of his wife in the form of a centrefold from a porn magazine.

Candy and Flaherty don't come off as well, though Candy does have a couple of funny moments. In one sequence, a spoofy rehash of the Tony Curtis/Sidney Poitier dilemma in *The Defiant Ones*, Candy is handcuffed to a large black man who happens to be an arsonist and an escaped convict. In his funniest scene, Candy is on one side of a closed door while the man to whom he is handcuffed has athletic sex with a woman on the other side of the door. In another scene, as the drummer for a nightclub dance revue, he fends off a small army of sex-crazed women rampaging onto the stage.

The most original scene in *Going Berserk* could have been lifted straight out of "SCTV." The cult leader tries to brainwash Candy by forcing him to watch an episode of the squarest of all 1950s TV shows, "Father Knows Best." In this version, Jim Anderson (originally played by Robert Young and portrayed here by Flaherty) is a sadist who tricks his children and assaults his wife. (To the delight of nostalgia buffs, Elinor Donahue, who originally played one of the daughters, takes the role of the mother originally played by Jane Wyatt.) In the most surreal touch, reprising one of his classic SCTV sketches, Candy pops up as Beaver Cleaver, blood-spattered in this case.

And blood-spattered was the way Candy felt by the time he was finished making *Going Berserk*. Universal opened the film without press screenings, and it immediately sank like a stone. Looking back at the debacle a few months later, Candy insisted that the original *Drums Over Malta* script was funny even if Universal didn't think so. According to Candy, Universal kept asking for *Porky's* and *Animal House*, though *Drums Over Malta* was not remotely like either of those gross-out youth comedies. With bitter sarcasm, Candy would mimic the Universal executives: "You're TV people. You don't know films yet. And you're Canadian. You'll learn. Norman Jewison has learned."

*The* same year *Going Berserk* was released, Candy had a tiny but delightful cameo in a movie that was more favourably received by the public: *National Lampoon's Vacation*. This was an amiable, episodic road movie directed by Harold Ramis, with Chevy Chase as the upbeat patriarch of a family from a middle-American suburb on a car trip from Chicago to California. Their destination: the Wally World theme park (read Disneyland) outside L.A.

The movie is a relaxed, softheaded social satire, at times aimless and bland but with a number of amusing highlights along the way. John Candy has only a few minutes of screen time, right near the end, but he manages to be wonderfully funny as a nervous security guard at Wally World.

Candy didn't realize it at the time but *National Lampoon's Vacation* was the beginning of one of the most important relationships of his life. The script was written by a fellow from Chicago named John Hughes, who only a few years later would give Candy a role that would change his life, in another comedy about travelling across America—*Planes, Trains and Automobiles*.

Eventually, "SCTV" exacted a kind of revenge for *Going Berserk*. It took the form of a sketch in which various actors who didn't get the part—including Jack Klugman and Stewart Granger—are shown auditioning unsuccessfully for the Paul Newman role in *The Verdict* while the director, Sidney Lumet, looks on. Martin Short does a wicked lampoon of David Steinberg, turning the lawyer in *The Verdict* into a world-class whiner.

Waving his arms, he goes on about how upset he is to have lost his star witness. Then he implores the judge: "Why don't you like me? What did I do to you? I'm charming, I'm cerebral, I dress well." Finally he adds, using a favourite laugh-getting phrase from Steinberg's old comedy routines: "All I have to say to you, judge, is...BUGA BUGA!"

In an aside, Steinberg/Short whispers: "Mr. Lumet, I couldn't resist adding that last line. I really do think it will play." Which was no doubt what Steinberg said on the set of *Going Berserk* when cast members questioned the dreadful dialogue.

This did put Steinberg's career as a movie director on indefinite hold, but in the mid-1990s, he achieved success as the regular director of the hit TV sitcom "Mad About You."

After shooting *Going Berserk*, Candy returned to Ontario to spend part of the summer with Rose and Jennifer. The three of them, along with Keema, their yellow Labrador, had moved into what Candy envisioned as his dream house. The property included a pond and a barn, and was set on ten acres of farm-land near the village of Queensville, about an hour's drive north of Toronto.

Candy had been combing the real-estate ads of the Toronto papers for months when he began shouting to Rose: "Honey, I found the place! I found the dream house!"

He went to see it without an agent, and immediately agreed to pay the asking price.

What happened after that became material for one of Candy's favourite anecdotes.

"I couldn't figure out why the ground was so soggy," Candy would explain. "It was squishy even when the weather was real hot. So I said to my neighbour: 'Is yours like this?' He said: 'No, you live in the swamp area. You knew that when you bought it, didn't you?' I said, 'Oh, yeah, yeah, of course I did. That's why I bought it.'"

To solve the problem, Candy had the entire property trenched. While the work was being done, he felt as if he were

living in a mudhole. It must have seemed like making *Stripes* all
over again. When the job was done, he was thrilled with the
result but had to come to terms with the fact that he would not
be able to recover all the money he'd spent on the rescue operation if he ever decided to sell the property.

Before long, a few special Candy touches had been added.
There was a satellite dish to pull in as many TV signals as possible on Candy's giant-screen set. There was a pond stocked with
trout to make fishing a gratifying experience. And, most distinc-
tively of all, there was a big barn occupied by old cars—every
vehicle John Candy had ever owned and driven in his life.

In September, 1982, "SCTV" won the highest honour in commercial U.S. television—the Emmy. The award was for comedy-
variety writing, and the feat would be repeated a year later.
Eighteen people turned up on stage to accept the first Emmy—
more, indeed, than there were in the SCTV skit about "Hill
Street Blues" winning an award.

Later that night, after the telecast was over, the extended
family of "SCTV," including writers and cast members, gathered
in a posh suite in the Century Plaza Hotel. Quite a lot of
California wine had been swilled back by the time Michael
Short (one of the show's regular writers, and the brother of
Martin Short) organized a parlour game with the combative air
of "Firing Line."

The half-willing victim of the game was Andrew Alexander,
who found himself pinned against a conference table and
ordered to give truthful answers to the questions being fired at
him from the floor.

One of the queries was: "Which one of us do you like best?"
Another was: "When are you going to marry Diane?"

Diane Titmarsh, Alexander's long-time girlfriend, was not
present and had not been consulted, but under pressure,
Alexander, trying to bluff his way out, replied: "Next June."

The next morning, he was somewhat surprised to learn that
Titmarsh had been besieged by congratulations from witnesses
to the interrogation. In fact, the couple decided to go through
with the wedding the following summer.

Winning the Emmy gave "SCTV" a sense of being officially recognized by the U.S. television industry, but it didn't solve the problems Andrew Alexander was having with NBC. Alexander and the performers were desperate to move out of their 12:30 a.m. Friday-night time slot into the 11:30 p.m. Saturday slot occupied by the long-running but seriously troubled "Saturday Night Live."

The press could hardly have been more positive about "SCTV." "Smashingly funny, audacious and needlingly accurate," wrote James Wolcott in *New York* magazine. And the *Los Angeles Times* referred to it as "the best comedy show on TV— maybe the best one in TV history."

But sometimes it seemed to the people doing the show that the critics were the only ones watching. In fact, about five million U.S. viewers tuned in regularly, but few of them stuck it out until the show ended at 2 a.m. In Canada on the CBC the show had 400,000 loyal viewers.

Alexander's goal was to persuade NBC to let "SCTV" alternate with "Saturday Night Live." But he was caught in a catch-22 situation. "SCTV" was a bargain for NBC compared to other programs, but given the relatively small number of people willing to stay up until 2 a.m. to catch it, it was still too expensive for the numbers it delivered. Everyone agreed "SCTV" deserved a better time slot, but negotiations for a different arrangement dragged on for months without a happy resolution.

Peter Calabrese, an NBC vice-president, remarked in a published interview: "We know we've got the best comedy show on television. We've got to find a way to move it so it will be seen." Calabrese went so far as to suggest to the press that "SCTV" could indeed alternate with "Saturday Night Live."

That infuriated Dick Ebersol, executive producer of "SNL," who was also the producer of a rock show hoping to replace "SCTV" in its late-late Friday slot. Ebersol and his friend Brandon Tartikoff, NBC programming czar, took a dim view of Calabrese's comments. "SNL" was considered part of NBC's family, while "SCTV" was very much an upstart and an outsider.

Not long afterward, Calabrese left NBC. "SCTV" had lost its strongest supporter at the network, and its fate was sealed. Not even Guy Caballero could have botched matters as thoroughly as the high-paid jugglers at NBC who were letting TV's most original comic creation slip right through their fingers.

Meanwhile, "SCTV" was still on the air, having endured the departure of three of its stars—Dave Thomas, Rick Moranis and Catherine O'Hara.

Candy was in top form that autumn, doing some of the best work of his career, and clearly energized by the show's new recruit, Martin Short. In one of the most brilliantly surreal sketches ever done on the program, a kind of time warp occurs in the SCTV control room where Short as Ed Grimley, while operating switches, is confronted with a vision of Jackie Gleason as Ralph Kramden, ranting about that blabbermouth, Alice's mother. It is, of course, John Candy in a role he was born to play. Understandably confused, he mistakes Grimley for his pal Ed Norton, as the layers of illusion keep piling up.

Some of Candy's most marvellous work can be glimpsed on episodes of that most self-congratulatory talk show of all time, "The Sammy Maudlin Show." It hardly matters whether viewers ever saw the source of this scathing takeoff on the original Sammy Davis, Jr. talk show of the 1970s. Sammy Maudlin is a perfect satiric explosion of all overblown celebrity egos ever let loose on TV.

The Sammy Maudlin routines began on the original Global series of "SCTV," but they got better and funnier in the show's last years. The shamelessness of showbiz inspired Flaherty (as Sammy), Eugene Levy (as Vegas-style entertainer Bobby Bittman) and Candy (as Sammy's self-effacing second banana William B.) to dizzy new peaks of excess.

What gave the Sammy Maudlin sequences their cutting edge was the cast's daring habit of choosing targets that came close to their own experiences. In one episode, a jovial William B. makes reference to Sammy's drug-abuse past, then introduces a film clip of a congressional investigation into drug use. Clearly rattled, Sammy looks as if he would like to throttle William B. on the spot.

William B. emerges as a whimpering, pathetic buffoon when

he leaves Sammy's show after twenty-three years ("I had to go—
I was dragging the ratings down") to star in his own. William
B.'s show turns out to be such a humiliating fiasco that sched-
uled guests leave early rather than wait for their appearance.
Laughing nervously, poor William B. has to endure a conde-
scending lecture from a crusty eighty-five-year-old songwriter
named Irving Cohen (played by Martin Short as a composite of
Irving Berlin and Jule Styne).

"You never should have left 'The Sammy Maudlin Show,'"
the pontificating Irving Cohen tells William B., chomping on a
cigar with tremendous self-satisfaction and pronouncing every
syllable as if it were intended for court records. "It's a mistake
you'll live to regret. It's your funeral."

When William B. goes crawling back to Sammy Maudlin,
Sammy greets him with a big phony smile and warmly explains:
"You're back doing what you do best—setting up more talented
people like myself."

These episodes constitute some of the most brilliant satire of
show-biz ego ever created, in the same league as *Sullivan's Travels*,
the 1941 Preston Sturges movie, or *Singin' in the Rain*, the 1952
musical about the traumatic effect the introduction of talkies
had on Hollywood. They can be savoured even if you don't
know anything about the career histories of SCTV performers.
But a familiarity with the saga of John Candy's defection to "Big
City Comedy," and his subsequent return to "SCTV" gives this
cycle of Sammy Maudlin shows that much more edge. And they
seem just as fresh when you watch them more than ten years
later as they were at the time.

More and more, however, John Candy felt the time had
come to take his final leave from "SCTV." The all-consuming
grind of writing and performing the show was getting to him.
With Thomas, Moranis and O'Hara gone, he felt under more
pressure than ever to come up with new material. Yet Candy
didn't even have time to watch TV, and he felt that to do a show
satirizing TV without actually watching TV was a form of cheat-
ing. The troupe had to rely on recollections of shows they had
seen in years past. Sometimes they would even find themselves
satirizing shows that many of them had never seen.

Besides, Candy was frankly discouraged by NBC's handling of "SCTV." "We would have taken anything other than that 12:30 time slot," he told one interviewer. But what really annoyed him was NBC's way of putting together "best-of" SCTV shows. According to Candy, NBC wrecked the material by imposing disastrous running orders. "You can't just take a fifteen-minute piece over here and slam it next to another fifteen-minute piece over there. Each show was well thought out."

With Candy's departure added to those of O'Hara, Thomas and Moranis, "SCTV" had a smaller stable of stars, and that was one more argument used by NBC against Andrew Alexander. The fate of "SCTV" was so clearly precarious that in the spring of 1983, more than one hundred hardcore SCTV fans staged a rally outside Rockefeller Plaza urging NBC not to kill the show.

NBC offered a prime-time slot at seven p.m. on Sundays but Alexander felt it was a suicide mission. The show would be competing with "60 Minutes"; anyway, "SCTV" was designed for a late-night audience, not an early Sunday-evening audience. After an exhausting series of proposals and counterproposals, Andrew Alexander and NBC gave up on one another; "SCTV" had come to the end of the line on the network.

$\mathcal{A}$ few months earlier, there was a gathering of the clan when Andrew Alexander and Diane Titmarsh were married in Toronto. Andrea Martin, the compulsively punctual member of the family, was one of the first to arrive at the church. Joe Flaherty flew in from Los Angeles and showed up in a rented tuxedo, with the dignity befitting the super-responsible eldest brother of a large, eccentric family. Rick Moranis, whose feud with Alexander had become so blatant he wasn't invited to the wedding, was conspicuously missing. Among the familiar faces in the pews were Martin Short, Eugene Levy and Dave Thomas. John Candy and Catherine O'Hara, the usual punctuality-challenged members of the family, straggled in after the ceremony was under way.

"There's deep water running there," said Dave Thomas. "We grew up together, and when there are weddings and funerals in the group, we'll all show up at the church."

Afterward the celebration moved to the Boulevard Club, where everyone had a swell time and tried to overlook the fact that some of the most famous guests had hired lawyers to extract residual payments from the groom.

A week after the wedding, members of the old gang turned up again at the Old Firehall for a tenth anniversary bash for the Toronto wing of Second City.

Having made the break from "SCTV," Candy finally turned up on the show from which he had been notably absent. He was the guest host on the October 22, 1983, edition of "Saturday Night Live." Afterward he would tell friends how amazed he was that he could hardly walk a block in New York without being stopped by fans, whereas in Toronto, his home town, no one seemed to know who he was. That same season Candy became a frequent guest star on an NBC program called "The New Show."

In the fall of 1983 "SCTV" limped into a final season by moving to Cinemax, a U.S. cable channel. Cinemax had a modest 2.5 million subscribers and was unavailable to many of the people who might have been willing to pay for it in such areas as Brooklyn and most sections of Chicago.

SCTV's days at this point were clearly numbered. But when it was all over, there was enough material to be repackaged as 185 half-hours, which would move into the lucrative afterlife of syndication. "SCTV" was still on the air, sort of, but now group gatherings seemed like exercises in nostalgia for a phenomenon that was about to move into the past tense.

*Chapter 10*

# ALL ABOUT SPLASH

*W*hen *Splash* opened to critical acclaim in March, 1984, and immediately became Hollywood's box-office hit of the season, John Candy finally got the break that had been eluding him for years. Produced by Brian Grazer for Touchstone (a new division of Disney) and directed by Ron Howard, the movie delivered a romantic comedy with a novel twist.

A mixed-up young New Yorker named Allen Bauer—played by skinny, wide-eyed Tom Hanks—falls in love with a mermaid. The sea nymph, played by the spectacularly gorgeous Daryl Hannah, is a slinky, athletic-looking creature with long blond tresses. And despite winning performances by those two appealing stars, Candy just about steals the picture as the hero's good-hearted, wisecracking older brother, Freddie Bauer—a *bon vivant* bachelor who savours every unhealthy moment of his hedonistic lifestyle.

As Pauline Kael gleefully proclaimed in *The New Yorker*: "Ron Howard has a happy touch, and he's the first film director who has let John Candy loose. This gigantic, chubby Puck has been great in brief appearances, but the role of Freddie the playboy is the first role big enough for him to make the kind of impression he made in the SCTV shows."

After the nightmare film shoots Candy had experienced, his work on *Splash* was almost unbelievably smooth, painless and fast. The director was easy to get along with, and the star could not have been more pleased to be teamed with Candy.

"I was thrilled when I found out I was going to be working with the legendary John Candy," recalls Tom Hanks. In the late 1970s while in Michigan with a touring Shakespeare company, Hanks turned on the TV in his hotel room because he couldn't get to sleep. That's how he discovered "SCTV." It happened to be an episode in which Candy gave one of his most celebrated performances, as the title character in a parody of "Leave It to Beaver." "It was like hearing the Beatles for the first time," Hanks remarked years later.

The experience of working on *Splash* with Candy was so much fun, according to Hanks, that it hardly seemed like work at all. "It was just a gas."

Candy and Hanks would sit around Ron Howard's dining-room table reading the script and finding out where the laughs were. When improvements were needed, Candy assumed the actors would have to rewrite their own scenes. To his happy surprise, Candy found that as soon as a problem was identified, Lowell Ganz and Babaloo Mandel—who had been associated with Howard ever since their days as head writers of "Happy Days"—came up with a solution. They never failed to provide variations, alternatives and new jokes. Candy was dazzled.

Freddie was a wonderful extension of the John Candy known and loved by friends and co-workers—the jocular, debonair party boy who cheers everyone up and always wants to tell one more funny story and have one more drink. When Freddie goes to the gym to play racquetball with Allen, he takes along a cooler of beer, and appears on the court holding a beer in one hand and a cigarette in the other. (The gag is borrowed from Johnny LaRue, who posed as SCTV's resident exercise expert and worked out with a drink in one hand and a cigarette in the other.)

The story of how *Splash* reached the screen is almost as frenetic and cartoonlike a chase story as the plot of *Splash*, which features a mad scientist played by Eugene Levy who wants to perform sadistic experiments on the heroine. It began in 1978, when an inexperienced young producer named Brian Grazer got some development money from United Artists for a romantic comedy about a mermaid, and the noted satirist Bruce Jay Friedman was hired to write the script.

By the time the script was finished, United Artists was being run by Steven Bach, who liked the script and approved hiring a director. But Bach happened to be the guy who approved *Heaven's Gate*, Hollywood's most notorious flop ever, and he was fired before the mermaid movie could get out of the water.

Grazer's difficulties escalated when he learned that a much more powerful and famous producer, the veteran Ray Stark, also was planning a comedy about a mermaid. Stark's project was rumoured to be a vehicle for Bo Derek, and after a couple of scripts were drafted and rejected, Stark hired the most celebrated screenwriter in Hollywood, Robert Towne.

Grazer was having his own script problems. After ordering a rewrite of the Bruce Jay Friedman script, the new regime at United Artists got one it liked. The only problem was this version wasn't at all what Grazer had in mind. Grazer parted company with UA, and also parted company with Stan Dragoti, who had been chosen as director. Bizarrely, the way the dispute was settled was that each side retained the rights to its own version of the material.

When Grazer produced his first feature, *Night Shift* (1982)— a comedy about two guys trying to run a call-girl operation from a morgue—he got along so well with *Night Shift*'s director, Ron Howard, that Howard became interested in directing *Splash*. Grazer and Howard together approached Alan Ladd, Jr., of the Ladd Company (whose independent productions were released through Warner Brothers). Ladd gave the project a go-ahead. Grazer and Howard then hired their *Night Shift* writers, Lowell Ganz and Babaloo Mandel, to do a rewrite of Friedman's script.

It was all going smoothly until Alan Ladd learned that Ray Stark had signed Warren Beatty to star in his mermaid picture and Herbert Ross to direct it. Ladd decided to bail out. Instead of giving up at this point, Grazer hired agent Jeff Berg to pitch *Splash* to the studios. Berg had to convince one of them that Grazer and Howard—who gained credibility when *Night Shift* became a hit—could make their mermaid movie fast enough to beat Ray Stark to the screen. Berg made a deal with Disney, *Splash* went into production, and within months the film had been shot and edited.

Meanwhile Ray Stark spent a couple of million dollars on his mermaid movie but while Robert Towne was doing one rewrite after another, Warren Beatty and Herbert Ross went on to other projects. With the cameras rolling on *Splash*, Stark realized it was time to pull the plug.

Ron Howard had started acting as a child and was best known to TV watchers as Opie on "The Andy Griffith Show" and Richie Cunningham, the Fonz's sidekick on "Happy Days." Since the late 1970s, he had been making the transition into directing. He and Grazer would go on to form Imagine Films, one of the top independent production companies in Hollywood, and collaborate on many big movies, including *Cocoon* and *Apollo 13*.

Before *Splash*, some people were inclined to dismiss Howard as a lightweight, perhaps identifying him too closely with the character he portrayed on "Happy Days." But unlike some of the other directors Candy had worked with, Howard had a sure instinct for comedy timing. He knew how to set up a scene so the jokes would pay off.

When Howard sent Candy the script of *Splash*, Candy wanted to play the lunatic scientist. But Howard talked Candy into playing Freddie, and accepted Candy's suggestion that his pal Levy play the scientist. Candy transformed what could have been a straight man into a wisecracking, high-living cartoon—a sweeter-tempered version of Johnny LaRue.

Working with Howard and Hanks, Candy had a chance to show off the kind of intuitively sharp comic timing he had developed on "SCTV" but rarely had a chance to demonstrate in the movies, where the director rather than the performer is in control of the rhythm. Pauline Kael pinpointed a moment when Hanks says something and the audience is waiting for Candy to answer. Kael wrote: "His hesitation—it's like a few seconds of hippo torpor—is what makes his answer funny." Kael described Candy as "Falstaff at fourteen" and commented: "He doesn't add weight; he adds bounce and imagination."

*Splash* is not as consistently wonderful as its best sections make you hope it's going to be, because the enchanting romance gives way to emotional murkiness, and the slapstick chase elements become tiresome despite Eugene Levy's inspired nuttiness as the villainous scientist. But the movie still manages to leave you in a good mood—and eager to see more of John Candy. Unfortunately, in most of the roles he subsequently took, Candy would be unable to live up to the standard set by *Splash*.

Candy himself was rather incredulous about the film's achievement. Prior to its release, in an interview with Adele Freedman of the *Globe and Mail*, he spoke of it fondly but with oddly understated enthusiasm: "It's a harmless movie, a gentle little picture, a nice attempt by Ron."

Even after *Splash* earned great reviews and popular acclaim, Candy shrugged it off when I interviewed him for *Toronto Life*. "It wasn't Willy Loman (in *Death of a Salesman*) or King Lear," he told me. "People said 'Wow, you can really act.' Hell, I was just doing what I had been doing for years on 'SCTV.'"

That may have been true, but *Splash* was the Hollywood breakthrough Candy had been waiting for. As a result of its success, he signed a development deal with Disney's new Touchstone division that promised him a chance to create and control his own projects. The contract called for Candy to develop three projects a year in the capacity of writer/performer/creative producer.

Candy regarded the deal with a certain skepticism. "To develop, that's easy," he told Adele Freedman. "Now, if they'd guarantee me three to shoot, I'd be ecstatic. Development deals like this are a dime a dozen, really."

Still, Candy had hopes that at last he would be able to bring in some of his friends from "SCTV" and that they would be able to work with something like the creative freedom they'd had there. In the past, he was aware, their intelligence and need to work in their own way had made studio executives uncomfortable. Often the executives would treat them with a certain condescension. Their view seemed to be that the SCTV performers knew about TV but were inexperienced in movies; and that there must be something second-rate about them because they weren't as famous as their counterparts on "Saturday Night Live."

Candy was now on the verge of making serious money. His fee for *Splash* was $350,000, and his Disney development deal specified that he was to get $350,000 per film. As well, Candy hungered for the power over his own destiny that he sensed could go along with big fees. He liked to think that with his new clout at Disney, he was the guy who could finally spearhead the dream movie the old gang had always aspired to create together.

Around the time the Disney deal was being made, Ivan Reitman, who had hired Candy for *Stripes* and *Heavy Metal*, offered him a key role in his next movie, *Ghostbusters*, working alongside Bill Murray, Dan Aykroyd and the magnificent Sigourney Weaver. Things progressed so far that Candy even appeared in a *Ghostbusters* video. But Candy demanded a fee of $350,000, matching his Disney price. Reitman balked, and they had an unpleasant parting of the ways. Candy would never again work in an Ivan Reitman movie.

Reitman hired Rick Moranis to play the part originally meant for Candy, and *Ghostbusters* (which opened in the summer of 1984) went on to become one of the biggest-grossing comedies ever made. It might have looked in retrospect like a tremendous missed opportunity but Candy claimed a few years later that he had no regrets.

"Rick did a nice job with the part. Of course it would have been different with me, but I don't think it would have been right for me to lower my price for Ivan and then go back to Disney and collect a higher fee."

In the end, Candy's skepticism about the Disney deal turned out to be well founded. The company underwent a major transformation after Michael Eisner took over as Disney CEO in late 1984 and installed Jeffrey Katzenberg, his former cohort at Paramount Pictures, to run the film studio.

Almost any new Hollywood regime typically distances itself from the arrangements put in place by its predecessors. Moreover, it was part of Katzenberg's *modus operandi* to maintain absolute control of every detail of every project, and to give as little creative freedom as possible to writers, actors and directors. Candy's development deal was doomed the day Eisner and Katzenberg walked through the door. None of the films Candy planned for Disney would ever be made.

During this period NBC hired Candy as head writer for a new variety show pilot planned by Brandon Tartikoff. Tentatively called "Night Life" and described as a cross between "The Ed Sullivan Show" and "Saturday Night Live," the pilot was scheduled to be telecast in Saturday Night Live's time slot in early June. It was said that Tartikoff was thinking of cancelling "Saturday Night Live" and replacing it with "Night Life." However, nothing came of the idea. "Saturday Night Live" would survive into the late 1990s, and John Candy would never again return to the grind of a weekly TV show.

After the release of *Splash*, Candy checked into the Pritikin Longevity Center in Santa Monica (on the ocean, just west of L.A). The more successful he became as an overweight comic, the more often Candy was compared to his deceased friend, John Belushi. Added to this was the constant shadow of his father's early death. At thirty-three, John Candy was fast approaching the age at which Sidney Candy had a fatal heart attack, and his older brother, Jim, had already had a serious heart attack. John Candy feared he would not reach the age of forty if he kept up the lifestyle to which he had become accustomed.

"I suddenly realized I didn't want to be known as the guy I really tied one on with the other night," he told Susan Swan, who was writing a profile of him for *Toronto Life*.

Nathan Pritikin, the gaunt guru who ran the centre, was a true believer and a bit of a tyrant—a former engineer, who after being told he had terminal heart disease, invented his own radical method of clearing clogged arteries. His solution was a high-fibre, low-fat diet that included vegetables, vegetables and more vegetables.

Pritikin's rules were absolute: no meat, no caffeine, no alcohol, no tobacco.

Visitors to the Pritikin Center were expected to take long walks by the sea. For their dedication they saw fast results: not only weight loss but a significant lowering of their blood pressure.

Pritikin's followers were like born-again zealots, willing to spend hours reading labels at the supermarket and chopping peppers at home. The program became so fashionable among the prosperous and overweight that pilgrims flocked to the Pritikin Center, eager to pay a fortune so they could learn how to eat like starving peasants.

Nathan Pritikin's critics called him a fanatic and a lunatic, but his prediction that his findings would eventually be embraced by the American Medical Association and the U.S. Food and Drug Administration turned out to be largely true.

Candy not only spent a month at the Pritikin Center; he also convinced his mother and his brother to visit the Pritikin Center. For a time, at least, the experience changed the habits of the entire family. Thanks to his new regime—healthy eating and no drinking—Candy lost seventy-five pounds in a matter of months. In the past he had rationalized his weight by saying that his fans might not like him if he were thinner. Now he was adamant that he could be funny without being fat. He need not have fretted. The reality was that even with his weight substantially reduced, Candy was always going to come through as a performer of a certain bulk.

While Candy was at the Pritikin Center he got a phone call asking whether he would like to make a film with Richard Pryor, whose daring concert films had made him the most revered of all stand-up comics. The director was Walter Hill, who had earned praise for such action movies as *The Warriors* and *48 Hrs.*

"When?" asked Candy.

"The end of next month," was the answer.

"I'll be there," said Candy.

*Brewster's Millions* is a comedy with a one-joke structure. Brewster, played by Pryor, stands to inherit a huge fortune from a long-lost relative, but there's a catch. He has to spend a smaller fortune in thirty days without giving it away and without telling anyone the secret. He brings in his buddy Spike (played by Candy) to help him but does not explain to Spike what's really going on.

The material goes back a long way, to a novel by George Barr McCutcheon which had been turned into a stage play in 1907, and had been the basis for six earlier screen versions. The most recent was a 1945 movie with Dennis O'Keefe as a war hero returning to wed his home-town sweetheart (June Havoc).

What possessed Universal Pictures to commission a new version in the mid-1980s? It may have been the fact that a comedy with a similar plot gimmick, *Trading Places*, had turned out to be a surprising box-office winner in 1983. *Brewster's Millions* seemed like a startling departure for Walter Hill, who was known as an action director, but Hill had mixed action and comedy in *48 Hrs.*, and the result was a big hit.

The producers probably assumed that a reliable old vehicle could be successfully updated as long as they could get the most popular and gifted funnymen of the moment to appear in it. But Richard Pryor has the kind of genius that doesn't emerge unless he is turned loose, and as Brewster, Pryor is kept on a tight leash in the form of a contrived and not terribly plausible story.

Whereas Dennis O'Keefe had to spend a mere $1 million, Pryor is obliged to spend $30 million. That's inflation for you. The premise could have been given new satiric relevance if Brewster had been reconceived as a Hollywood player financing a movie, but the screenwriters (Herschel Weingrod and Timothy Harris) made the hero a minor-league relief pitcher who is also stuck (sigh) in the minor leagues of life.

The role of Spike, the hero's partner on and off the field, is such a feeble second-banana contrivance that Hill—a follower of "SCTV"—was surprised Candy was eager to accept it. When Candy came to visit him on the set of *Streets of Fire*, Hill told him: "I'd love to have you in the picture. I'm afraid the way the script stands there isn't much for you to do. But I'll do my best to expand the part for you."

Candy brought as much zest as possible to the underwritten role of the bewildered Spike, the catcher on Brewster's baseball team, who perceives his old friend's behaviour—renting and redecorating a palatial suite at the Plaza Hotel, investing in a scheme to carry water from the North Pole to the Sahara, hiring the entire New York Yankees team—as a series of wild pitches.

Candy had proved adept at playing the hero's funny sidekick in *Splash*, and here he fares better than Pryor, bringing a bit of bouncy euphoria to the strained proceedings. He conveys a wonderful kid-in-the-candystore spirit that must have been familiar to anyone who had ever been entertained by Candy on a film set or at a party. There's a delightfully silly moment where Candy gets to do a little dance up and down the steps of Brewster's Plaza suite. And the succession of expensive outfits draped over Candy's ample frame is a hoot.

But Candy couldn't save the movie. Pryor seems awkward, as the writers fall back on stale conventions—a subplot about corrupt politicians and a tiresomely moralizing speech from the hero's love object (Lonette McKee) explaining the importance of using money to help people. Hill tries to fill the void with crowded backgrounds and frantic activity, but the effect is exhausting rather than exhilarating. In the end, Hill felt Candy's part had not been sufficiently developed to take advantage of his talent, and he wasn't satisfied with the movie. But Hill and Candy became friends anyway.

"John Candy was a genuine person and a hell of a guy," says Hill, "and that's unusual. A lot of big movie stars aren't such likeable people."

In late July, *Brewster* moved to New York for location shooting. To celebrate the end of filming, Hill and Candy had dinner at a small Italian restaurant on the Upper East Side. For Hill it was an unnerving night.

Hill was very aware that Candy had been fighting to keep his weight down, following the Pritikin gospel all summer. So Hill was startled when Candy began ordering drinks. But he decided not to mention it. Candy was in a mood to celebrate. Both men had a few drinks, and Candy was in such entertaining form he had Hill laughing uncontrollably. After dinner they moved from one bar to another, and when they parted around four in the morning, Candy was flying high.

Afterward, Hill wondered whether he should have stopped Candy, but later when he mentioned it, Candy said he had already decided not to stick with the Pritikin regime. However, over the next couple of years Candy did return to the Pritikin fold at least for a while.

Candy's appetite for work was as voracious and excessive as his appetite for food and drink. If he had refused to work in any movie that wasn't up to the standards of *Splash*, he could have spent much more time at home with Rose and Jennifer and saved himself a lot of professional heartache—but inactivity made him too nervous. He felt insecure and incomplete when he was not working. He found it hard to say no, especially when there was a chance to work with people of note. No doubt this clouded his judgment and made him too quick to approve flimsy scripts.

Candy set a personal record by appearing in four Hollywood movies released in 1985, and for a while it seemed as if you would encounter him everywhere you went.

In the first of these movies to open, Candy had a cameo that took up only a couple of minutes of screen time. The film was *Sesame Street Presents Follow That Bird*—a road movie for five-year-olds in which Big Bird moves to Illinois, where he's placed in a foster home with a family of dodos. Then, deciding to get back where he belongs, Big Bird sets out to hitchhike back to New York.

This is a weird movie in which Jim Henson muppet creatures interact with human beings played by actors such as Chevy Chase, Sandra Bernhard and Paul Bartel. The juiciest roles belong to two of Candy's SCTV colleagues, Dave Thomas and Joe Flaherty—as a pair of goofy redneck villains scheming to capture and exploit Big Bird for profit. Candy plays the state trooper on a motorcycle who busts them and thereby secures Big Bird's safe passage. Candy even gets to say "Tell it to the judge" to Thomas and Flaherty, prompting Flaherty to burst into tears.

Candy returned home to enjoy the last part of summer, 1984, at the family farm. He and Rose were awaiting the birth of their second child. Christopher Candy was born that fall. And Candy found a way to stay close to home for a few months without giving up work.

In September, Candy and Eugene Levy got together to write the script for a one-hour TV comedy special, "The Last Polka," which was shot in various Ontario locations, including Kitchener during Oktoberfest and the Music Hall theatre in midtown Toronto (the site of the Shmenges' final concert). It was a way for Candy and Levy to go on working together, and it was also a way for Candy—who often put Levy's well-being near the top of his list of priorities—to help snap Levy out of the funk he had been in since the termination of "SCTV" the preceding spring.

"The Last Polka" is a mock documentary which purports to tell the tale of the Shmenge Brothers and their illustrious career playing "The Happy Wanderer" and other polka favourites. And this farewell bash for two legends who have decided to hang up their lederhosen also works as an entertaining send-up of *The Last Waltz*, in which Martin Scorsese used the occasion of The Band's melancholy farewell tour to look back on the history of a legendary rock 'n' roll group.

The joke in "The Last Polka" is that the same sort of attention is given two talent-challenged yokels—Yosh the clarinet man and Stan the accordion player. (The casting isn't arbitrary: Candy learned to play the clarinet in high school, Levy the accordion.)

"The Last Polka" traces the career of the Shmenges from their origins in the fictitious middle European country of Leutonia. We learn how they were influenced by Lionel Hampton and his vibraphone, how they spent their early years in Leutonian vaudeville, and how they got a break on a bowling show. Early in their careers, it is revealed, they were exploited by a shady impresario known as Colonel Tom Collins who took seventy-five per cent of their earnings. (Could this perhaps be a reference to some of the businessmen Candy had worked with as well as to the famous Colonel Tom Parker, who handled Elvis?)

The Shmenges, in turn, exploit other immigrant entertainers—such as a lounge lizard in folk garb, played by Rick Moranis, who sings truly horrendous renditions of old Jim Morrison songs. At the peak of their careers, Yosh and Stan Shmenge star in their own weekly TV polka show and acquire spinoff enterprises including a travel agency and a cabbage-roll take-out joint.

Then there's the group of three female singers, known as the Lemon Twins (Catherine O'Hara, Mary Margaret O'Hara and

Robin Duke) whose link with the Shmenges has a whiff of scandal, not just because the Shmenges spent so much time with women other than their wives, but because there were three of them.

The big unanswered question is why the Shmenges are retiring. No one seems to know the answer except Yosh and Stan, and they aren't telling. But it could have something to do with their ill-fated attempt to win new fans by putting on Day-Glo jackets and staging a rock concert. The event, which had to be called off for lack of an audience, is referred to as "the Plattsburg disaster."

If you're feeling glum, "The Last Polka" can cheer you up. It's a tickling demonstration of how Candy and Levy could come up with fresh and funny material even in an enterprise that sounded like an occasion for recycling old gags. On its own terms the show is a real achievement—proof of how funny these two guys could be without spending a lot of money as long as they had a free hand.

Yet there's a melancholy subtext, because we know it isn't only the Shmenges who are breaking up. There's a bitter-sweet sense that what we're really watching is the story of two old friends, Candy and Levy, trying to get back to the innocent good times they shared in their early days, trying to stay true to themselves and close to one another despite a lot of external forces driving them apart—especially the fact that one had become a movie star and one had not.

"The Last Polka" would not, as things turned out, be the last time John Candy and Eugene Levy worked together. It would, however, mark the last time they collaborated on a project they could both feel proud of.

# FLIRTING WITH DISASTER

*J*n November, 1984, John Candy travelled to the tiny, backward Mexican town of Tuxtepec (close to the Gulf of Mexico) to begin work on *Volunteers*, a social and political satire about the Peace Corps.

For Candy the personal cost of appearing in *Volunteers* was considerable, since it required him to be away from home during an important phase of family life. Rose was at the farm north of Toronto with their infant son, Christopher, as well as their four-year-old daughter, Jennifer. The backwardness of the location discouraged family visits, and geography made it harder for Candy to fly home for a weekend than it would have been if he had been working in a major U.S. city.

Nevertheless, Candy was anxious not to lose the momentum of his movie career, and he had high expectations for this movie. By reuniting him with Tom Hanks, *Volunteers* held out the promise of duplicating his triumph in *Splash*, where playing comic foil to leading man Hanks transformed Candy into Hollywood's great new jolly jester. Perhaps anticipating that *Brewster's Millions* would be a letdown for those expecting him to maintain his *Splash* pace, Candy counted on *Volunteers* to put him back on track as the screen's most lovable new funnyman.

Instead, *Volunteers* turned out to be a crushing disappointment, and inevitably raised troubling doubts in Candy's own mind as well in the minds of his critics about his ability to assess scripts and collaborators and make the right career choices. And these doubts would be magnified and intensified as Candy rashly got himself involved in several disappointing movies over the next two years.

Candy went to Mexico eager to begin work on *Volunteers* and renew his partnership with Hanks. As soon as he arrived in Tuxtepec, he inadvertently created a stir by inquiring: "Were those your elephants we passed on the way in from the airport?"

Nicholas Meyer, the director of *Volunteers*, had been fighting for two elephants, arguing that it would take a pair of the beasts to conjure the atmosphere of Thailand, where the story was set; to have only one, he claimed, would seem unauthentic. But Richard Shepherd, one of the producers, had been insisting the budget could not bear more than one elephant. The specimens Candy had spotted were with a circus that happened to be visiting the area. The Mexican elephants were immediately booked for the film, and the expensive single imported American elephant was cancelled.

If only all the problems of *Volunteers* could have been that happily resolved, perhaps the movie would have been a success.

On paper, *Volunteers* seemed to Candy and to other people a clever, promising script that had a lot of things going for it—surefire humour, exotic spectacle, even provocative political ideas. (Nicholas Meyer was known at this point for his terribly high-minded nuclear doomsday TV movie *The Day After*. Later, having climbed down from the moral high ground, he would be known as the director of *Star Trek VI*.)

While *Volunteers* was being made, those working on it seemed convinced they had a winner. Tom Hanks, for one, told people this was the most fun he had ever had as an actor. Nonetheless, it would go down as one of the low points in the career of Hanks (who a decade later would pull off the amazing feat of winning the best-actor Oscar two years in a row, for *Philadelphia* and *Forrest Gump*).

By the time *Volunteers* reached the screen in the summer of 1985, almost everyone realized something had gone terribly wrong. This was one solemn, draggy movie.

*Volunteers* had been in the works for six years before it was actually made; perhaps the vitality got drained out of it along the way. The idea was to make fun of American idealism, 1960s-style. The story is set in 1962, when John F. Kennedy's Camelot was in full flower. Tom Hanks plays a spoiled rich kid by the name of Lawrence Bourne III.

Fresh out of Yale, he finds himself facing a $48,000 gambling debt his father (played by that real-life Brahmin rebel George Plimpton) refuses to pay. To avoid being dismantled by an angry bookie, Lawrence runs off to join the Peace Corps in Thailand. Only he has no interest in the objectives of the Peace Corps; in fact, he behaves as if he were going to the Club Med.

Playing a young affluent jerk, Tom Hanks talks like Cary Grant, wears a white dinner jacket everywhere, and seems determined to redefine the phrase "ugly American." On the plane, this spoiled Yalie sits next to an irrepressibly gung-ho engineer from Tacoma, Washington—Tom Tuttle, played by Candy.

Tuttle natters on about his grandiose engineering schemes, remarking: "A challenge? You bet it is!" This excessively friendly nerd in a plaid shirt can't stop talking, much to the horror of the churlish fellow in the next seat.

Confronted by a planeload of yammering, naïve liberals, Lawrence Bourne III makes nasty cracks about his fellow volunteers and is soon despised by all of them. One of those most intoxicated with her own idealism is a young woman named Beth Wexler, played by Rita Wilson, who divides her time between rebuffing crude advances from Lawrence and reading *Profiles in Courage.*

(Predictably, Lawrence breaks down Beth's resistance before the movie ends. Less predictably, Hanks and Wilson, who met on the film, were married soon after they completed work on it.)

In Mexico the film-makers built a Thai village based on the Karen tribe of Burma's Golden Triangle. And maybe they got a bit too carried away with the logistics—which involved building the world's longest suspension bridge, more than two hundred and fifty yards long. A group of more than one hundred people from various parts of the world, including a number of Thai families, spent two and a half months in Mexico.

As Nicholas Meyer remarked, "It was like having a picnic on Mars. You couldn't go back for the salt."

The mission of these Peace Corps volunteers is to help a group of oppressed Asian peasants better their lot by building a bridge to civilization. In the course of the story, each Peace Corps volunteer becomes involved with a political group that has its own agenda. The moral: these villagers would be better off without help from Communists, drug-dealers, the CIA or young American idealists working for the Peace Corps.

After reading the script, Sargent Shriver, who was then director of the Peace Corps, complained that *Volunteers* was spitting on the American flag, and demanded changes. The changes weren't made, but by the time *Volunteers* was released, Shriver had moved on, and Peace Corps officials were ready to endorse the film. They didn't seem to mind if it was a lousy movie, as long as it was a clearly pro-American lousy movie.

For the first half-hour, *Volunteers* wavers between promising and tolerable. Hanks has some amusing zingers about both the volunteers and the Thai villagers. And Candy injects energy and spirit into the proceedings whenever he appears on screen— which is not nearly often enough.

At first Hanks makes snarkiness amusing, but after a while he undergoes a transition from being entertainingly insufferable to being just plain insufferable. In an underwritten role, Rita Wilson makes little impact, and, since there's rarely anyone on screen we like or care about, the audience becomes restless and alienated.

Candy might have been able to step into the breach, but the movie makes an almost unbelievable blunder by shaping the story in a way that makes his character disappear. After setting out to build a bridge across the river, Tom Tuttle is kidnapped and brainwashed by the Communists.

There are other big problems. The film's attitude to the villagers begins to seem patronizing, if not downright racist. Whatever there was in the script by Ken Levine and David Isaacs that drew favourable interest before the film was shot, and whatever director Nicholas Meyer thought he was doing with the material, in the end the movie becomes an embarrassment—a would-be soufflé that keeps failing to rise.

Candy does have a funny scene when he spouts Maoist rhetoric, but by the time he comes back into the proceedings, the bridge has been co-opted by guerrillas and black marketeers—and the audience has had to abandon all hope for salvaging this movie.

Stuck in a remote and utterly unalluring location, Candy managed to have some good times off screen. According to John Langley, who worked on *Volunteers* directing the second unit (and would later go on to produce the successful TV show "Cops"), Candy regaled his colleagues with stories and comic creations, played cards with the local masters, and kept everyone's spirits up. For Langley, being marooned with Candy turned out to be the start of a great friendship, and he would cherish the memory of one particular dinner with Candy as "the funniest evening I've ever spent in my life."

Living conditions, however, were no laughing matter. Candy was staying in a hotel room infested with cockroaches the size of golf balls. Partly to amuse themselves, Langley and Candy came up with the idea of doing a mockumentary about the making of *Volunteers.* They got the go-ahead and made a six-minute film, like an SCTV sketch, in which the stars are feuding and the film is threatened by backbiting. This spoof was aired many times on Home Box Office, which was one of the companies putting up the money for *Volunteers.*

One of Candy's best moments in *Volunteers* comes when he says what he misses most about home is tuna casserole with potato chips on top. In truth, during months in a remote Mexican village, Candy missed a lot more than tuna casserole. Not only was he separated from his family; as a result of being stuck in Mexico, he was conspicuously absent from a weekend-long bash in Chicago a week before Christmas celebrating the twenty-fifth anniversary of Second City.

The get-together was attended by three hundred people, including many of Candy's old friends and colleagues. Emotionally, it was a highly charged occasion. A scholarship fund was established to honour John Belushi, and the program of events included a series of private parties (including one at the home of Bernie Sahlins), a closed-door comedy marathon, and the taping of a commemorative TV special. Candy was represented by a pre-taped sequence.

While he was in Mexico, Candy got a call from Ned Tanen, then the president of Paramount Pictures, who said: "I've got a great script here that Carl Reiner will direct if you'll do it. He'll be calling you in five minutes."

To Candy, steeped in the history of television comedy, Carl Reiner was a minor god. Reiner's TV career had begun in 1950, when he became a writer and actor alongside Sid Caesar and Imogene Coca on "Your Show of Shows." He spent nine years there before going on to create, produce, write and act in "The Dick Van Dyke Show" in the early 1960s.

Then, after winning eleven Emmys, Reiner had begun writing and directing movies in the late 1960s, starting with the screen version of his autobiography, *Enter Laughing*. But by then he was perhaps too used to the conventions of TV. His movies tended to back away from troubling issues and heavy emotions, favouring instead a superficial treatment typical of TV sitcoms.

Reiner was most comfortable working with light comedy performers who had a background in television, including Dick Van Dyke, George Burns, Henry Winkler and Kirstie Alley. He became best known for the four movies he made with Steve Martin—the finest of which, *All of Me*, had just come out when Candy got his call from Reiner.

Candy later made a comedy routine of how eager he was to get this call: "This is Alan Brady from 'The Dick Van Dyke Show,' calling me in Mexico! And he's waiting to see if I'll do this movie. It took me about thirty seconds to say yes."

Candy assumed he was being offered another supporting role. He was flabbergasted when Reiner explained that Candy would have the lead—as a frazzled air-traffic controller, a blue-collar American family man who takes his wife and children on what turns out to be a disastrous beach vacation.

Reiner arranged to send the script to Candy in Mexico and promised they would have a great time working together. When the script arrived it seemed to Candy rather threadbare. And Candy was aware the movie was being hurried along on a precariously tight schedule, with production to start in March, so that Paramount could release the movie in hundreds of theatres in mid-summer.

Still, Candy was willing to overlook the negative factors. Reiner had always been one of his heroes, and this would be a chance to work with him. It would also be a chance to play a starring role in a mainstream comedy, and collect a star paycheque of $800,000. He and Rose needed some new furniture, and you could buy a lot of furniture for $800,000.

*Summer Rental* was filmed in a tremendous rush, to meet Paramount's deadline, and it was nobody's idea of a great movie, but it was a tolerable family comedy. It had solid supporting performances from Richard Crenna and Rip Torn. And it demonstrated Candy could play a sympathetic, ordinary character and still be funny. If the movie in the end was a little thin, well, in Candy's view that's because it was made in too great a hurry.

"It was a Guinness Book of World Records movie," he joked afterward. "We shot it in April and May and it came out in August. We didn't even have enough time to spend the whole budget."

Candy discovered that being the leading man is more exhausting than being the sidekick. "I was in every scene," he remarked. "I had to work every day, with no days off."

As for the responsibility, he admitted: "There's a lot of pressure because you know they're spending eight million dollars on the picture. I ain't Rambo, I ain't Schwarzenegger. I thought, 'Geez, what if they don't make their money back?'"

Actually, *Summer Rental* performed reasonably well at the box office. Candy knew it wasn't his best work, but there were some consolations. One was that he developed a warm relationship with Reiner, whom he had always revered from afar. Perhaps because he had such respect for him, Candy allowed Reiner to raise the delicate subject of Candy's weight. And Reiner did have some influence; he persuaded Candy to give the Pritikin diet another try.

Candy was grateful to Reiner for something else. Reiner was

the first director who made Candy feel he had a valuable role to play behind the camera, not just as an actor. That gesture proved to be an enormous boost for Candy's ego.

"Carl Reiner allowed me to be part of the process of making the movie," Candy told Brian Linehan a year later. "He showed me what he was doing, and explained technically what he was looking for."

Reiner took Candy to the editing room, solicited his input time and again, and kept asking the question that John Candy had always yearned to hear from his directors: "What do you think?"

*J*n the summer of 1985, with *Summer Rental* on movie screens across North America, Candy got the most unexpected honour of his life when he was chosen one of *Playgirl* magazine's ten sexiest men. The editors explained: "The shaggy moptop, dimpled cheeks, physical grace—nobody is sexier than this giant of comedy who turns us on with good humor."

Candy was more than a trifle embarrassed, and had to endure a lot of wisecracks from his SCTV friends.

Rose Candy, who almost never spoke to the press, was so pleased that she told Rob Salem of the *Toronto Star*: "It's a great ego booster. He may be a sex symbol, but he's *my* sex symbol."

Sex symbol or not, there was a growing perception that Candy had failed to live up to the promise of *Splash*. It was definitely time for another hit. Instead Candy made *Armed and Dangerous*—which was so bad that even devoted Candy fans felt it crossed the line. Critics and audiences who were fond enough of Candy to make allowances and put up with disappointing movies weren't willing to endure *Armed and Dangerous* uncomplainingly.

Candy's salary had soared to two million dollars for *Armed and Dangerous*. The project had been around for six years, and there had been about fifteen versions of the script. At one point it had been a vehicle for Belushi and Aykroyd, then Harold Ramis and Dan Aykroyd, then Aykroyd and John Candy (with John Carpenter to direct). When Aykroyd and Carpenter dropped out Candy was left with a contract and no movie.

In retrospect it's clear Candy would have been better off if

*Armed and Dangerous* had been cancelled. Ironically, it would have stayed in limbo if Candy hadn't insisted on pushing forward when the project was all but dead. Candy had arranged to rent a house in L.A. and take Rose and the children there for the summer of 1985, and he was upset at the prospect of cancelling his plans. If he had accepted the collapse of the film, he could have had a quiet summer with his family at their farm outside Toronto. But Candy was so upset by the loss of work that he made it clear to Columbia Pictures he was prepared to enforce his contract with legal action.

Finally, Candy asked whether the studio would be willing to go ahead with the movie if he could get his pal Eugene Levy to co-star with him and a new director could be found. The studio gave in to his pressure, and handed the assignment to Mark Lester, who was completely unsuited to it.

Elated that he was getting his way, Candy ignored all the danger signs that should have alerted him to the obvious. *Armed and Dangerous* had "disaster" written all over it, and he should have counted himself lucky to get a chance to escape from making it.

Candy plays a cop named Frank Dooley who gets fired when he is framed by two fellow officers who have been stealing TV sets. He takes a job as a security guard for the Guard Dog Security Company. His new partner is failed lawyer Norman Kane (played by Levy). Their boss (Robert Loggia)—a union czar with Mafia connections—is stealing from both the security guards and the companies they're supposed to protect.

As these two fight the criminal conspiracy, visiting some of L.A.'s strangest locations in their search for the culprits, Mark Lester simply turns up the music and wrecks a lot of cars. Though Lester had a background in action films, even the car chases in *Armed and Dangerous* are witless.

At one point in the film when the two guards are hiding in a porn shop, Candy has a scene in Divine-style drag while Levy wears a cycle jacket and leather pants with patches cut out to expose his bare buttocks. At first, Levy said there was no way he was going to appear on screen in those pants. But Candy and Lester laughed so hard when they saw him in this outfit that

Levy let himself be talked into doing the scene.

That behind-the-scenes anecdote suggests more fun than the movie ever delivers. Candy and Levy had done masterly team-work before, but here, although their smart friend Harold Ramis was officially co-author of the script, they fail to get any rhythms going, and there doesn't seem to be any chemistry between them. They're like two actors who had never met before. The script tries to get laughs out of Candy's bulk, making him climb a tree to rescue a cat. As an overweight vigilante cop, Candy represents what Dirty Harry might have become if he had been addicted to pizza.

David Edelstein pinpointed a central irony when he wrote in the *Village Voice*: "Both Candy and Levy do good shtik but they're working for the kind of people they had once ridiculed (on SCTV)."

In the *Washington Post*, Paul Attanasio commented: "It takes a director with a true genius for disaster to put together John Candy and Eugene Levy, the fine character actors Kenneth McMillan and Robert Loggia, and the delicious new comic actress Meg Ryan and come up with a movie without a single laugh in it. Indeed, who but Mark Lester could have pulled it off?"

After a string of botched comedies, Candy was taking some heat for his choice of roles, and his interviews were beginning to sound like exercises in damage control.

Even before *Armed and Dangerous* could be added to the list of felonies, Gene Siskel of the *Chicago Tribune* practically put Candy on trial when he interviewed him during the annual industry ShoWest convention in Las Vegas in March, 1986.

According to Siskel, if Candy's recent movies had turned out a little differently, he could have been the toast of the convention. Instead, said Siskel, each film was a critical and financial disappointment. "Together they have at least temporarily delayed Candy's move to the top of the movie-comedy heap," Siskel decided.

Discussing the strange ways the movie business worked, Candy was fond of quoting his agent, John Gaines: "My agent is always telling me, 'It's not called show art, it's show business.'"

A couple of weeks after the disastrous mid-summer opening

of *Armed and Dangerous*, Patrick Goldstein wrote in the *Los Angeles Times*: "Eighteen months ago if you had asked people in Hollywood to pick a hot new comedy star, you could always have spotted John Candy's name near the top of the list... What went wrong?"

The problem, as Candy explained it somewhat defensively to Goldstein, was that what a project looks like going into it sometimes has very little to do with the movie that eventually emerges.

"I'm always hearing about these great scripts," Candy observed. "But then they say, 'Oh, it needs a rewrite.' Then before you know it, there's another rewrite, and then it needs a little polish, and by the time that has been done, the script is almost unrecognizable."

By mid-1986, John Candy had good reason to be dejected. Two years earlier, riding the crest of *Splash*, he had seemed like the big screen's surest star of the future. That precipitated a burst of frenzied activity. On each occasion Candy had gone into a project with great expectations, only to find when it came out it was widely viewed as a letdown.

Being very sensitive to criticism, with a propensity to painful late-night brooding, Candy felt personally wounded by the failure of one movie after another. And this string of flops inevitably brought his lifelong vulnerability and insecurity right back to the surface. His sense of disappointment, defensiveness and betrayal reached epic proportions. For a while he seemed like a kid who'd had the lollipop snatched away at the last moment.

After the debacle of *Armed and Dangerous*, Candy's next appearance was a cameo in the enjoyably silly musical *Little Shop of Horrors*, based on a cheap, campy old sci-fi flick. Rick Moranis stars as Seymour, the assistant in a flower shop who tends a prize cactus named Audrey, which becomes a voracious, flesh-eating monster.

Candy turns up briefly as Wink Wilkinson, a manic deejay with a fevered imagination and a memorable hairdo. *Little Shop of Horrors* is more or less hijacked by the hilarious duo of Steve Martin as a sadistic biker-dentist and Bill Murray as his masochistic patient; pain for kicks has never been so funny on screen.

Candy has only one scene, when Wink interviews Seymour on his radio show, but he makes the most of it. We catch a glimpse of the scary, unpredictable quality that sometimes lies at the far end of an entertainingly over-the-top personality. This is a vivid demonstration of how effective Candy can be in quickie appearances.

Candy had another brief but memorable role in *The Canadian Conspiracy*, a seventy-five-minute, award-winning TV mockumentary about an alleged takeover of Hollywood by seditious forces from the great white north. Produced by Bill House (who had hired Candy for the children's show at the Poor Alex Theatre in 1972), it was written and directed by Robert Boyd (who went on to work on the "Kids in the Hall" TV show). Primary financing came from Home Box Office and the CBC.

The jocular premise: only through extreme American paranoia could the Canadian invasion of Hollywood be viewed as a threat. With tongue in cheek, the film presents Canadians the way Orson Welles presented Martians in his notorious *War of the Worlds* broadcast, and the way Senator Joseph McCarthy treated members of the Communist Party. What makes these new intruders so dangerous is that they look and sound just like Americans. Yet they are actually ruthless aliens spreading their subversive attitudes through a "harmless" form of popular entertainment.

One by one, various operatives—Margot Kidder, Anne Murray, Dave Thomas, Leslie Nielsen, Monty Hall, David Steinberg, Rich Little, Ivan Reitman, Morley Safer, Doug Henning and Lorne Michaels—deny there is any conspiracy. But a deadpan narrator rattles off the indictment and shows details of a plot going back to Mackenzie King and Mary Pickford. Eventually, the investigation leads to Mr. Big, Lorne Greene, who operated a school of broadcasting in Toronto circa 1950, long before he became America's favourite patriarch on NBC's hit show "Bonanza." Cornered in the deep ends of their California swimming pools Hollywood Canadians deny they've ever heard of Lorne Greene. Yet few are willing to explain how they got their "Greene" cards. And many stars are shown trying to hide their faces from the camera as they duck into waiting limos.

The breakthrough comes when a former agent turned stool pigeon spills the details of the plot. HBO wanted Candy to play this part, and House said he was prepared to offer whatever it would take to get Candy. But Candy's agent, John Gaines—who was widely known as a temperamental screamer—replied that in no circumstances would Candy play this role. Perhaps Gaines took a dim view of Candy spending his time on a low-paying, obscure Canadian TV project. Or perhaps, as House suspected, Candy wanted the gig to go to his pal Eugene Levy, who was not at the time overwhelmed with offers of work.

Once Levy was given the leading role, Candy agreed to take a smaller part as one of the celebrity conspirators. He was paid $500 and worked without a script, improvising his own material. In hilarious deadpan style, he explains to an off-camera interviewer that the principal difference between Americans and Canadians is in their footwear.

In the summer of 1986, Candy stepped up the Canadian invasion when he bought a huge, luxurious, eleven-room Spanish-style house in Brentwood, on Mandeville Canyon just north of Sunset Boulevard, and his family made a permanent move from Toronto. Before this, Candy had resisted living in L.A., saying he preferred to nest in Canada.

But Jennifer was ready to start school, the Toronto/L.A. commute was getting more difficult, and it was clear that L.A. was where most of Candy's work would be generated. This way the family could spend more time together without major upheavals.

Most of her friends and even her hairdresser were aware that Rose Candy was very apprehensive about moving to L.A. But once there she would get very involved in her local community and Catholic church affairs. And John Candy assured everyone they would have a cozy little group. Andrea Martin, Joe Flaherty and Martin Short all lived nearby. Candy felt sure Eugene Levy and his family would be next to make the move (but they never did). And after being introduced to Candy and going to lunch with him, Beatrice Arthur, the deep-voiced, big-hearted star of the TV sitcom "Maude," had offered to throw a big party welcoming the Candy family to L.A.

Moving to L.A. had become Candy's latest fix. Candy was joining the list of Canadian snowbirds for whom southern California represented the promised land, the ultimate escape, the big time and the last word in living well. But to a well-trained Catholic boy from East York, Ontario, L.A. had to represent something else as well—the devil's playground.

*Chapter 12*

# PLANES, TRAINS AND JOHN HUGHES

*A*n untitled script sent by John Hughes in 1986 seemed to John Candy like the answer to his prayers. As soon as he read the script, Candy's hopes were suddenly revived. He felt sure this was exactly what he had been waiting for.

"I just cried with laughter when I read it," Candy remarked several months before filming began. "It's like it was written for me, which makes a big difference. I could just see the movie in my mind."

For once Candy's high hopes turned out to be well founded. Hughes, the prolific independent producer/writer/director from Chicago, had made a name for himself with a string of popular brat-pack comedies but *Planes, Trains and Automobiles* wasn't about kids. This was a comedy about two mismatched business travellers, both trying to get home for a holiday weekend, who share a disastrous trip from New York to Chicago—with a long, unplanned layover in Wichita, Kansas.

Candy was to play the role of Del Griffith, a compulsively talkative salesman of shower curtain rings. Steve Martin was cast as Neal Page, a snobbish advertising executive who loathes being forced to spend time with a lowlife like Del. The script basically had only one joke but it was a shrewd one: with *Planes, Trains and Automobiles*, John Hughes had borrowed the premise of *The Defiant Ones* (Tony Curtis and Sidney Poitier handcuffed together) and turned it into a comedy—except that in this case it was class rather than race that divided the characters, and there weren't literally any handcuffs keeping them together—just psychological handcuffs.

Before starting work on the Hughes picture, Candy had to fulfil a commitment to Mel Brooks by playing a weird creature in *Spaceballs*. This was a sendup of *Star Wars* written and directed by Brooks, who was trying to repeat the huge success he had enjoyed in the 1970s with two other spoofs, *Blazing Saddles* and *Young Frankenstein*.

Candy plays a creature named Barf who is half man, half dog—a faithful sidekick to Lone Starr (the Han Solo clone played by Bill Pullman). Mel Brooks takes the dual role of President Skroob and Yogurt, and Rick Moranis is a childishly menacing figure known as Dark Helmet. The film is likeable, harmless and silly, but its wit is feeble.

The amount of money Candy was being paid for *Spaceballs* was the source of a running gag on the set. The way Candy liked to tell the story later, "Mel had never paid anybody except himself and his wife (Anne Bancroft) that kind of money. It was tough for him to part with it. He's actually a generous man, but he talks like Jack Benny."

Candy, who operated Barf's tail with a pushbutton hidden in his jumpsuit, prepared for the role by consulting his own yellow Labrador, Keema. With moveable ears that seem to be an extension of his upswept hair—suggesting built-in curlers—he looks a bit like Angela Lansbury as Mrs. Lovett in *Sweeney Todd* and a bit like Bert Lahr playing the Cowardly Lion in *The Wizard of Oz*. But this time, he's all dressed up with nowhere to go.

Candy was hardly ever known to sing, but the way he looks in *Spaceballs* makes you feel there should be a song coming on. If only Mel Brooks had given him a great silly music hall or vaudeville number like the one Lahr sang while on his way to ask the great Oz for some courage, perhaps Candy could have supplied *Spaceballs* with a much-needed blast-off.

Unlike Mel Brooks, John Hughes was the same age as Candy; they were both in their mid-thirties when they made *Planes,*

*Trains and Automobiles.* Audiences might have guessed Hughes was even younger, because he specialized in contemporary comedies about self-absorbed teenagers in middle America, and reinforced the prejudices of his target audience by caricaturing adult authority figures, especially parents and teachers.

Hughes was a hard-driving former advertising copy writer who had been remarkably successful in staking out his own turf. Four years earlier, Candy had an entertaining cameo role in one of the first movies made from a John Hughes script—*National Lampoon's Vacation.* In fact Hughes had done a kind of apprenticeship writing for the *National Lampoon* magazine. It was the success of the Lampoon movie and of another Hughes-written movie, *Mr. Mom,* that positioned Hughes to produce and direct his own projects. Seizing the opportunity, Hughes quickly built a small empire.

Movies that Hughes not only wrote and produced but also directed included *Sixteen Candles, The Breakfast Club* and *Ferris Bueller's Day Off.* And though no one talked about John Hughes as one of the greatest directors in the history of cinema, Hollywood was mightily impressed with his apparent Midas touch.

Typical Hughes characters were teenagers living in the kind of comfortable, all-white Chicago suburbia where no one ever ran out of milk and cookies. They were the indulged, precocious children of baby boomers, less concerned with the world's most pressing political and economic issues than who was taking whom to the prom, and what to wear. Hughes seemed to have little use for anyone over nineteen.

While Hughes could be criticized for sentimentalizing and pandering to his constituency, and for falling back on facile conventions, he did show flashes of talent and a fresh way of looking at familiar situations. Hughes had a great ear for lingo, catching the way these kids really talked when they were hanging out at the mall. He also had an instinct for finding and shaping young talent, notably Molly Ringwald. And the knowing selection of music on his soundtracks augmented the feeling of authenticity.

Perhaps it would be stretching things to compare an early Hughes movie to such classics about adolescent groups as

Federico Fellini's *I Vitelloni* or Jean-Luc Godard's *Masculine-Feminine*, but at first there was reason to hope that John Hughes might be capable of painting a truly original and resonant portrait of middle-class American teen life in the 1980s. However, after only a couple of years Hughes movies began to seem like sausages coming off an assembly line—a midwest precursor of "Beverly Hills 90210."

Hughes was a workaholic who churned out movie after movie quickly and often glibly. Perhaps because his life experience was too narrow to provide material for his prodigious production schedule, Hughes began repeating himself and relying on trite formulas. He wrote so many scripts that he couldn't direct them all and so developed protégés—Howard Deutch and Chris Columbus—to direct them for him. A weakness for puerile dramaturgy became distressingly evident in films like *Ferris Bueller's Day Off*.

Besides, there was so much recycling from one Hughes film to another that the entire Hughes organization began to seem like an exercise in cultural self-cannibalization. The Hughes machine would reach a kind of crescendo a few years later, when, by dropping the age of his central character from teen to subteen and putting a gimmicky new spin on his familiar tale of the stress that travel causes within an ordinary American family, he would create the most lucrative comedy in Hollywood history. The title—*Home Alone*—was proof of his marketing genius if not his film artistry.

*T*he story of *Planes, Trains* is a travel nightmare. A Chicago-bound flight is diverted to Wichita. Stuck in a blizzard, passengers are obliged to rely on other means to reach their destination. Given the holiday squeeze, these two unlikely companions are forced to share a motel room. After thrashing around in the same bed for a night, they rent a car, then wind up on a bus. Getting to Chicago has never seemed so perilous.

Covering his loneliness by chattering on and on, while cracking his knuckles as if to punctuate the clichés coming out of his mouth, Candy's Del Griffith is a relative of Tom Tuttle, the Peace Corps engineer who latched onto Tom Hanks in *Volunteers*. But this time Candy's cuddly pest—sporting a K-Mart wardrobe and a Charlie Chaplin pencil moustache to offset his mountainous flesh—is placed at the centre of the movie and programmed to win the hearts of the audience, especially when he sings a rousing version of the Flintstones theme song on a crowded bus.

Given the storyline of *PTA*, as it was nicknamed by those working on it, the movie had to be shot in a variety of locations, including New York, Chicago, Los Angeles and various points along the way. Cast and crew spent weeks on the road. Filming took place from February to May. Paramount planned to release the film in late November for the 1987 U.S. Thanksgiving weekend. Hughes was on such a tight schedule he had to delay the release of a movie he had shot previously, *She's Having a Baby*, until 1988 because he didn't have time to edit it.

According to Andy Lipschultz, the unit publicist on *PTA*, Candy was extremely gregarious and very popular with cast and crew alike. Seemingly tireless, he could do take after take after take of the same scene without complaint. One night Lipschultz was playing the saxophone in his motel room when there was a knock at the door. It was John Candy, who had to know who was playing the sax, and wanted to share the experience.

Candy earned the goodwill of almost everyone who worked on the movie, from journeymen technicians to his celebrated co-star. Despite being clearly the more established performer, Steve Martin did not seem to mind letting Candy walk away with the picture. The script invited the audience to side with Candy's character, and Martin was remarkably generous about playing second banana in this case, despite his top billing.

Speaking after Candy's death, Martin told Janet Maslin of the *New York Times* that in the course of making the film, the two lead actors did a lot of ad libbing. A decade later, Martin was still overcome by the brilliance of one touch Candy came up with.

He was referring to the moment at the end of the film when Martin goes back to the train station and finds Candy there alone. Candy explains that after his wife died, he would just travel around and attach himself to people during the holidays. "But this time I couldn't let go," he confesses.

Steve Martin's eyes filled with tears as he told Maslin this story about his deceased co-star.

The material isn't much more than a thin, artificial formula for gags, but Candy and Martin establish such an engaging Laurel-and-Hardy chemistry that even those who notice the limitations of John Hughes and his world-view may find themselves succumbing.

"This is Candy's bustout performance, the one where he puts it all together," wrote Hal Hinson in the *Washington Post.* "Candy has never been more boisterously cracked."

But Candy wasn't merely funny in *PTA*. For a change, he had an acting showcase, and he delivered a touching performance. What makes the picture special is that Candy goes way beyond formula comedy to create an affecting and memorable portrait of a blabbermouth so desperate to be liked and accepted that he worms his way into the lives of strangers.

To create this character, Candy daringly drew on an element of his own personality—the part of him that loved being on film sets because it was a way of meeting new people and turning them into friends. These co-workers became appreciative audiences for Candy's celebrated private comedy monologues, which were even more wildly hilarious than his public performances.

You can't help sympathizing with Candy's Del when, after a particularly awkward night sharing a motel bed, his snobbish room-mate tells him off. However, some of us may cringe when Candy retorts with a speech about the dignity of little people that even Frank Capra, that shameless master of populist manipulation, might have considered excessive. It was as if Hughes wanted to persuade someone that this wasn't just a light comedy, it was his own personal *Death of a Salesman.*

There were a few dissenting critics, but even David Denby, who panned *PTA* in *New York* magazine, admitted: "The movie has one bright, nasty insight going for it: that someone like Martin's executive, who has fought his whole life for status and defines himself by his taste, would experience sudden intimacy with a social inferior as an unspeakable violation of everything he stands for."

Whatever the critics thought, *Planes, Trains and Automobiles* was embraced by the movie-going public from the moment it opened on screens across North America on November 25, 1987—taking in ten million dollars at the box office during its first five days in release.

*Planes, Trains and Automobiles* proved to be a milestone for Hughes. It demonstrated that he could make a film about adults and still have a hit, and thereby liberated him from his self-created teen ghetto. For John Candy it proved to be even more of a benchmark.

This was the movie that changed Candy's life and made him, at long last, a genuine Hollywood star. At first, Candy was thrilled about this development. But within a couple of years, the pressures of stardom would begin closing in on him, causing a major strain. For a while, it would be great to have the recognition and the money he had always craved. But then it would no longer seem so great, and he would come to feel that the best times of his life were the days when he and his sharp-witted pals were unknowns working at Second City for a couple of hundred dollars a week.

After *PTA*, John Candy's life would never be the same. It wasn't just that he had become at last what he had always wanted to be—a movie star. It was that he was a particular kind of movie star. Millions of people who thought of themselves as ordinary slobs adored him, because this overwhelmingly unglamorous guy was one of them, making their kind of life count for something by putting it up there on the big screen.

Creating a common-man hero as lovable as Chaplin's Little Tramp, Candy had accorded validation to a lot of people who went to see this movie in suburban malls. They recognized themselves in his performance, which made them want to honour Candy and be a part of his success. They felt connected to him, as if he were a close personal friend. But this kind of adulation, though Candy had always dreamed of it, was as hard to handle as neglect.

After playing Del Griffith, John Candy could never go out in public without being mobbed by devoted fans. Movie-watching America had fallen in love with him, and not even a string of third-rate movies could shake that allegiance. From the moment *PTA* opened, John Candy had a big new problem to cope with:

the consequences of getting what he had spent much of his life wishing for.

Shortly before *PTA* opened, there was a high-spirited evening at Candy's Brentwood home. The guests included Graham Chapman, of Monty Python fame, who had flown in from England to discuss a film he and Candy were planning to make together. The film, which Chapman had written in collaboration with Monty Python colleague John Cleese, was called *Ditto*. It was a comedy about a man who throws himself into a duplicating machine and copies himself. Chapman wanted to direct the film with Candy in the leading role.

Candy, who was again in a Pritikin phase, loved to cook for friends, especially pasta, and on this night he and Rose whipped up an elaborate but healthy pasta dish of which Candy was very proud. Present at the dinner besides Chapman and Candy's two children, Jennifer and Christopher, were Catherine McCartney, who had come from Toronto to help negotiate the deal, and Jon Slan, president of Paragon Films (who like Candy had recently moved his family from Toronto to L.A.).

Slan was a prospective producing partner. That Canadian connection gave Candy a rationale for getting McCartney involved in the deal. Long after moving to Hollywood and hiring high-profile Hollywood agents and managers, Candy continued to give her a piece of the action, as a gesture of loyalty to someone who had helped him get started in show business.

There were a lot of funny stories told that night. Candy was doing his best to cheer up Chapman, who seemed depressed. It wasn't clear until later that Chapman had been terminally ill at the time. At the end of the evening, Candy screened *Planes, Trains and Automobiles*.

Several of those interested in working on *Ditto* felt it needed a rewrite, and Bob Dolman (an SCTV writer who had until recently been married to Andrea Martin) was brought in to work on it. But the project wound up on indefinite hold because Chapman didn't like Dolman's suggested changes. By the fall of 1989 Chapman would be dead, a cancer victim at the age of forty-eight.

*A*fter the phenomenal success of PTA, Candy developed a close ongoing relationship with John Hughes. Even before the film was released, he had done a cameo appearance (uncredited) for Hughes in *She's Having a Baby*, which was released in early 1988. And Candy became a kind of good-luck charm for Hughes, as if even a token involvement by Candy was a good omen for any project.

*The Great Outdoors*, a Hughes movie directed by Howard Deutch, reunited Candy with his old friend Dan Aykroyd. (This was the third of four movies Candy and Aykroyd made together.) Allegedly based on the recollections by Hughes of a camping trip he once took to Wisconsin, this was thin material that seemed to recycle *National Lampoon's Vacation* (a Chicago family on an ill-fated holiday) and *Planes, Trains and Automobiles* (two incompatible guys forced to be together).

Shot in the fall of 1987 near Bass Lake, California, and released in the early summer of 1988, *The Great Outdoors* was at best a family programmer for a broad constituency seeking innocuous hot-weather diversion.

Candy and Aykroyd are teamed as antagonistic brothers-in-law getting on one another's nerves during a family vacation at a lakeside resort. Candy plays a sweet, slightly dopey guy named Chet, who brings his brood from Chicago for a getaway in the north woods. Aykroyd is the obnoxious Roman, who arrives uninvited (in a Mercedes sedan with the licence plate ROMAN 1), bringing his entire dysfunctional family—and ruins everything.

Chet loves rural serenity; Roman sees every acre of unspoiled nature as a potential condo development or toxic-waste dump. The level of cute humour is epitomized by a running gag about raccoons, with their grunts translated into humorous English via subtitles.

Leeches get into the rowboat, and a bat gets into the cabin. Candy gets to tread water and fool around on water-skis. His most memorable challenge, though, was playing a scene with a 1400-pound grizzly bear named Bart.

"It was one of the most frightening experiences of my life," Candy confessed when the filming was over.

The scene required Bart to run after Chet. In order to get him to do that, Bart's trainer stood in front of Candy with food. Candy was wearing a green parka; all the bear could see was this big green thing in front of him blocking his food.

"I know I impressed a lot of the film crew," Candy joked. "They didn't know I could run that fast."

When the movie came out, there were those who thought Candy should have run fast after he read the script.

"The raccoons will have a better time than the audience," quipped the *New York Times*.

*Hot to Trot*, a Warner Brothers comedy also released in 1988, featured the voice of John Candy but not his face. That's because Candy shared acting duties with a sleek four-legged creature in the role of a talking horse named Don. Why would Candy consent to be in a feeble barnyard sitcom? No doubt he had fond memories of Donald O'Connor in the *Francis the Talking Mule* movies.

Besides, Candy was shrewd enough to realize it would be less time-consuming and less taxing to star in a movie if you didn't have to worry about make-up, costume and hair. He wouldn't have to show up on shooting days; he just had to go to the sound lab and record his lines and hope that the animal trainers had taught the horse to move its lips when words were supposed to be coming out.

Comedian Bob Goldthwait plays Don's owner, a stupid stockbroker who relies on Don for hot tips, and has a troublesome stepfather played by Dabney Coleman with horsey buck teeth. Among the big jokes: Don's horse family hangs a human shoe over its door; and when Don introduces the family to his human pal, one of them wants to know what it's like having sex facing your partner.

Candy does a good job of humanizing Don, but *Variety* summed it up brutally: "*Hot to Trot* is dog food. Box office should be nil."

Thanks to *Planes, Trains and Automobiles*, Candy was free to choose his projects carefully. His price per picture had climbed to three million dollars. The mystery is: Why did he go on appearing in so many bad movies if he could afford to say no?

Some people in Hollywood blamed Candy's agent, John Gaines of the Agency for Performing Arts (who would die of AIDS in 1993). But Candy read the scripts and in the end decided which movies to do and which movies not to do. He was restless when he was between projects, and didn't really want time off. He felt most truly at home on a film set; he thrived on long hours and enjoyed the camaraderie with cast and crew. Besides, the shadow of his father's early death gave him a need to build up a nest egg for Rose, Jennifer and Christopher in case they had to go on without him.

Then, too, each fresh project was like a new toy in which Candy could invest his hopes. When a movie failed, it was a depressing blow, and to get out of his funk, Candy needed a new challenge to pour his energy into. Starting a new movie was like the up phase in a manic/depressive cycle.

Candy was especially optimistic about *Who's Harry Crumb?*—filmed in Vancouver in the spring of 1988 and released in February, 1989—because he felt it represented a turning point in his career. In many of his Hollywood movie experiences, Candy had felt frustrated and powerless. Scripts that had seemed good when he read them were rewritten several times, and movies that had seemed promising turned into embarrassing fiascos.

*Who's Harry Crumb?* was supposed to be different. It was being produced by Arnon Milchan, whose credits included such reputable movies as *Once Upon a Time in America, The King of Comedy* and *Brazil.* Candy and Milchan had become friends, and the movie was being tailored to Candy's talents.

*Crumb* was to be filmed in Vancouver, and Candy would be working with many old friends. The director was Paul Flaherty (an SCTV alumnus and Joe Flaherty's brother), and the cast included Joe Flaherty, Valri Bromfield and Stephen Young. And with a credit as executive producer, Candy had a hands-on role.

During his stay in Vancouver, Candy was in a buoyant mood. For once he was doing a movie where he had some control and his input was welcome. When Catherine McCartney paid a visit, Candy took her to a little restaurant he had discovered. When they arrived, there was hardly anyone in the place,

but within half an hour the place was packed with other customers who seemed more interested in John Candy than what
they were having for dinner.

Candy was feeling gregarious, basking in the enhanced
celebrity status *PTA* had brought. After a while he moved into
the kitchen, and took over cooking and bringing out orders. The
party went on well past the normal closing time, at which point
Candy invited the staff of the restaurant to his hotel suite, where
the talking, laughing and drinking continued into the night.

When *Who's Harry Crumb?* was finished, it turned out to be
a serious letdown. It's an amiable comedy with Candy as a bumbling detective who thinks he's a brilliant sleuth, and comes up
with all the wrong answers while trying to foil a gang of rogues
who have kidnapped an heiress. Candy has some mildly entertaining moments, and he gives a graceful performance, but the
film suffers from having only one main character, and it never
gets past being a Pink Panther knockoff.

There are too many gags about broken furniture, booby-
trapped cars and Harry's dimwittedness. It would take a better
director than Paul Flaherty—who shows little evidence of comic
energy or precision timing—to make sparkling comedy out of
this tame, derivative script.

Trevor Evans, the CBC producer who had hired Candy in
1974 to appear in children's shows, was with Candy and
McCartney the night Candy wound up cooking in the restaurant kitchen. CBC executive Carol Reynolds had asked Evans a
year earlier if he could get Candy to star in a TV special. Candy
had come up with a concept: He wanted to entertain Canadian
Army troops in Germany or Malta, in the style of Bob Hope.
He would do sketches on war subjects, like having people during
the War of 1812 go to Buffalo to shop. He would use Canadian
guest stars such as k.d. lang and Michael J. Fox.

But the project was too costly for the CBC, and discussions
dragged on for more than a year. By then the CBC was no
longer underwriting shows on its own but working with co-pro-
ducers. Evans delivered the news that Candy would have to
bring in a U.S. co-producer or put up a large portion of the budget for the show from his own company.

Candy resented what he took as a rebuff, and went so far as to tell Evans he would never work for the CBC again. But six months later, he would host a gala evening at the Just for Laughs comedy festival in Montreal, which was produced as a CBC special. And Candy continued to have friendly dealings with Carol Reynolds.

"John Candy Entertains Canadian Forces Abroad" wasn't the only TV special dreamed up by Candy but never produced. For several years he worked at getting the old SCTV gang together for one last show, and in 1986 he told Brian Linehan he was optimistic about doing a one-hour reunion special to be aired on CBS in prime time. Candy called all the old cast members and asked if it would be possible. Most said they would never want to revive the series but would like to do a one-time event.

But when they began discussing details, the arguments began. Candy had already promised some of SCTV's old writers they could be involved, but Eugene Levy and Catherine O'Hara felt strongly if it was going to be a one-occasion, one-hour show, the performers should do all the writing themselves. Candy was irritated by their attitude. Besides, trying to co-ordinate schedules was an exercise in frustration.

The SCTV reunion was beginning to look like the impossible dream, as wistful and impractical a notion as the widespread yearning for one more Beatles concert. Those cheeky kids who used to regale us tweaking the nose of the show-business establishment had long since staked their separate claims in the system they used to lampoon, and it was too late to get back to where they once belonged. They had ventured too far down that long, winding road—the one that led to the gigantic letters spelling out the name of the entertainment capital against the backdrop of the Hollywood hills.

*Chapter 13*

# SUNSET BOULEVARD

The big change in John Candy's life, the way Martyn Burke remembers it, began the moment Candy shook hands with Bruce McNall at the Great Western Forum on October 6, 1988, the night Wayne Gretzky made his debut as a member of the L.A. Kings hockey team before the home-town fans. As the team's owner, McNall basked in Gretzky's glory that season, and as McNall's new best friend, Candy basked in the glory of Gretzky's proudly smiling owner.

"From then on I began to see a lot of changes in John," recalls Burke, a novelist, film-maker and screenwriter from Toronto who had known Candy since 1975. "He was clearly making an effort to be more like Bruce. At times I got the feeling he actually wanted to *BE* Bruce McNall."

There were certain similarities between the two men, Burke had noticed. They were both big chubby guys about the same age with similar social backgrounds, and they both worked hard to seem gregarious on the outside when in fact deep within both there was a feeling of painful shyness.

John Candy was taller than McNall and rarely wore suits but in other ways he and McNall were almost mirror images. Both had risen—despite social backgrounds of little distinction, bleak nowhereseville upbringings, and school peers who regarded them as social misfits—to positions of considerable fame and eminence. They even had similar smiles.

What did these two see when they looked at one another? In Candy, McNall must have seen a popular movie star who was also an avid hockey fan as well as a Canadian like Gretzky—all of which translated into someone who could help boost the image of the Kings.

To Candy, McNall was a mover and a shaker—a smart operator who shaped his own destiny. By contrast, Candy saw himself as a mere performer who was at the mercy of the players who ran the system. In McNall, Candy saw someone he could emulate and thus find a way to gain control of his own career.

According to journalist Kevin Cook, who chronicled McNall's misdeeds for *GQ* magazine, McNall had a mesmerizing effect on people. "McNall radiated success, and he was very friendly. People genuinely liked him and enjoyed shaking hands with him. He not only revitalized the Kings franchise but created an aura of Hollywood glamour around them. He conveyed the promise of pleasure and excitement: with Gretzky, the Kings were going to win a lot of hockey games, and everyone was going to have a lovely time."

McNall had a block of seats reserved for his VIP friends, and before long Candy was invited to McNall's box, way up behind the opposing team's goal looking down the full length of the ice. After his first visit to the McNall box, Candy returned to section twenty and told Burke: "I hate sitting up there. I can't stand McNall's seats."

But as time went on, that's where he sat all the time.

McNall's private party went on before the games and after the games. He started a tradition of holding small private dinners in the Senate club (a dining lounge) at the Forum. There was always an E-shaped table, and the seating was carefully orchestrated. The more important you were considered, the closer you sat to McNall.

At first there were typically about twenty guests at these dinners, but gradually over a few years the size of a routine gathering grew to double that number. Among the celebrities often included were: Goldie Hawn and her mate Kurt Russell, Tom Hanks, Kevin Costner, Sylvester Stallone, Arsenio Hall, Barry

Bonds, Woody Harrelson, Michael J. Fox.

McNall's chief financial officer, the fiercely unpopular Susan Waks, was a regular as was Jane Cody, McNall's wife at the time. And there was usually a smattering of bankers and financiers McNall was trying to impress. Even Ronald and Nancy Reagan spent an evening at the Forum as McNall's guests.

The joke about Candy was that even after he was made honorary team captain of the Kings, no one could be sure whether he was fully committed to the Kings or still rooting for his old hometown favourites, the Toronto Maple Leafs. As an extension of the joke, Candy even had a hockey sweatshirt made up that was half L.A. Kings and half Toronto Maple Leafs.

Within a year Candy was so much a part of the McNall entourage that he sold his old season's tickets to Burke. The change of seating was something Burke regarded as a symbolic gesture that signalled big changes in Candy's life.

According to Burke, despite his star status, Candy didn't truly consider his film work respectable, and the one thing he craved above all was to be taken seriously. Candy was looking for a way to validate himself—to do something he considered honourable. Burke saw McNall unwittingly turn the key and unlock the door to Candy's psyche; as Burke watched in horror, all of Candy's demons proceeded to spill out.

"I could see John comparing himself to Bruce and becoming more unhappy with whoever and whatever he was," says Burke. Just where this was leading would not become clear until two years later, when Candy, in partnership with McNall and Gretzky, would become co-owner of the Toronto Argonauts football team and return to his home town as a kind of Great North clone of McNall. Candy had a tendency to want to do too much; after he met McNall that tendency accelerated dramatically. Before long, Candy was surrounding himself with flunkies, the way McNall did.

And extending his own weakness for extravagance, Candy got into the McNall-like habit of looking at every problem as if it could be solved by spending exorbitant sums of money. Candy bought expensive art, and furniture he didn't need. He acquired an expensive family vacation house in Lake Arrowhead (two hours from L.A.) which he hardly ever occupied. He built a state-of-the-art fitness centre for himself in his guest house, but rarely got around to using it.

"In order to understand why John turned himself into an owner and a tycoon," explains Burke, "you have to look at how tremendously influenced he was by McNall. He adopted the same credo: Enough is never enough.

"Whenever John got something or achieved something, after a very short time, he would decide that it wasn't sufficient; he had to go on to something else. This craving got so extreme that every achievement became like a drug addict's short-term fix. There would be a quick burst of euphoria, and then he would be plunged into deep despair again, and so he'd start looking for the next fix."

Before this time Candy had a small townhouse office on Montana Street in Brentwood, very near where Nicole Brown Simpson would be murdered a few years later. In those days, Candy's company, Frostbacks, was a small operation like those of many actors who had achieved enough success to develop material to showcase their talent, and then make deals with studios to have these movies produced. But following McNall's example, Candy began using Frostbacks to pursue a wildly varied range of activities, including a radio show hosted by Candy and a cartoon series featuring Candy's voice and personality.

A few months after meeting McNall, Candy took his hockey-fan buddies Burke and Young to see a building he was thinking of buying in Santa Monica. It was a huge place with ten times as much space as Candy had in his Brentwood office. It was more like McNall's headquarters.

"What do you need all this space for?" Burke and Young asked. "After all, you're an actor, not a conglomerate."

"You don't understand," replied Candy. "We're going to make this into a big production company very actively involved in a whole range of projects."

Soon they began to see what he meant. Candy didn't buy the building in Santa Monica, but he did buy a very large office building on San Vincente Boulevard north of Wilshire near his home. Once he had moved into it, he hired enough assistants to fill it, and embarked on a McNall-like series of schemes and deals. There were not only movies but "Radio Kandy" (the weekly radio show), a Saturday morning TV cartoon show called "Camp Candy" with Candy as a comical head counsellor and various projected TV specials.

Late one night Claire Burrill got a call from Candy saying they must work together again. Burrill had started as Candy's lawyer and wound up handling Candy's affairs in the early 1980s before being dropped in 1985. Now he was being wooed back to take over Frostbacks and turn it into a major enterprise.

Burrill accepted the challenge, starting in January of 1989, as Candy was about to start filming *Uncle Buck* in Chicago and "Radio Kandy" was beginning an eighteen-month run.

Some may have wondered why Candy wanted to become enmeshed in such a complicated set of business affairs when it would have been easier for him to sit back and accept offers of huge fees to appear in movies set up by other people. In fact it was of great importance to Candy to feel he was in control, that he was playing a creative role behind the scenes, that he was a player. It was gratifying for him to have a lot of people working for him and answering to him even if that forced him into a job—CEO of Frostbacks—for which he was ill-suited. In Candy's mind, all that was a necessary part of really making it in Hollywood.

The imperative to forge his own empire was motivated partly by Candy's feelings of frustration and helplessness when he was just a hired actor, albeit a high-paid one. Just before the escalation of Frostbacks, Candy had the experience of doing a commercial movie gig for a fee of three million dollars, and it was understandable why it did not leave him with a feeling of satisfaction.

*Speed Zone!* was the third movie in the *Cannonball Run* series. Hollywood producer Al Ruddy had had the film in development for years before he made a deal with Montreal producer Murray Shostak, who had come up with a way to do it by taking advantage of Canadian tax-shelter incentives.

The story had the same old premise as the two *Cannonball Run* pictures made earlier in the 1980s. There was an illegal cross-country road race with a huge cash prize and a make-your-own-rules competition. Only this time the pros were out of the running and it was up to amateur drivers to fill their place.

The picture afforded another opportunity for stunts and sight gags plus a chance to show off a lot of flashy sportscars and some handsome scenery.

The cannonball movie craze had begun in 1976 with the release of two movies—an action film called *The Gumball Rally*, and a spoof entitled *Cannonball*. Then in 1981 Ruddy and Raymond Chow cooked up *Cannonball Run*, with Burt Reynolds, which was a baffling box-office hit—thus leading to a dismal 1984 sequel, *Cannonball Run II*. *Speed Zone!* brought the cycle to a merciful conclusion.

Candy's involvement was absolutely crucial, as far as the producers were concerned, so they were willing to accept his three million price-tag on a movie with a total budget of sixteen million dollars. His participation gave the movie authentic Canadian credentials while at the same time attracting a substantial pre-production sale to a Japanese distributor. Candy was not only a Canadian with box-office clout in the U.S., he was also hugely popular in Japan. So important was the Japanese money that some of the actors, notably Brooke Shields, were hired specifically because of their appeal in the Japanese market.

But Candy did not seem to regard *Speed Zone!* as simply a grab for quick money. According to Vivienne Leebosh, who was hired by Shostak to be the associate producer, Candy was very high on the project, and got quite involved in shaping the script and choosing some of the actors.

The script was written by Michael Short, one of Candy's old SCTV colleagues. The director, Jim Drake, was urged on the producers by Candy's agent, John Gaines. Since Drake's experience was mainly in TV comedy, Candy was able to wield a great deal of influence over him. And Donna Dixon, Candy's leading lady, got the part at Candy's suggestion.

Much of the filming was done outside Montreal, but additional shooting had to be done in Arizona and Los Angeles. The producers ran into a lot of problems. They were under pressure to complete principal photography before December 31, 1988, to comply with Canadian tax-shelter regulations. Early snow in Montreal caused the budget to skyrocket. As a result, everyone wound up fighting with everyone, and the film-completion guarantors moved in to take charge, protecting investors from being stuck with an unfinished movie.

"The Cannonball is history," barks Peter Boyle as a demented police chief named Spiro Edsel. After *Speed Zone!*, it was.

As the story begins, it seems the illegal, high-stakes road race has been done in by Chief Edsel and his law-and-order ilk. So the pros quit, and it's left to a bunch of cheerful amateurs—John Candy and others—to take over, roar across the country in their funny cars and cross the finish line in time to collect some loot.

Eugene Levy plays one of his crazed nasty guys—an abusive fellow with a sweet, kooky girlfriend (Donna Dixon) who talks like Marilyn Monroe (for reasons never explained) and is thinking of changing her name from Tiffany to Norma Jean. She is rescued by Candy and, in the film's funniest scene, is at his side feeding him movie-trivia questions when Candy, pursued by a fleet of police cars, off-handedly puts his car into reverse at a high speed. Before the movie is over, in the name of chivalry, Candy gets a chance to punch out Levy.

The cast includes Joe Flaherty, Tim Matheson, Jamie Farr and the Smothers Brothers. But the high-profile talent is mostly wasted on a fast trip to nowhere in particular. Candy does have a few amusing moments, but he's on cruise control most of the time.

Seeing Candy at the centre of a recycled old movie may remind SCTV aficionados of that old sketch when Candy as Dr. Tongue and Levy as Woody Tobias, having taken on the Jon Voight and Dustin Hoffman roles in an appalling sequel to *Midnight Cowboy*, come face to face on a panel discussion with Pauline Kael (as impersonated by Mary Charlotte Wilcox), who demands to know what possible reason they would have for doing it. They're a little hesitant to admit the obvious—that they're doing it because they thought they had a chance to make a killing.

Now only six years after performing that sketch, Candy found himself in the position of the characters he used to satirize on

"SCTV." What would he say if he met the real Pauline Kael and she asked him why he was doing movies like *Speed Zone*? It's hard to imagine Candy had really conned himself into thinking he was going to get anything out of *Speed Zone!* above and beyond a cheque for three million dollars.

Candy had appeared in an embarrassing number of bad movies, and cumulatively they had exacted a toll. Though almost every star gets stuck in some turkeys, Candy had been in much more than his share of them, to the point that appearing in stinkers was one of the things he was known for. Amazingly, though, Candy survived being in movies that would have killed other careers. There was something about him that made the public want to forgive him. This or that movie may have been a dog, but they still loved John Candy.

Could he have made better choices? No doubt. Would it have been preferable if he had worked less frequently but more selectively? Probably—but it would be naïve to think that any intelligent observer could tell in advance which movies were going to turn out well and which ones badly. Unlikely as it may seem that a genuinely witty *Cannonball Run* movie could be made, who's to say it was absolutely out of the question? Hollywood movies were at best a glamorous crapshoot. Anything could happen.

According to Bernard Sahlins, the Second City guru who had discovered Candy back in 1973, the problem lay in the specific form of lunacy known as going Hollywood.

"When he hit it big in *Splash*," explains Sahlins, "it was the right kind of role for John—reactive." (Sahlins meant that Candy's work was framed by his character's relationship to Tom Hanks.) "Then with the usual Hollywood insanity they started throwing things at him that were wrong for him—leading-man things. There are very few people who can keep a career perspective in the face of this kind of temptation. Rose was a great anchor and stabilizing influence, but finally you find yourself surrounded by advisers who tell you only what you want to hear. John enjoyed making a lot of money and feeling universally loved and being Johnny Toronto. And maybe he couldn't help himself. People in Hollywood live in some other world—rarified and remote. It's hard to say no. That's why Hollywood people keep failing upwardly.

"When you have power there's no one to thrust the truth on you because you're so powerful and most of the time you don't want to hear it. And if you're also famous, you can't go out to eat without fifty people looking to see whether you're using the right fork. In defence, you are forced to lead an artificial existence. At first you are pleasantly surprised when you walk down the street and people mob you. Then after a while when they mob you, you're irritated. But if they ever stop mobbing you, then you get really upset. You're caught in an absurd and deadly syndrome."

According to Martyn Burke, Hollywood was a funhouse where John Candy got lost. "When you become successful in Hollywood, you have money, power and fame all being thrown at you. If you go after all of it at once, Hollywood will destroy you. John was too scattered and unfocused to make good choices. He got involved in a huge range of activities that would have been beyond anyone's capacity to handle. By the time he had to apply the brakes, it was too late. The wheels had come off."

Candy was painfully aware of the bind his star status had put him in, and had spent a lot of hours feeling depressed and miserable when some of the clinkers came out and were badly received. The worst times were long nights at his Brentwood home, when he would sit in front of his giant-screen TV set brooding, drinking and eating large quantities of junk food. (By 1988, he had abandoned the Pritikin regime.)

Sometimes, in a melancholy or sentimental mood, he would place calls to old friends he had lost touch with, such as Charles Northcote and Sheldon Patinkin, as if he were reliving the good old days and trying to find a way to get back to them. Life at the top was not turning out to be quite as wonderful as Candy had imagined in the days when he used to spend so much time and energy trying to get there. Now that the initial elation had worn off, he was beginning to discover that having stardom was in some ways more problematic than the frustration he had known in the past feeling constantly on the verge of it and waiting for the magic moment to arrive.

One of the big items on Candy's ever-lengthening list of

grievances was Tri-Star's abysmal marketing campaign for *Who's Harry Crumb?*, released, in a manner of speaking, in the spring of 1989. Candy had gone to the trouble of preparing an ad campaign and handed it to the studio. But Tri-Star executives rejected it, saying they had their own. According to Candy, there was very little evidence of it.

"I had to rent my own billboards," he complained incredulously afterward. Tri-Star purported not to believe in billboards.

Obviously, Tri-Star had lost faith in *Harry Crumb* before it was released. Opening it was just a matter of going through the motions. After a few weeks, the movie had vanished without a trace.

Doing a weekly radio show might not make a lot of sense economically, but at least Candy could have a good time doing it. In a way, the radio show represented a return to the fondly remembered past, when Candy and his SCTV colleagues were just a bunch of wisecracking kids operating with almost no money and enjoying the freedom of putting their shows together any way they felt like it.

"You're listening to Radio Kandy!" Candy's listeners were informed at the top of the show. "What else have you got to do?"

His weekly two-hour show, starting in January on Sunday mornings at eight o'clock, was syndicated by Transtar Radio Network and carried on close to three hundred stations in the U.S. and Canada.

On the first show, some listeners were startled to hear California traffic reports delivered by a certain Commander Wes Steel, who was allegedly surveying the roads from a B-52 bomber and shooting at stalled cars.

Candy had played disc jockey before, hosting a ninety-minute program in Canada a couple of years earlier, mixing jokes and old rock songs. The same producer, Toronto ad man Doug Thompson, was packaging the new show.

"Radio Kandy" was above all a showcase for Candy, reflecting his humour, his taste in music and even his choice of friends. Candy's old pal Valri Bromfield appeared regularly as a teen pop idol. Joe Flaherty was also a regular. And from time to time there would be visits from Edith Prickley (Andrea Martin), the McKenzie Brothers (Dave Thomas and Rick Moranis) and Ed Grimley (Martin Short).

The show made its debut on the air just when Candy had gone to Chicago to start filming *Uncle Buck*—produced, written and directed by John Hughes. Arrangements were made for Candy to record his material at a studio in Chicago and send the tape to L.A., where the show was packaged.

This coincidence no doubt led Candy to invent one of his best bits in *Uncle Buck*. Candy as Buck is alone in the kitchen of his brother's suburban house on his first morning of being responsible for his nieces and nephew. As he starts to cook breakfast, he fantasizes about being a radio deejay and begins barking out patter. Then he hears LaVern Baker singing "Tweedlee Dum, Tweedlee Dee" and, while cooking eggs, sings along and bops around the kitchen until he's apprehended by his difficult, scowling teenage niece, Tia.

This is the kind of wonderfully silly detail that can cheer you up when you see it and make you break into a smile every time you recall it afterward. In the end it was the accumulation of such moments in many movies and TV sketches that made John Candy beloved by millions of fans.

Buck is the eccentric relative whose most attractive feature is his availability to fill in on short notice. He is asked to move in and take over when an emergency forces his brother and sister-in-law to travel without their children. From the moment he arrives, Buck gets drawn into domestic combat with fifteen-year-old Tia (Jean Kelly), who regards him contemptuously as a nerdy imbecile. Tia has to learn, along with the rest of us, that Buck is not quite the childish lowlife he seems.

*Uncle Buck* turns out to be far from a great movie, but Candy is both funny and touching in it, giving one of his most winning performances. Unfortunately, there's a price to be paid for the pleasure of watching Candy in top form; the audience has to suffer through a lot of groan-provoking John Hughes contrivances. Hughes reaches rock bottom in a scene at the younger niece's school when he uses the principal's facial deformity as a way of making the audience loathe her.

Buck not only manages to protect Tia from her no-good boyfriend and her sister from those hateful school authorities but also feeds pretzels and beer to the family dog, sorts out a problem he has had with his long-suffering girl friend (Amy Madigan), and forges a relationship with his eight-year-old nephew (Macaulay Culkin in his debut) through entertaining banter.

The Hughes script is an improvement on *The Great Outdoors* but not as good as *Planes, Trains and Automobiles*. Yet afterward you can forget all that and remember the beautiful vaudeville timing of Candy and Culkin, or the endearingly funny spectacle of an ill-prepared outcast learning family values while munching frosted flakes and trying to vacuum up the mess on his clothes.

No wonder the part and the actor were made for each other. In truth there was more than a trace of Uncle Buck in Candy's real life. Certainly at times, surveying his luxurious surroundings in Brentwood, Candy must have wondered what he was doing there. At heart, he was still a guy more comfortable snacking on frosted flakes straight from the box, like Buck, than being offered caviar canapés on a silver tray at some elegant soirée in Beverly Hills. And as Candy explained in interviews, he found the basis of Buck's relationship with his nieces and nephew in his own relationship with Jennifer and Christopher. The essential point was not to talk down to the kids, but to treat them as equals.

During the making of *Uncle Buck*, Candy was as much of an overgrown kid off the set as on. One night he went out with Tarquin Gotch, an Englishman who had moved to Chicago to supervise the music on the soundtracks of Hughes' movies and wound up as an executive producer. As Gotch recalls, he was in Candy's limousine when Candy spotted a bar he liked and suggested they go in. The two had a fine time, as several hours rolled by. Candy just kept telling one great story after another. He befriended a couple of other people at the bar, and it became sort of a party.

The next morning at the crack of dawn Hughes was on his way to the set planning a busy day including two scenes involving Candy. He had the radio on in his car, and heard a phone-in show.

A listener called in and said, "You'll never guess who I've been with all night. I was with John Candy at this bar, and he was in such great form they kept the place open most of the night."

Hughes was livid. He phoned Candy to express his displeasure. Hughes claimed Candy could not possibly be in shape to do the scenes as required. Candy took the position that Uncle Buck was SUPPOSED to be a bit dishevelled. Hughes wasn't mollified. He cancelled the scenes for the day and told Candy to pull himself together and get some sleep.

Candy and Hughes made up after this tiff, but it turned out to be a sneak preview of a more serious falling out the two would have two years later.

Candy and Gotch, however, remained good friends for the rest of Candy's life whether or not they were working with the Hughes organization. "John Candy was a sweetheart," says Gotch. "If he was nice to you, it was because he liked you, not because he was impressed by your powerful position and how useful you could be to him. That's fairly rare in Hollywood. He was happiest when he could hang with the team. He liked being on a film set because then he knew what he was going to be doing at all times. And sometimes he would agree to a project which a more hard-headed operator would reject, just for the sake of an old friendship. He liked to be surrounded by people he felt comfortable with. He had his favourite driver, his favourite stand-in, and his favourite hair stylist."

All told, Candy appeared in eight John Hughes movies. He had leading roles in four of them and cameos in four others.

In *Home Alone* (produced and written by Hughes, directed by Chris Columbus) Candy provides a witty high spot. Catherine O'Hara is stranded at an airport trying to get back to Chicago after the family has gone to Paris and inadvertently left Macaulay Culkin home alone. To the rescue comes this guy from a midwest polka band played by Candy. No doubt his funny riff on the polka side of showbiz was created by Candy as a spinoff from his Shmenge Brothers material. He's equally funny when, driving through the heartland, he tries to make her feel better by telling her the grotesquely funny story of a kid who was accidentally left behind at a funeral home—and instead makes her feel worse.

Candy was on the set of *Home Alone* for only one day, and did almost all his filming in one amazing twenty-two-hour marathon shift. Candy constantly amazed Columbus with his stamina. He was happy to do take after take after take, often improvising.

When Hughes asked Candy to be in *Home Alone*, he offered him a tiny piece of the movie's profits. Candy graciously declined, saying it was only a cameo and he would do it as a favour. He had no idea that this tame, routine comedy would strike a nerve with middle America and take in a staggering $270 million—making it the third top-grossing movie in Hollywood history.

Candy had turned down a small fortune. But he felt so sure he would have an ongoing collaboration with John Hughes that he made plans to buy an apartment in Chicago. In fact, he would make only two more movies with Hughes. In one of them, *Only the Lonely*, he would have a chance to test himself as a serious dramatic actor. In the other, *Career Opportunities*, he would brighten a dreary film, playing a confused corporate recruiter who accidentally offers a cushy executive job to a candidate not actually qualified for anything but part-time night cleaning.

Though Candy often floundered in starring vehicles, he was almost always brilliant in quickie roles, which provided a chance to show off the satiric sketch skills he had perfected on "SCTV." And Hughes was smart enough to take advantage of the fact that in Candy he had not only a leading man but also Hollywood's king of cameos.

# Chapter 14

# NOTHING BUT TROUBLE

*F*or a brief time it seemed as if a good dose of stardom might be the magical cure for John Candy's lifelong insecurity. Instead, it served eventually only to intensify his anxiety. In truth, probably no amount of acclaim and reward could ever have been enough to alleviate his self-doubt.

When he was younger and less famous, Candy's eagerness for approval had been one of his most likeable qualities. Now it often seemed to have turned into a seething resentment toward those who failed to give him the recognition he craved.

One of Candy's outbursts was prompted by his anger at Bette Midler, who was about to star in *Stella*—an ill-advised remake of the 1937 Barbara Stanwyck tearjerker *Stella Dallas*. *Stella* was to be filmed in Toronto for Disney, and Candy was expecting to be offered the role of Stella's boyfriend, ultimately played by John Goodman.

Charles Northcote, who was in L.A. around that period on business and spent time visiting Candy, got an earful on the subject. Candy and Northcote, who had been Shriners together in the play *Creeps* eighteen years earlier at Toronto's Tarragon Theatre, had resumed their friendship after a lapse of several years.

They were having a lovely time catching up, and Candy had proudly showed Northcote some of the touches he had added to his Brentwood mansion. There were two guest houses behind the main house, which housed a playroom, a state-of-the-art workout gym for Candy, and a wonderful pottery studio for Rose. And there was an amusing touch in the yard that was pure Candy. He had installed two newspaper street boxes—one for the *Toronto Star*, one for the *Toronto Sun*.

Candy seemed like a relaxed, amiable host until the subject of *Stella* came up. Bette Midler, Candy complained, had had the nerve to demand Candy audition for the part, which he considered an indignity. He refused. Northcote was taken aback by the intensity of Candy's fury as he told the story.

"How dare she?" ranted Candy. "Who the fuck does she think she is?"

He sounded like a wounded animal. Then the moment passed, the anger vanished like a brief summer storm, and Candy resumed being the good-natured, bantering master of revels who always showed his friends a good time.

But that explosion of rage was far from an isolated incident. In 1989 and 1990, a number of people around Candy began to notice that the dark side of Candy's psyche was becoming more apparent. He was becoming increasingly suspicious and curmudgeonly. He was obsessed with the notion that everyone was taking unfair advantage of him.

Candy's old friends cherished him so dearly they were willing to forgive odd behaviour. In the words of Monica Parker, part of the community of actors and writers who had made the move from Toronto to L.A.: "John could drive people crazy, but I don't know anyone who didn't like him. People cared deeply about John and felt very protective. He was so self-destructive his friends thought, 'If we didn't take care of him, who would?'"

Loyal buddies liked to recall the fun and good times they'd shared with Candy, when he assumed the task of cheering everyone up with one hilarious story after another. But Hollywood had changed Candy, exacerbating his frailties and using his best qualities—his need to be liked, his generosity and big-heartedness, his sensitivity to other people's feelings—as weapons against him.

Sometimes Candy didn't seem to like himself as much as others liked him. The more upset he was, the more he would neglect to take care of himself—smoke too much, drink too much, eat too much, stay up too late. He had always feared he would die before reaching the age of forty, as his father had. Now with his fortieth birthday in sight, his behaviour had become more alarming than ever. He had abandoned Pritikin, and his weight was spiralling upward.

Increasing amounts of Candy's time and energy were taken up with carrying on vendettas. There was a lawsuit arising from Candy's stay in Chicago during the filming of *Uncle Buck*. Candy had become discontented with a house he had rented, and moved to another—refusing to pay for the first one. The owner took him to court.

Soon after Candy returned to L.A., the *Herald-Examiner* announced he had enrolled in a Nutri-System class in Beverly Hills. Mitchell Fink reported that Candy had signed up for a program in behaviour modification, weighing in at four hundred pounds with the stated goal of losing one hundred pounds.

"Does he really think that after losing one hundred pounds he'll be light?" the *Herald* asked gratuitously.

A month later, the *Herald* printed a retraction. "It was all rumour," was all the *Herald* had to say by way of explanation. "We heard from Candy's attorney."

In an interview with Robert Blau of *Cable Guide* conducted on the set of *Uncle Buck* and published in July, 1989, just before the film's release, Candy explained some of the things that were making him disgruntled. Candy had a few especially bitter words about some of the people he had encountered in the movie business.

"Hollywood is the best and the worst of what everyone thinks," Candy said. "There are wonderfully talented young people, and then you meet the scum of the earth. I wouldn't want my kids near them. I've worked for some of them. They're in bushes and under rocks."

The more famous Candy became, the more people made demands and offers—movies to make, dinners to attend, charities to support, business deals to get involved in. And the more he felt he couldn't afford to trust anyone. Stardom had given him the opportunity to surround himself with people who would say what he wanted to hear—and to cut himself off from those who might say things he did not want to hear. It also intensified his paranoid tendencies.

Candy was especially wary of money men in showbiz. He had been conditioned by his skirmishes with Andrew Alexander in the old days. Now Alexander had moved to L.A. and opened a comedy club in Santa Monica (a failed experiment which closed after a few years). A lot of the old Second City performers had appeared there, but Candy was a notable exception. He was battling with Alexander over royalty payments again, and the two were not speaking. Candy had escalated the quarrel by bringing a lawsuit against Alexander. By this point both men were multimillionaires, and the dispute was less about anyone's need for money than about getting even and proving who was right.

Candy was increasingly embattled, and not only against Alexander. One old pal Candy lost through a nasty business fight was the Canadian producer Jon Slan. Candy and Slan had set up three TV specials for Home Box Office. When Candy changed his mind and backed out of the contract, Slan was stuck with the pre-production expenses that had been run up on the project. But they continued to work on a movie for Universal— a comedy called *Boys in the Bus* about a dreadful announcer on cable TV.

That deal fell apart when Candy, who was supposed to get a two-million-dollar fee, demanded half of Slan's relatively modest producing fee as well. Slan tried to be flexible and generous by suggesting a sixty/forty split, but Candy rejected the offer. The two men never spoke to one another again.

Claire Burrill's days running Frostbacks were clearly numbered. The things that Candy wanted to do through Frostbacks were taking up a tremendous amount of Candy's time and they weren't worth it. Candy had two options. He could make two movies a year, earning six million dollars for perhaps twenty-three weeks of work. Or he could pursue all the projects he was interested in through Frostbacks and wind up making a fraction of the money he could command as a movie actor.

Candy began making negative comments about Burrill to

others and at the end of the year, Burrill's contract was not renewed. As far as Candy was concerned, if the wheels were coming off Frostbacks, Burrill had to go.

Candy had a new best friend who was soon to become a key player at Frostbacks. Bob Crane, son of the murdered actor with the same name (of the long-running TV show "Hogan's Heroes"), was an entertainment journalist when he met Candy in the mid-1980s. They hit it off immediately, and Crane's published articles took such a gentle, sympathetic tone they almost had the ring of press releases. In 1989, when Candy agreed to do the *Playboy* interview, the interview was conducted by Crane aboard an airplane—and there was nothing in the published article that might upset Candy.

Although Crane would not officially be named vice-president (development) of Frostbacks until 1993, he was already close enough to Candy by early 1990, when *Delirious* was filmed, to have his name listed under "special thanks" in the end credits.

*Delirious*, an MGM production which sat on the shelf for a year before being released in August of 1991, seemed at the outset intriguingly offbeat, offering a change from the kind of frantic, broad comedy roles Candy was used to being offered. Now, for once, Candy had a chance to play the romantic lead in a gentle comic fantasy. The role: Jack Gable, the writer of a TV soap opera, who is clearly a descendant of James Thurber's famous daydreamer, Walter Mitty.

The script was by Lawrence J. Cohen and Fred Freeman, who, twenty years earlier, had written one of Candy's favourite movies, *Start the Revolution Without Me*. Candy had always wanted to work with them, and here was his chance. The director of *Delirious* was Tom Mankiewicz, who had directed Tom Hanks and Dan Aykroyd in the 1987 film *Dragnet*.

After one week of filming on location in New York's Central Park, *Delirious* was shot mostly at an estate outside Santa Barbara, just two hours north of L.A. Candy had a good experience doing the film, and earned the friendship of many colleagues in the cast and crew, including Mankiewicz and his two leading ladies, Mariel Hemingway and Emma Samms. But when the movie was released more than a year after being completed, reaction ranged from indifference to hostility.

What went wrong this time? *Delirious* has an enticing premise. Jack Gable gets into a traffic accident and then wakes up inside his own soap opera, where all the characters have become real. He's in the fictional town of Ashford Falls, stuck inhabiting the character of a Wall Street shark.

For the first twenty minutes, *Delirious* has some enjoyable low-key charm, and the tacky showbiz environment provides a bit of humorous vulgarity. Candy is sweetly likeable in the role of a well-meaning bungler, and has a few amusing encounters with Mariel Hemingway as an unknown trying out for a role in the soap, and Renée Taylor and Jerry Orbach as a monstrous pair of producers.

But once the movie executes its main plot twist, *Delirious* completely loses its way. The characters and story of the soap are utterly devoid of interest; the plotting is klunky and convoluted. Just like the character he portrays, poor John Candy is a man trapped inside banal material.

"I'm in hell and my punishment is spending eternity on my own show!" wails Jack. Anyone trying to get through *Delirious* knows what he means. But Candy does manage to inject one very funny moment in a scene with Robert Wagner (playing himself). "You can't die," he exclaims in astonishment. "You're Robert Wagner!"

*Delirious* had a test preview in San Francisco in October, 1990, and was scheduled to be released in March, 1991. Not so fast, said MGM-Pathé Communications Co., putting the picture on indefinite hold because the company, facing a cash-flow crunch, could not come up with seven million dollars needed for prints and advertising. This was only months after Las Vegas mogul Kirk Kerkorian had sold MGM/UA to Pathé Communications Corp. Since then, several movies had performed poorly at the box office, and the company was in desperate need of a hit.

According to an article in *Variety*, Alan Ladd, Jr., then running the MGM studio, was at odds with other executives, who wanted to release all the company's movies regardless of budget shortfalls. Ladd had not spoken to Pathé corporate chief

Giancarlo Paretti for months. Paretti was preoccupied trying to get additional financing from Credit Lyonnais, the huge nationalized French bank that put up the money for Pathé's takeover of MGM/UA.

The sad truth about *Delirious* was that there was no conceivable way it could help save MGM. And it certainly couldn't do much for John Candy's career, either.

But in Tom Mankiewicz, Candy had found a loyal ally. "John had a big hurt inside him," Mankiewicz recalled after Candy's death. "He was always trying so hard to be everything to friends and family and was constantly afraid he was letting people down."

Once, Mankiewicz recalled, he and Candy were trying to make their way out of a building. It took more than half an hour, because the place was crowded with people who wanted Candy's autograph. "He didn't want to hurt anybody's feelings," said Mankiewicz.

*T*he reason Candy hated to hurt anyone's feelings was that he felt so terribly, deeply wounded when anyone hurt his feelings. Martyn Burke knew that, and he understood there was no subject Candy was more touchy about than his weight—which was simply an unmentionable subject in Candy's sphere.

Nevertheless, in late 1989 and early 1990, Burke and Stephen Young had talked about how alarmed they both were about Candy's escalating weight. Other friends had also made hushed comments.

A few months earlier, Burke experienced a flash of fear about Candy's weight. On a Sunday afternoon, four people—Candy, John Langley, Burke and Burke's friend Kelly Michels—had driven one of Candy's cherished old convertible cars to Malibu with the top down. After spending the afternoon at the home of Arnon Milchan (the producer of *Who's Harry Crumb?*), they ran out of gas on the way home.

Kelly took the wheel and the three hefty guys began pushing the car to the nearest gas station. All of a sudden Burke became horribly aware of Candy huffing and puffing and not being able to catch his breath. Burke had a premonition at that moment:

John Candy was going to have a heart attack and die.

Candy was laughing and enjoying the humour of the situation when Burke yelled: "Stop pushing the car, John. Let us do it."

Burke and Young were torn. On the one hand they were loath to stick their noses into what was clearly a carefully guarded private section of Candy's life. On the other hand they loved him as a brother and genuinely believed that failing some intervention, he was in serious danger.

Burke, who had spent much of his career as an investigative reporter with a relentless, bulldog style, was not known for his tact, and there came a moment in the spring of 1990 when he felt the time had come to raise the forbidden topic.

Burke was in Candy's kitchen in Brentwood one evening a few months before Candy's fortieth birthday. There was a gathering of people who worked for Candy along with a couple of friends, including Burke, Stephen Young and Bob Crane. Rose, Jennifer and Christopher were out of town.

"John's staff were bringing in pizzas, cases of beer, everything fattening. I remember John was drinking and eating huge amounts of pizza while at the same time telling me how all the men in his family had died or had disabling heart attacks around the age of forty."

Burke took the opportunity to tell Candy he was very worried about his weight, that it was crucially important for Candy to shed some pounds.

Candy froze at the mention of his weight, and with some awkwardness changed the subject. Burke knew that Candy could sometimes turn against old friends, and he knew it was about to happen to him.

In mid-summer, when John and Rose were with their children at the family farm north of Toronto, Burke called. He and Candy had been trading messages. Rose answered the phone.

Burke seized the opportunity to raise the touchy issue again. "You know, Rose, we're getting very concerned about John's weight, especially after what he told us about heart attacks in his family."

According to Burke, there was an eruption of wrath and

antagonism at the other end of the line.

"Oh, please don't start on the weight thing," Rose Candy said. As far as she was concerned, John was fine, there was no problem. "I just don't want to hear about it," she said.

Rose Candy was not drawn to show business, and she opted out of many of her husband's professional relationships, preferring to focus on Jennifer and Christopher, their house and activities at their local Catholic church. Nevertheless, she had become a kind of gatekeeper, influencing who of the many people trying to make a connection with John Candy would succeed and who would not.

Candy hated to say no to anyone; whenever he was asked for anything he would almost always say yes. Given the pressures of stardom, he needed other people around him who could step in and say no after he had said yes.

But there were certain people Candy could never refuse, no matter what advice he was getting, and one of them was Dan Aykroyd. Thus it was inevitable that Candy would be in *Nothing But Trouble*—a stupefyingly dreadful comedy that marked Aykroyd's debut (and quite possibly his simultaneous swansong) as a director.

Though *Delirious* was far from a success, it looked like *Citizen Kane* compared to this other comedy Candy filmed the same year.

The premise: a couple of hip New Yorkers played by Chevy Chase and Demi Moore turn off the main road while speeding through New Jersey and wind up in a hell-hole called Valkenvania, inhabited by vampires and other weirdos. Aykroyd, barely recognizable under piles of make-up, plays an especially creepy justice of the peace.

*Nothing But Trouble* expired quickly when released by Warner Brothers early in 1991—but not before the *Hollywood Reporter* predicted it would make everyone's ten worst list. *Box Office*, another trade paper, was less kind, advising: "Eat poison before you are forced to sit through it."

The only good news from Candy's point of view was that he seemed less implicated in the movie's failings than his co-stars. It's hard not to cringe in embarrassment for Aykroyd, Chase and

Moore. Yet Candy, playing a cop who nails the visitors for speeding, comes across as an innocent bystander. (You get the subliminal message he might prefer to nail his celebrated colleagues for dragging him into this mess.) And he's harmlessly sweet in a second role, appearing in drag as the creepy JP's mute, unlovely daughter. Somehow Candy emerges from the wreckage without a scratch, like the sole survivor of a highway crack-up.

It had not been a good year for John Candy, but he did have one positive experience in 1990. In the fall Candy went back to Chicago to star in what would turn out to be his last movie for the company run by John Hughes. It was while making this film that Candy marked his fortieth birthday; perhaps that milestone helped bring something out of him he hadn't achieved before.

*Only the Lonely*, written and directed by Hughes protégé Chris Columbus, charted a significant new direction for Candy. The picture had some comedy, but this was mainly a serious drama with Candy as the leading man. He plays a thirty-eight-year-old Chicago cop named Danny Muldoon who is so tied to the iron apronstrings of his tyrannical, fiercely possessive mother that he almost lets her sabotage a promising romance.

Columbus had written the script several years earlier, basing it on his memories of Italian guys on the South Side of Chicago who couldn't seem to leave home until their parents died. The script was considered too uncommercial until *Home Alone* made so much money that any Chris Columbus film became bankable. The character was changed from Italian to Irish to make the fair-haired, fair-skinned Candy plausible in the role.

To beef up his film's Irish credentials, Columbus offered the role of the mother to Maureen O'Hara. O'Hara had retired in 1971, after making her mark in *How Green Was My Valley*, *Miracle on 34th Street*, *Rio Grande* and *The Quiet Man*. She hadn't made a movie in twenty years, though she'd had offers. This time, at the age of seventy, she said yes.

Candy and O'Hara struck up a mutual admiration society while filming *Only the Lonely*. O'Hara insisted on meeting Candy before deciding whether to accept the role. As she told the story later, when she did meet Candy it took her less than thirty seconds to make up her mind to say yes.

When shooting began, Candy was given a star trailer and O'Hara had a smaller one—until Candy asked the producers to give her a big trailer like his. When they said only one was available, he gave her the big one and squeezed his hulking frame into a small one. Eventually the producers came up with two big trailers, one for each of them. Candy liked to think the Hughes organization had given in to his tactics, but Tarquin Gotch insists there really was only one big trailer available when shooting began, and a second one really did become available later.

Luckily, the chemistry between Candy and O'Hara comes through on the screen as well. It's what keeps you watching a picture that isn't quite the gem it thinks it is. The script is too much like an update of *Marty*, that much-acclaimed ode to banality, and it's too full of adorable contrivances—always on the verge of being trite and cloying. In other words, this is basically a John Hughes movie even though Hughes is merely its producer, not its writer or director.

Nevertheless, Candy gives a startlingly persuasive dramatic performance that brings out the sweetness in him. And the mother/son sparks between O'Hara and Candy are so vivid that even though we know we're supposed to root for Danny to stand up to this bigoted, domineering monster, our heart isn't in it. As Rose Muldoon, O'Hara makes such a spirited comeback that we relish every tantrum.

As Danny's girlfriend, Theresa—the backward daughter of an undertaker—Ally Sheedy is stuck being dull and virtuous. It's a no-win situation. Candy's scenes with Sheedy don't have the juice that his scenes with O'Hara have. And when Theresa walks off into the sunset with Danny, we can't help feeling that life with her is going to be a lot less lively than life with mama.

After wrapping the movie, Candy went home for the holidays. He had been ducking calls from Stephen Young, assuming Young would have the same message as Martyn Burke on the subject of Candy's dangerous weight and unhealthy lifestyle. Young decided this communications breakdown was no reason why he shouldn't give Christmas presents to Jennifer and Christopher Candy as usual.

When he dropped off the gifts, the door was answered by a
maid. Young could see that John and Rose Candy were home,
but they chose not to come to the door or invite him in. This
was consistent with Candy's attitude that any friend who hurt
his feelings should be cast into purgatory. And if the friend happened to be motivated by concern for Candy's well-being, and
was trying to stop him from destroying himself—well, from
Candy's point of view, that was no excuse.

# Chapter 15

# TOUCHDOWN FEVER

*B*rian J. Cooper, an accountant from New York turned sports promoter, received a startling call at his Toronto office from Bruce McNall one day in the fall of 1990. McNall had become acquainted with Cooper through their mutual ally Wayne Gretzky, whom Cooper had known for a decade. Now Gretzky and McNall were turning to Cooper for advice about the idea of buying the Toronto Argonauts football franchise in the Canadian Football League.

As owner and president of Hollis Communications, based in Toronto, Cooper had a number of large corporate clients, such as John Labatt Ltd. and Seagram Canada. He also organized Gretzky's annual celebrity tennis tournament. Since Gretzky's move to Los Angeles in 1988, Cooper had been introduced to McNall and had spent some time hanging out with the two of them.

McNall had already talked to Cooper about looking for opportunities in Toronto, especially the possibility of a National Basketball Association expansion franchise, but Cooper was taken aback when McNall called to ask what Cooper thought about the Argos.

Harry Ornest, the hugely unpopular owner of the Argos, was sick of fighting with officials of SkyDome, where the Argos played, about restaurant concessions, and he put the team up for sale. The Argos had been troubled since moving to the Dome in 1989. They were drawing on average only 32,000 fans per game.

Cooper gave McNall something less than a ringing endorsement for the purchase of the Argos. He knew the market-place, and he knew the problems; he had seen what had happened, or failed to happen, in recent years. But McNall was confident he could turn a losing franchise into a profitable one through a little razzle-dazzle, just as he had done with the L.A. Kings.

McNall pushed ahead aggressively, insisting the team was a good buy. The next thing Cooper knew, he had a call telling him McNall and Gretzky had decided to go ahead and buy the Argos, and were bringing John Candy into the deal as a third partner. The price was five million dollars. Candy put in one million dollars and became a twenty per cent owner. McNall was the majority owner.

"Well, if you've made the decision, we'll have to see whether we can make a go of it," said Cooper. "This is a fickle market-place. You're going to have to invest."

The way Candy told the story, he had phoned his friend McNall to congratulate him on buying the Argos. Instead of accepting Candy's good wishes, McNall replied: "I want you to be involved. Get out your chequebook."

Candy got excited but then had to persuade his own financial advisers it was a good idea. "I have accountants who think I'm insane," he joked in a TV interview with Valerie Pringle on CBC's "Midday."

As for Wayne Gretzky, he and Candy genuinely liked one another. Gretzky was very appreciative of Candy's raucous sense of humour. They liked to hobnob, swapping hilarious yarns about their adventures on the road, and they sometimes played golf together. Each was flattered by attention from the other. The Argo deal gave them an excuse to spend more time together.

Soon Candy was needed in Toronto for the first of countless public appearances to promote the Argos. Brian Cooper, who was hired as chief operating officer of the Argos, had set up a press conference for the three new owners.

McNall, Gretzky and Candy rolled into town, trying to sweet-talk the press with promises of reversing the fortunes of the woeful Argos and even rejuvenating the entire Canadian Football League. They wanted to get the community interested in the Argos again; they wanted to attract families to the Dome and make sure everyone went home feeling entertained. They promised fun, good times, and lots of glitter.

Candy, who had started to grow a beard for his next movie, *Once Upon a Crime,* set to work on advertising, including TV spots, to stir up more interest in the Argos. And, he told the press, he planned to call on some of his celebrity friends, including Dan Aykroyd, for help.

*Once Upon a Crime,* Candy's last starring role for the next two years, was another one of those movies Candy should have said no to. But the picture was being touted as a big career opportunity for Candy's friend Eugene Levy, making his directing debut. Candy felt he had to do the picture for Levy. It would be the fifth and last movie they made as a team (not counting two made-for-TV films).

Produced in Europe by the Italian-born mogul Dino De Laurentiis, *Once Upon a Crime* was a remake of a 1960 Italian farce about six tourists who have come to Monte Carlo to make money at the casino, only to become suspects in the investigation of a murder. None of them has committed the crime, but they all act guilty.

Frank Yablans, a prominent Hollywood producer and former head of Paramount Pictures, had called De Laurentiis to request the rights to remake it as an American movie.

The reply: "Thanks for the idea, it's a good one."

After seeing the film, one has to wonder: Was it really such a good idea?

According to De Laurentiis, "The moment we saw Levy we knew his style was exactly what the piece needed."

The only problem was convincing Levy it would be hard enough to direct the movie without being one of the main actors. Levy settled for a cameo role as a casino cashier. De Laurentiis told Levy to make a fast-moving film and not take it too seriously.

"Pressure is one thing I never allowed myself to feel," said Levy at the time. "Thinking about the responsibility of doing a major movie with big stars could bring a grown man to his knees—so I didn't think about it."

Candy gets top billing, but his role as a compulsive gambler seems minor compared to those of Richard Lewis and Sean Young as an unemployed actor and a woman recently jilted. Also in the cast: Cybill Shepherd, Giancarlo Giannini, James Belushi and George Hamilton.

The script, by Charles Shyer and Nancy Meyers, is a flimsy contraption that relies on such plot devices as a lost dog. It's meant to be a delicious romp in the manner of a Pink Panther comedy, but it has no style or rhythm. There must have been a lot of people in the audience who felt Richard Lewis was expressing their sentiments exactly when he delivered the line: "When is this thing going to be over?"

*Once Upon a Crime* is the sort of idiotic bad movie Candy and Levy used to spoof unmercifully in their SCTV days. The SCTV version would have cost a lot less and been a lot funnier. Candy appears to be on automatic pilot throughout the proceedings. At least the movie gave him an excuse to spend some time in Rome and Monte Carlo. Afterward he told a colleague he should have known better, and this was the last time he would ever make a movie as a favour to a friend.

While he was still in Rome finishing *Once Upon a Crime*, Candy started to work on TV and radio spots to promote the Argos. By the time he arrived in Toronto, there was already an outbreak of Argo fever. That's because the new owners grabbed newspaper headlines by signing the hottest player in U.S. college football, Notre Dame's Raghib (Rocket) Ishmail for $18 million (including $4 million up front).

The idea was to create a frenzy of hoopla building up to opening day. McNall was trying to repeat the success he had bringing Gretzky to Los Angeles. But there was a big difference between Wayne Gretzky and Rocket Ishmail.

"The trick Bruce did with Wayne," notes Brian Cooper, "was using a star to turn everyone in L.A. into a hockey fan. He wanted to try the same thing with Rocket. But Wayne was the athlete of the decade, whereas Rocket was just an unproven collegiate talent. And Rocket had a personality that wasn't really amenable to being put on public display."

Candy may not have realized what he was getting into, but in fact he was abandoning a major Hollywood career in order to become a glorified cheerleader for his home-town football team. Some of his Hollywood friends thought it was a form of career suicide.

Whether he was conscious of it or not, this seemed to be Candy's way of turning himself into a clone of Bruce McNall, and at the same time becoming Johnny LaRue for real—the party-loving big star come home to run the football team, drive around in limos and entertain friends in the palatial club owner's box at the Dome.

Psychologically Candy and McNall had a few things in common. Both had powerful yearnings, going back to painful experiences they had in high school, to be macho heroes on equal footing with star athletes. Both had such a strong need to be well liked that they put great effort into being extravagantly generous and saying what they felt other people wanted to hear. And both had a strong capacity for self-delusion.

However there was one huge difference: Candy was ethical where McNall was crooked. But Candy was too eager to go along on McNall's joyride. What he failed to see—perhaps because he didn't want to look too closely—was that McNall's affairs were already mired in corruption when Candy went into business with him. Though he claimed assets of $133 million, McNall was just a simple-minded salesman who depended on clever accountants to cook up shady deals so complex even the experts at Merrill Lynch and the Bank of America couldn't understand them. Little did the bankers or John Candy realize that within the walls of the sleek Century City office of McNall Sports & Entertainment, McNall and his top employees were taking millions in perks and payoffs out of the company coffers even while negotiating newer and bigger loans to make the payments on the old ones.

In a way, McNall's story was a modern re-enactment of the *Wizard of Oz*. Because he was thought to have superhuman powers, people projected onto him their yearnings and aspirations. McNall's mystique would eventually turn out to be merely

smoke and mirrors, but for a few years, his aura had suggested
the wealth and splendour of Oz. The yellow brick road was
crowded with people who wanted to meet him, hoping a little
of his magic would rub off on them, and some of them were
people with very big names.

McNall's baronial style set the tone for the new football
regime in Toronto. The Argos spent $250,000 doing over the
box, and Candy brought in his interior designer from L.A. to
work on it. The chairs were king size, in the Candy/McNall
manner. There was room to accommodate twenty-five or thirty
guests.

McNall and Gretzky flew in and out of Toronto hastily, but
John Candy lingered and became the heart and soul of the Argos.
He engineered a deal with the CBC; in exchange for plugging the
Argos, the CBC would get Candy plugging CBC shows.

Candy became so carried away in his enthusiasm for creating
Argo promotion that he was seriously talking about bringing in
a film director from Los Angeles, as if a thirty-second TV spot
were an epic on the scale of *Lawrence of Arabia*.

Before the season started, Candy went to New Orleans to play
one of the lawyers in Oliver Stone's much-ballyhooed political
thriller *JFK*, which advances the view that the 1963 assassination
of President Kennedy was the result of a political conspiracy, not
the act of a lone gunman. The school year had already ended, so
Rose, Jennifer and Christopher all went to New Orleans for a
couple of weeks.

Candy knew he needed to spend more time with Jennifer and
Christopher. Having lost his own father at a young age, he felt
he had no script for being fatherly. And he was away from home
so much that Rose had to do much more than her share of par-
enting. He tried to make up for his absence by bringing his own
irresistible exuberance to occasions like birthdays. When he was
away from home, Candy talked to his children on the phone a
lot. When the family was together in Toronto or L.A., he enjoyed
taking them to sporting events. But there was no question that
his commitment to the Argos would take him away from his
family to an even greater extent than his movie career had.

Candy had just a small part in *JFK*, but he was nervous about it, as it was a dramatic role in a serious movie. In fact, Candy comes across well in a wonderful scene with Kevin Costner, who plays the fearless hero, Jim Garrison (the investigator who challenges the Warren Report and makes a personal crusade of uncovering a conspiracy). Hiding behind sunglasses and devouring a plate of crab, Candy depicts Dean Andrews, a drawling good-ole-boy lawyer who pretends to know a good deal less about the plot to kill JFK than he actually does know. Candy demonstrates a relish for acting here, but given the fact that this was a controversial movie with an all-star cast and a marathon running time, his fine performance was lost in the crowd and mostly overlooked.

Indeed, it was almost cut out of the film. A trailer with Candy in it had already been released when Oliver Stone decided to edit Candy out. Candy was devastated when he heard about this. Stone's decision also upset Costner, who argued vehemently with Stone and persuaded him to put the scene with Candy back in. In the end, Candy received a handwritten letter of apology from Stone.

Candy came to the Argos' opening hoopla straight from New Orleans. He even wore his *JFK* outfit—a 1960s suit with hat and sunglasses—to a blast-off party for four hundred guests at the funky Horseshoe Tavern in Toronto the night before the first game of the season. The idea was to create a media frenzy with a celebrity-studded event to publicize the Argos. A high point of the party was a performance by the Blues Brothers featuring Candy's pals, Dan Aykroyd and Jim Belushi. Among the celebrity guests were movie director Norman Jewison, SCTV alumni Martin Short and Dave Thomas, and Candy's *Delirious* co-star, Mariel Hemingway. (Belushi and Hemingway had been flown in for the occasion on McNall's private 727.)

Bret Gallagher, an engaging young sports and film promotions consultant hired by Cooper to line up exciting half-time entertainment for Argo home games, wound up being Candy's assistant as well. Gallagher was supposed to be booking stadium anthem singers, arranging liaisons with the corporate world and generally revitalizing the stadium atmosphere. But a big part of his job became arranging Candy's media blitz and accompanying him on his rounds.

Gallagher often found himself taking Candy to radio stations, sometimes at five o'clock in the morning, not only in Toronto but also in Winnipeg, Regina and Edmonton. Why? The strategy was to raise the level of interest right across the league.

One morning when they were on their way to a radio station, Candy told Gallagher: "I hope none of the movie chiefs are watching, because I don't promote my movies this much."

In fact, Candy gave up more than a year of his movie career for the Argos. Why did he care that much? Well, he had done more than forty movies and a lot of TV shows. But running a football team seemed like exciting fun, and a novel experience. And it appealed to the boyish dreamer in John Candy—the kid who had played football for the Neil McNeil high school team and sat in the stands at Exhibition Stadium to cheer for his beloved Argos.

Besides, Candy wanted to do something for Toronto and become the toast of the town; above all, he wanted to be taken seriously—to be regarded as a man who could make things happen rather than just a funny guy.

For the opening game, 41,000 fans turned out, and were treated to more than a football game. The Blues Brothers, with Dan Aykroyd and Jim Belushi, performed at intermission. John Candy and Mariel Hemingway also got into the act. There was lots of glitter and noise to liven up the Dome—marching bands, special effects, Hollywood stars on the sidelines.

Unlike his two partners, Candy did not disappear after opening day. "John was the most generous man you could ever meet with his time and money," recalls Brian Cooper. "He was wildly creative, and for a while he seemed to be practically running the CFL. He would devote endless hours, attend almost every game, go to meetings of the board of governors. We'd go to Edmonton on a small private plane. He'd try to break the blackout rule, he'd do a media blitz like you would not believe, and he'd be with the players during meal breaks, offering encouragement.

"Then after we'd won the game, we'd wind up at a restaurant

until four o'clock in the morning. John had such a sharp wit, he would provide entertainment for everyone in the place. All he had to do was raise an eyebrow and the whole room would be in hysterics. Finally he would go into the kitchen, drink in hand, and take over making dinner so the cooks could take a break."

Candy would also cook pasta feasts for the Argo inner circle at his Newmarket home. Watching Candy push meat into the pot, Cooper was reminded of Clemenza in *The Godfather.*

Kelvin Prunester, one of the Argos' tackles, became Candy's personal trainer. Though Candy worked out, he did not combine exercise with diet. During his time with the Argos, Candy's weight moved beyond 300 pounds, possibly as a result of compulsive, nervous eating linked to stressful problems he was going through during this period. Sometimes, especially when moving through a crowd, he would be unable to catch his breath and would have to stop for a rest.

Throughout that first season, Candy was ever-present—waving to the crowd, talking to fans, giving pep-talks to the players, driving around town in a limo with pennants sticking out of the back of the car, turning up on one talk show after another. The Argos, a franchise previously known for drowning in mediocrity, put on a show every game. And on the field, with the help of the Rocket and star quarterback Matt Dunigan, the Argos became the Cinderella team of the year—and went on to win the Grey Cup.

Yet even during this triumphant season, not everything was great in the front office.

"We were winning but we were paying big-time," says Brian Cooper. "We all assumed Bruce had very deep pockets, but there just wasn't enough money coming in. I got tired of ducking creditors. Once when I was out at a restaurant, I was confronted by a printer from Scarborough who said, 'You owe us five thousand dollars.' I know how to juggle money when necessary, but we were running all the time at a negative cash flow. It got to the point where I had to put my foot down and insist on some equity from the owners. Bruce put a little bit more money in after that, but it was never enough."

Meanwhile, even while cheering the Argos on during their march toward the Grey Cup, Candy was increasingly beset with anxiety. While his movie career was on hold, Candy left his long-time agent, John Gaines, and signed with Guy McIlwaine at International Creative Management, a much bigger talent agency.

The announcement was coupled with news that Candy would co-star with Rick Moranis in a comedy called *Going Fishing* for Disney's Hollywood Pictures. But the movie was never made, and Candy's stay at ICM lasted less than a year. The defection of Candy was a major blow to APA, which had a small list of clients. In the fall of 1993, Gaines's partner, ex-Montrealer Marty Klein, had a fatal heart attack. (Candy attended the funeral.) Gaines died of AIDS three weeks later.

In October, Gallagher accompanied Candy on a swing through the rubber-chicken circuit of the CFL. Candy was a special guest, helping to draw crowds at a series of fund-raising dinners for individual CFL teams. This was all part of the strategy that to strengthen the Argo franchise it was necessary to bolster the whole league.

Gallagher did the advance work—figuring out how to get Candy in and out of each venue, where he was going to sit, and so on. He was also careful to make it clear to the local organizers that there would be no autographs. According to Gallagher, if Candy started signing them, the result would be bedlam because everyone in the place would want one.

But during the Blue Bombers dinner at the Winnipeg Convention Centre, while Candy was sitting at the head table, the radio disc jockey who was chosen as emcee announced to the crowd of two thousand fans that anyone who wanted Candy's autograph should start lining up. Gallagher knew Candy hated to say no to his fans, and he could see that Candy was sweating, so he plotted a quick getaway, enlisting the help of security police and busboys to whisk Candy away just before the stampede of autograph-hunters.

In November, when the Argonauts played the Winnipeg Blue Bombers in the CFL's Eastern Conference play-off final, Candy was not able to attend the game. But he had arranged to watch the game at his Los Angeles home via a special satellite hook-up.

On the Friday before the game, Martyn Burke was at home in Santa Monica when he got a memorable phone call from John Candy. They had been estranged for more than a year since Burke took Candy aside to express concern about his weight. Now Candy was calling to attempt a reconciliation.

Candy made some flattering comments about *Ivory Joe*, Burke's recently published novel, and told Burke the two of them ought to find a way to work on a project together. Then he issued an invitation.

"You've got to come over on Sunday. Wayne and Janet Gretzky are coming to watch the game with Rose and me, and it's going to be great. We'd love you to join us."

Burke could tell that Candy had been drinking, and he knew that after a few drinks Candy was prone to become sentimental and brood about rifts he felt badly about. Burke also knew that Rose Candy was less forgiving, and wondered what she would say when John told her about these plans.

After hanging up the phone, Burke recounted the conversation to his companion, Laura Morton, and told her: "John will probably call tomorrow morning and cancel."

Around nine-thirty the next morning, there was an awkward and embarrassed call from Candy. All the arrangements had been changed. The invitation for Sunday was off. "We'll have to do it some other time," said Candy before abruptly terminating the conversation.

As soon as the Argos won the Eastern final, trouncing the Winnipeg Blue Bombers 42 to 3, Candy began preparing for Grey Cup weekend in Winnipeg. He and his family could have arranged more luxurious accommodation, but the players were staying at the Sheraton, so that's where Candy insisted on staying, along with Rose, Jennifer and Christopher.

"It was a blast," recalls Bret Gallagher. "We had a ton of events planned. But John couldn't attend the Grey Cup gala the night before the game, because we knew he would have been there all night signing autographs."

During the big game on Sunday, November 24, Candy was beside himself with excitement—and the Argos did not disappoint him. On a snowy field they capped their miracle season by beating the Calgary Stampeders 36-21 and winning the Grey Cup for only the second time in forty years. It was a highly emotional day for John Candy—the fulfillment of one of his most fervent dreams.

"When we won the Grey Cup, everybody loved everybody," Brian Cooper remembers. "There were tears in John's eyes. It was like something out of a feel-good movie: The famous comedian buys a football team in his home town, and in the first year they go out and win the league championship. Only this wasn't a movie—it was real life."

# Chapter 16

# JOHN'S GALLOWS

*I*t was Queen Elizabeth who called 1992 her "annus horribilus." For John Candy the year was just as replete with nasty twists and turns. Despite the excitement of winning the Grey Cup the year before, trying to keep the Argos afloat turned into a frustrating exercise. With the team's losses mounting just when he was faced with increased pressure from his creditors, Bruce McNall's enthusiasm for Canadian football had waned, leaving Candy to brood about whether his friend and mentor had led him into a cul-de-sac and then abandoned him. Candy was caught in a tough spot; in order to stay loyal to the Argos, he had to distance himself from McNall, whose neglect was hurting the team.

The Argo bubble began to burst soon after they won the Grey Cup. To Candy, money was always secondary. But that view was not shared by McNall. The fact was that the new owners had lost well over three million dollars in their winning 1991 season. Attendance had averaged 36,000, and there had been only one sell-out crowd of 50,000—for the Eastern final.

In 1992 the new owners were facing the prospect of more losses. During the off-season, McNall threatened to end his involvement with the Canadian Football League over a dispute about the Argos' lease at SkyDome.

As if all that weren't distressing enough, Candy became

embroiled in a nasty and embarrassing public argument about the expenses for his goodwill tour. The CFL office received a bill from McNall for $225,000 and at first balked at paying it.

According to McNall, the CFL had agreed to pay Candy's expenses, and the amount was well within reason. "We could have asked for two million dollars," said McNall, who was livid that the league appeared to be reneging on a commitment. "This is a man who makes a lot of money. Ordinarily he would earn millions of dollars for that amount of time."

The CFL eventually paid the bill, but the incident left a sour taste. And a more distressing long-term problem had become apparent: a lot of mistrust was building up between John Candy and Bruce McNall. In the beginning, Candy was full of admiration for McNall's habit of doing everything first-class, as if money were never a problem. But money soon became a problem.

"Bruce would say one thing and people in his organization would say another," says Brian Cooper. There seemed to be people working for McNall—especially his chief financial officer, Susan Waks—who had more control of the purse strings than McNall did. Nobody at the Argo front office was fond of Waks; "a pitbull in a dress" was Cooper's description of her. Candy had more trouble with McNall's staff than he did with McNall.

"Certain conditions weren't being met to keep the Argos afloat," says Cooper. "John did what he could to make it work, but he wasn't the majority owner, and he wasn't calling the shots. I could see he didn't necessarily agree with all the moves that were being made."

In 1992, the Argos stumbled both on the field and off. Attendance dropped to an average of 31,000. The appeal of Rocket Ishmail had fizzled. By mid-season Wayne Gretzky was making no secret of the fact that owning the Argos had stopped being fun.

"He hates losing," said McNall, referring to Gretzky. "He loses his temper a lot."

Argo quarterback Matt Dunigan signed with the Winnipeg Blue Bombers for more money. Candy was upset that McNall let him go. Argo head coach Adam Rita was fired.

Less than a year after winning the Grey Cup, the three Argo owners were scraping bottom. They couldn't seem to do anything right. The Argos just kept losing, and the fans just kept staying home. For John Candy, it would be an understatement to say that owning the Argos no longer seemed much like starring in his own feel-good movie.

Not only were the Argos floundering, but Candy's Hollywood career seemed to be in limbo while he poured his energy into the Argos. Candy was paying a price for his obsession with the Argos. He was discovering that even a strong position in the movie capital begins to unravel when you fail to give it the focus and concentration needed to maintain it. No wonder Candy was increasingly subject to panic attacks during which he would perspire profusely. He was as heavy as ever, and he was seeing a psychotherapist.

Old friends compared notes anxiously. Was Candy, as one of his best friends told mutual acquaintances at a gathering of Canadian expatriates in L.A., paying the price for burning the candle at both ends, and in the middle as well? Was he severely plagued by paranoia, as others surmised? Were alcohol and drugs at the root of his problem? Had stardom turned out to be the most difficult cross he had ever had to bear? Was he becoming more isolated than ever, using his expanding staff as a buffer zone between himself and the rest of the world?

Candy often referred ironically to his habit of punishing people who had, in his view, committed an offence. "I have a place called John's Gallows," he would remind Brian Cooper or Bret Gallagher when they seemed to be moving into dangerous waters. "Would you like to spend some time in John's Gallows?"

In an interview with *Parade* magazine, Candy spoke about his confusion and his changing attitude: "In my earlier days, I put people on such high plateaus, thinking they must know what they're doing. I was just a young actor, what did I know? I put so much faith in others because I didn't have enough confidence in myself. Before, I didn't deal well with the loss of people, especially my father. But I've come to terms with that and with the little boy—me—he left behind. For the first time, I'm comfortable with myself."

Candy also spoke candidly about his changing views of money and the things it can buy. "It took me a long time to learn what is really valuable in life," he said. "I went through a period of real acquisitiveness—buy this, buy that, get the most expensive car. Hell, get two of them! All these things, as if owning lots of stuff said a damn about who you really are and what your life really means. Maybe I've finally learned what happiness is: my family, my wife, my kids. We're only here a short time. Let's enjoy it, whatever happens. We love each other. That's all that matters."

Although he was trying to present himself on that occasion as a man who had found peace of mind, Candy continued to be extremely troubled much of the time. He had become more reclusive, and when he did go out, he was often accompanied by bodyguards.

John's Gallows was getting to be a crowded place. In February, 1992, John Langley was added to the list of old friends from whom Candy had become estranged. Langley and Candy had been buddies ever since late 1984, when they had been stranded together in Mexico working on *Volunteers*. They had tried developing several film and TV projects together over the years, but none ever came to fruition.

Still, they had stayed in touch, going to sports events together from time to time and exchanging gifts. Occasionally they would go out to a bar, though Langley sensed that boys' nights out represented an aspect of Candy's life of which Rose took a dim view. And Langley had been in the car with Candy and Martyn Burke that Sunday afternoon in 1989 when they had run out of gas on the way back from Arnon Milchan's place in Malibu.

Langley and Candy had once gone on a fishing expedition, and Langley went to Florida to help Candy make some arrangements for his mother, who was planning to spend the winters in Fort Lauderdale. Candy wanted to make sure his mother would be safe and secure. Langley—who, as executive producer of the popular TV drama series "Cops," had great relationships with police forces all over the country—offered to help through his contacts with Fort Lauderdale police and real-estate agents. Langley had a friend who was the sheriff of Fort Lauderdale, and at Langley's request, Candy lent some support to the sheriff's re-election campaign.

Now Langley had reached a milestone—the one hundredth episode of "Cops"—and was celebrating with a big party at 72 Market Street, a fashionable restaurant in Venice, California. Langley had invited his friend John Candy to the party, and he really wanted him to be there. But Candy didn't show up. Instead he sent Bob Crane. Langley was so hurt and angry that he gave Crane an earful, knowing every word would be repeated to Candy.

"I guess it's okay for me to fly to Florida to help John with his mother," said Langley with bitter sarcasm, "but he can't be bothered making a half-hour drive to attend my party."

After that, Langley lost touch with Candy. In retrospect, Langley would blame himself for the breach, feeling he had spoken in a fit of pique, and that if he had been a bigger man he would have realized Candy had problems Langley didn't know about that made it painful for him to attend events like the "Cops" party.

In April a bizarre report about Candy appeared in one of the L.A. newspapers. Candy was suing a dog trainer in Los Angeles Superior Court, claiming he had paid $19,000 for a German shepherd that turned out to be seriously ill. Candy's suit charged the trainer with fraud and breach of contract, and sought to recover the price of the dog.

Around this time, Toronto producer John Brunton of Insight Productions was trying to organize a John Candy tribute. The idea came from Norman Jewison, who wanted to create an event like the American Film Institute's televised lifetime achievement award dinner as a fund-raiser for the Canadian Film Centre.

At first Candy said, "Why would you pick me? Surely you can find someone more worthy."

Brunton and his associates all said they were sure Candy was the best choice; he would be a magnet to attract a lot of high-profile people. After thinking about it for a while, Candy called back to say: "Couldn't we turn it into a breakfast? You could just give me a plaque at the back of Fran's."

Brunton couldn't help chuckling. Fran's Toronto coffee shops, which had hardly changed since the 1950s, were about as unglamorous as you could get—the sort of place where Uncle Buck would feel at home.

But after fretting about it, Candy began moving in the opposite direction, escalating the tribute into a mega-event. He would like to hold it in the biggest possible venue—SkyDome. Dan Aykroyd and the other guys from the Blues Brothers could fly up in a private jet; Steve Martin would also appear.

"Suddenly it had gone from being something small in a back room at Fran's to a bigger production than *Gone With the Wind*," recalls Brunton. By this time Carol Reynolds of the CBC and former SCTV producer Patrick Whitley (now working for the U.S. cable service Showtime) had also become involved. A huge TV deal was in the works.

Candy called Brunton and said: "Johnny, I think you better come to L.A. and talk. I've been thinking about the tribute."

When he got to L.A. Brunton, who had known Candy years earlier, discovered that going out to a public restaurant or bar with Candy to have a discussion was no easy matter. According to Brunton, other Hollywood actors who were considered celebrities—Robert DeNiro, for example—would be left alone when they were seen in public, because there was something intimidating and unapproachable about them. But John Candy seemed the most approachable movie star of all time. He had the common touch—working-class appeal. People felt they knew him, and it mostly didn't occur to them that they were invading his privacy. Nor was Candy capable of sending out the message that he would prefer to be left alone; he preferred to have his fans believe he was always receptive, even grateful for their attention. When he was spotted, the whole room would turn into a tizzy.

That's why Brunton and Candy wound up having their talks at Candy's private bar in the Frostbacks office on San Vincente. It was a memorable hangout; Candy had gone to great trouble and expense to have a large section of the carved mahogany bar from the Irish pub in *Only the Lonely* transported from Chicago to L.A. and installed in his office.

After they had talked through all the plans for the tribute, Candy finally decided he couldn't go through with it. "It's too embarrassing to have all this attention directed at me," he told Brunton. "It's just not my style."

*C*racks in the Candy image were evident to some observers in June when Candy appeared on a panel at the Banff Television Festival in the Canadian Rockies. Monica Parker, whom he had known since his early stage days in Toronto, was on the same panel. Though they both now lived in L.A., they rarely crossed paths. Yet if they were not exactly close friends, they were still warm acquaintances. During the panel discussion, Parker was distressed to find Candy uncomfortable, ill at ease and alarmingly unrelaxed. Still, Parker suggested they have dinner, and Candy agreed.

"He looked terrible, and I felt really badly for him," recalls Parker.

She was looking forward to having dinner and chatting in a less stressful environment. But keeping their dinner date proved to be impossible.

"You could always ask John for anything, and he would always say yes," remarks Parker, "but the more famous he became, the more people there were around him saying no. At Banff there were flanks of henchmen to walk him wherever he went. There was an amazing phalanx of people around him at every moment.

"When it came time for dinner, he wouldn't answer his phone, and he wouldn't come out of his room [at the Banff Springs Hotel]. And there were people handling him who wouldn't let me get to his room. I felt awful, because he had made this commitment to have dinner with me, and then obviously he just couldn't handle it. And I was absolutely horrified to realize that the funny, happy-go-lucky friend I cherished had turned into this paranoid, scared, demon-plagued man."

Candy spent much of the summer in Toronto, often occupying the club-owner's box at SkyDome along with his entourage. It would be an understatement to say the Argos were not in form to win another Grey Cup. They finished the season with six wins and twelve losses. One of the less painful matches of the summer was the Rose Bowl—a combination touch football game and birthday party for Rose Candy that her famous husband gave every year at their farm. John Candy always played quarterback.

*I*ronically, just as Candy was becoming more apprehensive about appearing in public, he was offered a chance to play a character who took reclusiveness to preposterous lengths. Candy was seriously considering doing the film version of Paul Quarrington's novel *Whale Music*. He had even made calls to France to discuss it with his old friend Bill House, now a senior executive with the government film agency Telefilm Canada, while House was at the Cannes festival.

The central character in *Whale Music* has more than a passing resemblance to Brian Wilson, the large and weirdly withdrawn member of the Beach Boys pop group. The film was to be produced by the Toronto-based Alliance Entertainment Corp. Candy drove up to the Briar country resort north of Toronto to discuss the project with Quarrington, Alliance CEO Robert Lantos, producer Steve DeNure and director Richard Lewis (not the actor of the same name).

Candy knew Brian Wilson, and he had read Quarrington's book in galleys before it was published. Both he and Rose Candy liked the book. Candy had agonized for some time about the project; he was drawn to it, but he was also afraid of it. In the end, he backed away from it, and Maury Chaykin was cast in the role. The story of a famous, overweight performer who becomes so paranoid that he refuses to budge from his house was perhaps a little too scarily close to home for Candy.

In September, after the family returned to L.A. for the beginning of school, Candy flew to Toronto to join old colleagues for a benefit show called "Friends of Gilda" at the Elgin Theatre. Organized by producer Marlene Smith, it marked the twentieth anniversary of *Godspell*'s Toronto opening, with Gilda Radner in a key role. At the same time, this was a posthumous celebration of Radner's career and a fund-raiser for the Genesis Research

Foundation, providing money to fight ovarian cancer, which had claimed Radner's life.

Others participating in the evening included Martin Short, Dave Thomas, Eugene Levy, Andrea Martin, Rosemary Radcliffe, Jayne Eastwood, Robin Duke, Gerry Salsberg and Marvin Hamlisch. The show was taped for telecast later, and Perry Rosemond was enlisted to direct it.

"I hadn't seen John in fifteen years," Rosemond says. "There seemed to be a necessity on his part to make me feel he was the still the same guy I used to know. He was eager to demonstrate that all this film stardom hadn't gone to his head. I was the director, and he showed a lot of deference; he was just a humble performer. There was a feeling in the group that their days together in Second City had been the best time of their lives and could never be duplicated."

During the show, Candy did a deadpan comedy monologue explaining his coolness to *Godspell*, the show that transformed Gilda Radner in 1972 from an unknown to the favourite funny girl of Toronto theatregoers.

"I'm supposed to tell you why I hate *Godspell*," said Candy in his driest, most mockingly long-suffering manner. "You see, I was never in *Godspell*. And for the past twenty years I have been reminded of that at every function we go to where these people start singing 'Day by Day.'"

What Rosemary Radcliffe remembers about that evening was the great stress of putting the show together because of the unspoken pecking order according to who had become most famous. When the show ended, most of the performers were on one side of the stage, huddled together congratulating one another. Then she noticed Candy, who was way over on the other side of the stage by himself, pacing nervously. He was more gargantuan than ever, and he seemed unhappy and preoccupied.

Radcliffe walked across the stage to join Candy, and asked him: "John, would it be possible for me to get your autograph for my son?"

She tore a piece of paper off the wall, and Candy scrawled: "To Max Stohn, best wishes and good luck for always, your friend John Candy."

Radcliffe gave Candy a big hug. Perhaps she even sensed this would be the last time she would ever see him.

Candy's next scheduled public appearance in Toronto turned into a shambles that left a trail of bitterness on all sides. Candy had accepted an invitation to be the host of the Academy of Canadian Cinema's Genie Awards, the Canadian film industry's version of the Oscars, in late November. The show was to be telecast live on the CBC.

At first, recalls Maria Topalovich, executive director of the Academy, everything was great. Money was no problem. "Candy was wonderful, and there was no problem about anything. The whole show had been written around him."

Then a week before the show, a full-page ad (placed by the CBC's promotion department) ran in *Playback*, a Canadian film industry trade paper. It had a large photo of Candy. "To host the Genies, we got the biggest star we could find," said the accompanying text. "We'll get you a star so unbelievably, incredibly big, you won't believe your eyes."

When someone sent a copy of the ad to Candy, he was furious. His contract specified that he had approval of all promotional photos, and that provision had been clearly violated. According to Topalovich, the ad was placed by someone at the CBC without the knowledge of the Academy or Milestone Productions, producers of the show. The CBC claimed it was an oversight.

In Candy's view, it was an act of treachery that could not be overlooked or forgiven. "I talked to him and his handlers in a conference call," Topalovich recalls. "He wasn't mad at me but he expressed tremendous anger at the CBC. He demanded an apology from the CBC. By the end of our talk, he said he wanted to think about it."

It took the CBC a couple of days to come up with the apology—someone in authority was sick—and by then Candy wasn't even returning calls from Topalovich. It was clear Candy had backed out of the show, and the Genies were in big trouble.

The show was saved by Leslie Nielsen, who had been host of the Genies the previous year and agreed to do it again on almost no notice and despite the obvious fact that he was not the Academy's first choice. The script had to be completely rewritten at the last minute.

Ironically, Candy drew far more attention to the *Playback* ad than it would have received had he ignored it. When the incident became news around the world thanks to an item on CNN, Candy began to worry that it could have a harmful effect on projects he was trying to finance.

Several years later, Topalovich was still bothered by Candy's over-reaction. "He caused a lot of trouble and could have done serious harm to the whole Canadian film industry," she said. "If it hadn't been for Leslie Nielsen, the Genies could have gone under."

*A*round this time, Candy came up with an idea for a one-hour mainstream TV comedy special. It was called "Bram Stoker's John Candy Special," a spoofy reference to the 1992 movie *Bram Stoker's Dracula* (directed by Francis Coppola). The concept involved Candy being host of a show-within-the-show, supposedly telecast live from the moon.

For this special Candy was reunited with Jason Shubb, one of the associate producers of "SCTV" in its Edmonton phase. Candy and Shubb thought they had a deal with NBC Productions, but the project expired in a complicated tangle of agents and attorneys.

According to Shubb, it was a brilliant concept, and Candy was taking great joy in developing it. When the deal fell apart, he was extremely upset and took it as a personal rejection.

There were other tantalizing projects on Candy's back burner—a screen adaptation of the novel *Confederacy of Dunces* and a film biography of Fatty Arbuckle, the silent comedy star who became the tragic, innocent victim of a Hollywood scandal.

Candy was hoping his flagging career could be revived by another collaboration with John Hughes, the writer/director of *Planes, Trains and Automobiles* and *Uncle Buck*. But by early 1993 the relationship between Candy and Hughes had cooled. Candy was wounded and perplexed by the deep freeze he was getting from Hughes.

Candy had been confident his association with Hughes would be ongoing. But it had become unglued over the past year. A series of projects they had planned to do together failed to materialize—for a variety of reasons. Candy was set to play yet another blue-collar hero trying to get home for Thanksgiving in the film *Dutch*. The movie was made, but not with Candy.

There was supposed to be a cameo for Candy in *Home Alone 2*, but negotiators for the two sides failed to come to terms. The same thing happened on *Dennis the Menace*. Candy and Sylvester Stallone were supposed to play a pair of neighbours in another movie, but according to Candy, Hughes pulled out.

Candy—who was extremely sensitive about anything resembling rejection—was crushed and upset when Hughes stopped returning his phone calls, Tarquin Gotch remembers. Candy and Gotch (who had defected from the Hughes company and was using office space at Frostbacks, thanks to Candy) swapped stories about what seemed like baffling behaviour on the part of Hughes—how one day he would treat you as his best friend, and the next you would be exiled to Siberia, without a word of explanation.

The timing of the rift was unfortunate, because there was an urgent need for Candy to revive his Hollywood career. For the first time in fifteen years, he had not starred in a movie for an entire year. (However, he made one cameo appearance in *Boris and Natasha* and another in *Rookie of the Year*, in which he played a sports announcer covering the Chicago Cubs.) And in August Candy had set industry tongues wagging when, less than a year after leaving Gaines and Klein, he dropped Guy McIlwaine at ICM and signed with another high-powered agent—Ron Meyer at rival CAA (who three years later would be chosen by Edgar Bronfman as the new president of MCA).

Luckily for Candy, a comeback vehicle had been offered to him: Disney's *Cool Runnings*.

# JOHNNY TORONTO

*C ool Runnings*, filmed and released in 1993, marked the first commercially successful Hollywood movie John Candy had starred in since *Uncle Buck* four years earlier.

The story was drawn from one of the most bizarre episodes in the history of the Olympic games. In 1988, an unlikely team of Jamaican bobsledders who had never seen snow defied the odds and earned worldwide acclaim.

A movie based on that saga had been in the works for several years and was almost made a couple of times, only to have the plug pulled. Producer Dawn Steel finally got the cameras rolling in two locations—Calgary and Jamaica.

Candy plays Irv, the coach, the catalyst for the Jamaican athletes to achieve their personal best. At first he doesn't believe they are capable of being bobsled racers.

"From my character's point of view," Candy observed in an interview promoting the film, "these guys are a joke. They'll never succeed. We're in Jamaica. There are no sleds here, no snow. They have no idea what a bobsled is. Yet they're determined."

Irv gives the Jamaican athletes a two-week trial. Then, impressed by their energy and drive, he determines to help them reach their goal. At first the film-makers had thought of Irv as a dramatic rather than a comic role, but when Candy was suggested for the part, they changed their mind.

"John was the biggest surprise to us," said Dawn Steel. "Once he read the script and said he wanted to do it, we couldn't picture anyone else in the role."

In fact Candy gives the picture a likeable spirit. As director Jon Turteltaub explained: "It was important for me that Irv wasn't a goofy, funny guy. He's hardened, tired, angry and bitter, and has come to Jamaica to escape from something in his life. John loved playing the part, and he was able to balance the comedy and the heart."

This being one of those alarmingly heartwarming, wholesome Disney outings for a mainstream family audience, the movie has its buffoonish side, featuring bar-room brawls and gags about guys from the tropics doing pratfalls when they encounter ice. The moral struggle in *Cool Runnings* is as rigged as the 1919 World Series. Yet despite its formula of shameless post-Rocky uplift, the film is watchable; patches of it are even enjoyable.

Candy does the best anybody could with big speeches such as: "If you're not enough without a gold medal, you're not enough with it." And (on having been barred and disgraced in the past): "It's quite simple, really. I had to win. When you make winning your whole life, you have to keep on winning."

Dawn Steel went so far as to suggest that the reason Candy connected emotionally with the role was that there was a bit of Irv's story in Candy's film career. "Irv was a guy who won medals and then made mistakes and wasn't welcome any more. In some ways John felt that way also. He had an extraordinary body of work, yet he felt out of the core of Hollywood decision-making."

*Cool Runnings* (released in the fall of 1993) was a box-office hit, and it gave Candy's career a needed boost. As things turned out, it was also the last John Candy movie that would be embraced by the public.

As the Toronto Argonauts floundered through the 1993 season on their way to an embarrassing final record of three wins, fifteen losses, John Candy—busy making a Hollywood comeback—was spending less time with the Argos. But he was still loyal to the team and the dream of leading them to glory, and he frequently occupied the club-owner's box during Argo home games at SkyDome.

Candy's disenchantment with Bruce McNall had become apparent, at least to members of the Argo inner circle like Brian Cooper, who recalls: "When John had had enough, he sort of divorced himself from Bruce at one point. I would present a plan, and John would say, 'Do what you want.'"

Around the same time Candy was becoming increasingly disaffected with McNall, he was enjoying reconciliations with another mogul who played a major part in his life—Andrew Alexander. In 1985 Alexander had purchased the original Chicago Second City operation along with exclusive worldwide rights to the name from his former partner, Second City founder Bernard Sahlins. Then in 1992, after the failure of his Santa Monica club, Alexander moved from Los Angeles to Chicago.

Bret Gallagher—who left his Argo job to work as Candy's assistant—had inadvertently raised an unmentionable name one day when an "SCTV" rerun was on in Candy's hotel suite. Watching the credits on the show, he asked: "Who's Andrew Alexander?"

Bob Crane, who was in the room at the time, giggled and shot Gallagher a look that indicated he was crossing into dangerous territory. But Alexander had already initiated a series of deals that would lead to his being called back from the gallows.

Candy and Alexander had been battling for years, most recently through a lawsuit over royalty payments. But Alexander hated being regarded as the bad guy; he wanted to be liked and appreciated as the godfather who put "SCTV" on the air and thereby launched a lot of major careers. Alexander had suggested compiling a comedy video called *The Best of John Candy*. It was his way of extending an olive branch—and provided a way to end the lawsuit Candy had launched while making both sides feel they were winners.

Meanwhile Candy had heard that his old friend Joyce Sloane, who had been with the organization for twenty-five years, was rumoured to be in danger of losing her job once Alexander returned to Chicago. Candy could be fiercely loyal to old friends, especially if he felt they were in need of protection. That gave Candy a reason to make contact with the Second City office, and Alexander seized on the opportunity to bolster the rapprochement. Sloane would be kept on in a part-time consulting role. Moreover, Alexander had a tempting offer that would turn antagonists into allies.

By 1993, Alexander had decided to seek a licence for a specialty comedy channel in Canada—and he invited Candy to become his partner. It was a shrewd idea—at once strengthening his application to the government regulatory board which had the task of granting licences, and at the same time giving Candy a good reason to make peace.

"There was a fence to be mended, and they did it on their own," says Gallagher. "Look what Andrew was offering. He was setting up an application for a comedy channel, and he was willing to let John be one of the owners—just like Guy Caballero. They resolve the dispute about royalties. John's friend gets her job protected. And as a sweetener, they release a video of John Candy's best SCTV sketches."

Indeed, the rapprochement was so complete that after spending years as the man John Candy loved to hate, Andrew Alexander would be chosen to deliver his eulogy.

In the fall of 1993, work was keeping Candy in Toronto rather than Los Angeles, so Rose and the children stayed on at the Ontario farmhouse through the fall school term rather than returning to L.A.

In October, Candy signalled a major career change when he filmed the made-for-TV-movie *Hostage for a Day*. The script had been written for him by his Frostbacks employee Bob Crane and Crane's wife, Kari Hildebrand, along with Peter Torokvei. It's a lightweight comedy about a browbeaten print-shop owner, Warren, who stages his own kidnapping in order to thwart his domineering, spendthrift wife and her mean-spirited father.

When Crane suggested Candy could direct as well as star, Candy jumped at the chance to direct—but decided he couldn't handle it if he were also playing the main part. So in the central role written for Candy, he cast George Wendt (who had played Norm on "Cheers" for eleven years, and whom Candy had known since 1973, when both worked in Chicago at Second City). Candy contented himself with a juicy cameo as a KGB agent with a thick beard and a thicker accent, and his brief appearance on screen gives the picture a needed jolt of energy.

Financed by the Fox network (in the U.S.) and WIC (in Canada), *Hostage* had a four-week, twenty-day shoot, using Woodbridge (a Toronto subdivision with monster homes) and the beguiling Haliburton cottage area.

The filming of *Hostage* began with the shadow of death over it. Just before shooting started, Kari Hildebrand—who had been fighting cancer for months—was found dead one morning by her husband, Bob Crane, at the guest house on Candy's Queensville estate, where they had been staying during pre-production work on the film.

Candy handled everyone working on the film with extraordinary affability and generosity, realizing that this was his chance to treat actors the way he had always wanted to be treated by his director. During the shoot, Candy showered the cast and crew with gifts—flowers, hats, jackets. Candy had always been known for his generosity to co-workers, but this time the flamboyance and extravagance also bore more than a touch of Bruce McNall's baronial style of showmanship.

The set of *Hostage for a Day* was an ongoing love-in. Candy hired several of his old Second City friends—including Robin Duke (as Warren's greedy wife), Don Lake, Peter Torokvei and John Hemphill—for the cast. He chose Ian Thomas, brother of Dave Thomas, to write the music for the film. And, tipping his hat to the SCTV past, Candy even set the story in the fictional town of Melonville.

In interviews to promote the film, Candy said he found it gratifying that for once he did not have to take the heat for the mistakes of others. "What was so rewarding in this venture," he told a group of TV critics, "was that I had the control. I'll take the blame, and if it does well, I'll take the credit. I enjoy being in that position."

Unfortunately, there wasn't a whole lot of credit to go around when *Hostage for a Day* finally reached the air after Candy's death. It's genial enough, with some sweetly funny touches, but too softheaded, scattered and absurdly far-fetched to deter couch potatoes from zapping to another channel.

One night Candy entertained a group in his box at the Dome, partly to celebrate his forty-third birthday, and partly as a farewell party for his colleagues on *Hostage*.

Bill House attended the party along with his friend Linda Muir, the costume designer on *Hostage*. Candy was affable and welcoming, but House was alarmed by Candy's appearance. Not only was he heavier than ever, but House recalls, "Candy did not look at all well, and in particular his hair looked diseased."

Candy wanted to talk to House about Telefilm Canada and the prospects for producing comedies in Canada. House couldn't help noticing that throughout the discussion, Candy drank one beer after another and chain-smoked Rothman's cigarettes. It would be the last time House saw his old friend.

In November, Candy made his final public appearance when he and Eugene Levy shared the job of emcee at a benefit concert at SkyDome to celebrate the twentieth anniversary of Concert Productions International. They introduced Blue Rodeo, Simon and Garfunkel, and Gordon Lightfoot. Between emcee duties, Candy returned to his box to watch the show. He told one of the guests he was beset with anxieties, had a hard time sleeping, and was prone to fall asleep in the middle of the day at his desk. But, he said, his deceased friend Gilda Radner had appeared to him in a dream. "Don't worry, John," she told him, "everything is going to be all right."

Gilda could not have been more wrong.

In November, while still editing *Hostage*, Candy began work on Michael Moore's satire *Canadian Bacon*. Moore had become a minor celebrity in the late 1980s because of his surprise hit, *Roger and Me*, an impudent documentary about General Motors plant closings in Moore's Michigan home town. Owing to Moore's habit of playing fast and loose with the facts for comic effect, the film was notorious as well as successful.

*Canadian Bacon*, which aimed to be irreverent and provocative in the manner of *Dr. Strangelove* (Stanley Kubrick's black comedy about nuclear doomsday), was to be Moore's first non-documentary feature film.

Candy took the role of Bud Boomer, the excessively zealous redneck sheriff of Niagara Falls, N.Y. The U.S. defence industry, enduring rough times after the end of the Cold War, sees Canada as a good prospect for official enemy status. Even the President is persuaded that invading Canada would raise his standings in the polls.

But it's Candy's Boomer who takes matters into his own hands and launches an assault on Toronto. It seemed like a delicious premise for the comedian who had been known to friends in Chicago and L.A. as "Johnny Toronto," and had lived up to that nickname by becoming co-owner of the Argos.

Without Candy, Moore would likely not have been able to make *Canadian Bacon*. Before Candy committed to it, Moore had run into a wall of resistance from potential backers.

"The feeling in Hollywood was that it was too anti-American, not the sort of movie people wanted to take a date to," Moore told me just before the movie's North American premiere at the 1995 Toronto Film Festival.

Moore had been turned down by virtually everyone. Then Candy read the script, discussed it with Moore over breakfast in Detroit, and announced he wanted to do it. What drew him to the project was the fact that it offered something akin to the spoofy roles he used to play on "SCTV."

Candy was bankable (because of *Planes, Trains and Automobiles* and *Uncle Buck*), so within two weeks, Moore had a deal to make the film under the banner of Propaganda Films on a budget of twelve million dollars.

This demonstrated an important rule of the game: what matters in Hollywood is not how good your script is but whether anyone thinks people will pay money to see it. Once Candy was signed up, others signed on: Alan Alda, Bill Nunn, Rip Torn, Rhea Perlman.

For once in a Hollywood movie, Toronto got to appear as Toronto instead of a stand-in for New York or Chicago. The denouement occurs when Candy and his troops conquer the CN Tower. Climbing the stairs of the Tower was no easy task for

Candy at his weight, and he facetiously suggested Moore could build a set replicating the monument instead of using the real one. It was a running gag that no other actors had ever shot a scene as high up in a freestanding structure.

As long as Candy was around, the film set had the atmosphere of an endless carnival. "The rock and roll was always coming out of his trailer," says Moore. "There were always jokes and stories and music and old western movies on the VCR. His door was always open, and it wasn't the usual movie star scene. John's visitors included high-school chums and working-class people. There was never an invisible fence that said 'I'm a star and you can't come near me.'"

In late November, Candy's friend Dan Aykroyd came for a few days, bringing a special treat for Candy—Virginia smoked ribs. Aykroyd also made a cameo appearance in the film, playing a cop with the Ontario Provincial Police.

Candy had clearly bounced back from recent woes, and his co-workers were treated to a return appearance of the exuberant, ebullient John Candy from the good old days. This was a generous, benevolent Falstaff who treated each film set like his personal tavern, ensuring that his colleagues' needs were being met and that every day's filming was enriched by fun, laughter and good times.

The successful release of *Cool Runnings* gave him a lift, and so did the chance to direct *Hostage for a Day* and feel, as he never had before, completely in control of a project. After doing hardly any movie work in 1992, he had taken on an exhausting schedule in 1993, but this made him more content. On a film set, he was at home and in his element, and the work left less time for brooding. At the same time, he was able to do the work while living at home, surrounded by Rose, Jennifer and Christopher. The work kept his mind off his health problems and the continuing collapse of the Argos.

During the filming of *Canadian Bacon*, Candy demonstrated again the qualities that made him one of the most popular stars with movie crews. He always went out of his way to befriend the ordinary workers in non-glamorous jobs. Each of them was invited to his trailer for a drink and a chat.

One day Candy left the set to visit a sick child in hospital—
Gerry Salsberg's twelve-year-old son Zachary, who had cancer.
Candy turned up at the astonished boy's bedside bearing a
boxload of John Candy movies on video.

Instead of buying Christmas presents for the cast and crew of
*Canadian Bacon*, Candy donated $10,000 in their names to
charities for hospitals and deprived children.

"That made a lot of us feel good," says Walter Gasparovic,
the second assistant director on the picture. "None of us needed
more hats and jackets."

Candy's loving attention was especially welcome because,
according to people who worked on it, *Canadian Bacon* was far
from a happy set. Moore kept the details of day-to-day filming
plans vague, and there was constant tension which occasionally
erupted in screaming arguments between Moore and his director of photography. And Moore was involved in ongoing warfare
with executives of Propaganda. He claimed they were trying to
force him to soften the political satire.

"Five weeks into the shooting, the film company had not
given me a single pay-cheque," recalls Moore.

It was Candy who came to his rescue. As soon as Candy
learned what was going on, he called his agent in Los Angeles
and demanded that Moore be paid. Within hours, Moore
received a phone call from the business affairs department of
Propaganda to inform him that a cheque was being delivered to
his agent. For a guy used to being shunned by GM's Roger
Smith and other big authority figures, the protective clout of his
new collaborator was as startling as the spectacle of the CN
Tower being captured by Americans.

*O*ne year after it was shot, *Canadian Bacon* was on the shelf and
the subject of nasty arguments in the trade press. Polygram
Filmed Entertainment, which oversees Propaganda, had planned
to release *Canadian Bacon* through MGM/UA, but the film was
delayed and then dropped from the release schedule. In
December, 1994, an executive of Propaganda told *Variety* the
film's test screenings had been very disappointing.

An enraged Michael Moore retorted: "What they found out

was that teenagers who hang out in malls and don't know the name of the governor of California don't get the film. But Baby Boomers in major cities do get it and love it. So now we know our audience."

After having its premiere at the 1995 Cannes Festival, *Canadian Bacon* was given a limited theatrical release in September, 1995, through Gramercy Films in the U.S. and Polygram in Canada. It drew mixed reviews and disappeared from theatres within weeks.

Candy has some good moments, but *Canadian Bacon* fails to live up to its promise, and comes off as a potentially clever fifteen-minute skit agonizingly stretched out to fill ninety minutes. Bits that may have looked brilliant on the page are strained in execution, perhaps because Moore doesn't know how to work with actors. You find yourself staring at the screen and saying: "That's a funny idea. How come I'm not laughing?"

Still, *Canadian Bacon* would seem like a masterpiece compared to Candy's final movie, the dismal *Wagons East,* shot in Durango, Mexico, in early 1994.

Just before Christmas, 1993, John Candy put in a gruelling all-nighter at a film lab working until dawn on the final cut of *Hostage for a Day.* After spending what turned out to be his last Christmas with his family, he would make a problem-filled trip to Mexico.

Candy made no secret of the fact that he was not looking forward to *Wagons East.* He told Walter Gasparovic that he hadn't been feeling well. His knees were giving him trouble, his weight was up, his waistline had expanded to an amazing sixty inches, and he felt tired all the time. Gasparovic asked Candy why, if he was feeling tired and unwell, he planned to go ahead with *Wagons East.*

Candy's answer: "Three million dollars."

The experience of making *Hostage for a Day* had given Candy such a high that he wanted to develop a new career as a director. And he felt that his *Wagons East* fee would buy him the freedom to do that.

He had also agreed to an acting gig in a high-profile Hollywood movie to be made after he finished *Wagons East.*

Steven Spielberg—who had not worked with Candy since *1941* fifteen years earlier—was planning to make a movie based on the comic strip *Little Rascals*. Spielberg had called Candy personally to ask him to be in it.

Meanwhile, Candy continued to brood about the Argos, partly because some of *Canadian Bacon* was shot at the CN Tower, right next to SkyDome.

It just doesn't seem to work, Candy ruefully confided to Gasparovic, when pals get involved in a joint enterprise. "Friendships don't lead to good business partnerships," said Candy.

Still, Candy had not yet come to terms with the fact that Bruce McNall was about to unload the Argos—though the signs were visible, if Candy had been willing to read them.

During their SCTV salad days, Candy and his dear friend Eugene Levy had done a spoof called "The Mirthmakers" in which Candy as Orson Welles visits Levy as super-rich entertainer Bobby Bittman at his ostentatious Beverly Hills mansion, and they feed the audience the hilarious whopper that great comics have to sacrifice themselves so that the audience may laugh, and that this obscenely prosperous star would gladly trade places with someone who is poor but happy.

Not many years after performing in that sketch, Candy now found himself living something close to Bobby Bittman's life. But to Candy's frustration, the creative freedom he assumed would go along with fame and money had not. In fact, the more he hobnobbed with the great and famous, the more difficult it had become for him to be true to his own comic instincts—to stay loose and stay funny.

Now, trying to live out a boyhood dream of leading his hometown sports team to glory, Candy had come close to turning himself into one of those Hollywood sharks he used to love lampooning—a tycoon munching pizza in the back seat of a stretch limo.

# Chapter 18

# OUT OF BREATH

*I*n January, 1994, right after the holiday break, Candy made
his way to Durango, which had a lot of Hollywood lore
associated with it. Durango was a dusty western town in the
dead centre of Mexico, a twelve-hour drive from the U.S. border. In an earlier era it was favoured by such directors as John
Ford and John Huston because of the variety of landscape—
mountains, rain forest, desert—within an hour's drive. But its
importance as a film location more or less ended when the
Hollywood western died.

Candy wasn't thrilled to be making *Wagons East*, and if he
had to do it, he would have preferred filming it in Arizona, as
the producers had been considering before they chose the
Mexican locale.

Carolco, the company producing *Wagons East*, had made
some extremely successful movies, including *Terminator 2, Basic
Instinct* and *L.A. Story*. But lately the company had landed in
deep trouble, its financial restructuring and impending collapse
a subject of frequent headlines in the trade papers.

Candy had long had a deal with Carolco, and after a pro-
tracted period of not being able to come up with a project to
consummate the deal, Carolco was getting close to the point
where it would have to pay Candy millions for not making a
movie. To prevent that from happening, Carolco latched onto

*Wagons East*, which had previously been in development at MGM and then fallen into the Hollywood purgatory known as turnaround.

The comic premise of *Wagons East* is suggested by its title. Fed up with bank robberies, dust and the overwhelming boorishness of life in the boondocks, the pioneers of a western town decide to turn around and go back east en masse. To lead them they choose a reluctant wagonmaster, played by Candy—and run into the fierce opposition of powerful railway barons who consider this development bad for business.

Candy had agreed to star in *Wagons East* based on a very slim outline, but was unhappy with the finished script. Though he considered bailing out, the case of Kim Basinger—who faced bankruptcy after losing a case in which she was sued by the producers of *Boxing Helena* for defecting from the film—had made stars more cautious about going through with that sort of threat.

New writers were brought in to do last-minute revisions, but Candy could detect very little improvement. According to one insider, "They spent $100,000 a week on new writers and wound up with three additional jokes."

*Wagons East* would eventually emerge as a feeble, one-joke effort that should have gone straight to TV. Both Candy and his co-star, Richard Lewis, seem to operate at half their usual energy level. Candy, more bloated than ever, seems both dazed and enervated. He looked disconcertingly like Orson Welles in *Touch of Evil*, though no one says to him, as Marlene Dietrich said to Welles in that film, "You're a mess, honey. You've been eating too much candy."

But at least he has one marvellously funny moment. At a bar full of settlers eager to hit the road, Candy proclaims: "We leave at dawn." There's a pause while a second thought passes through his mind. Then he shrugs and wavers: "Noonish."

Like so many of Candy's best lines, it was something he improvised on the set. But it's hardly enough to turn the movie into a triumph and send him out in a blaze of glory.

*I*n retrospect many people would say that a man who was more than one hundred pounds overweight and had a family history of heart disease should not have been allowed to work in a place noted for its high altitude. And some of Candy's colleagues would later recall that Candy often had trouble catching his breath while he was in Durango.

Candy gained an alarming amount of weight while he was in Mexico.

A few years earlier in an interview Candy had explained his weight problem. "My metabolism is slow, so exercise is very important. I can eat a normal 2000-calorie diet and put on weight. I know what I have to do if I want to lose weight and stay healthy—eat a proper diet and exercise. All I've got to do is apply it."

But applying it was just what Candy found impossible. Candy's days in Mexico were filled with high anxiety, and in periods of great stress, he tended to go on compulsive eating binges. On the set of *Wagons East*, Candy would make a show of bringing diet drinks and carrot sticks to his trailer, but he also stocked up on beer, candies, chips and cookies—supposedly for visitors. Even while he talked about the necessity of losing weight, he consumed immoderate portions of tacos, burritos and fried chicken.

The producers were worried that Candy might not be able to finish making the film. The script called for him to be on a horse much of the time, but his hips were in such bad shape that often a double had to be used.

Candy flew to Los Angeles for two days and consulted doctors, who recommended a hip-replacement operation but said Candy would have to lose a substantial amount of weight before he could have surgery.

Added to his health problems, Candy had to contend with a great deal of stress while he was in Mexico. First there was the Los Angeles earthquake in mid-January which put many people on the film into a state of jitters. Phone contact was almost impossible, and days went by before some people could reach their loved ones in L.A. Candy was frantic about Rose, Jennifer and Christopher. As it turned out, they were fine.

Then in February Candy was shaken to discover his beloved Argonauts were on the verge of being sold. Eight months earlier, McNall had asked Brian Cooper to put the team on the block. Cooper felt badly about keeping this information from Candy, but Cooper was caught in a tricky situation. He had an excellent rapport with Candy—the two enjoyed trading sharp-witted barbs—but he was essentially working for McNall, and Cooper's long-term loyalty was to the third owner, Wayne Gretzky, who had brought him into this situation in the first place.

Cooper was flown to Los Angeles to look at the numbers on the Argos and develop a presentation for potential buyers. In mid-season, months before the club was sold, Cooper—embroiled in a dispute with McNall over money he was owed—left the Argos.

"Wayne knew about the plans to sell the team," recalls Cooper, explaining Gretzky's dilemma. "Bruce was his employer and also his partner in an investment that wasn't doing well. Wayne is an astute businessman, first and foremost. He was losing a fair amount of money. And he realized the basic fact of this market-place: It wasn't going to get better."

It was made clear to Cooper that Candy—who was known to be emotionally committed to sticking with the Argos—was not to be told the team was up for sale. "John had no idea what was going on," says Cooper. "He would have been very upset with me. I would have been on my way to the gallows for sure. I felt like a bit of a traitor."

By mid-1994 McNall would stand exposed as a fraud artist of gigantic proportions whose phony claims tricked some of the world's leading banks into giving him hundreds of millions of dollars which he could never repay. His veneer of success led great and famous people to covet his invitations—until he was convicted on two counts of bank fraud, one count of mail fraud, and one count of conspiracy.

A spectacular flimflam man eventually forced to sell off all his assets while facing a lengthy jail term, McNall at the end of the road would bring to mind a legendary Christmas Eve segment of "Street Beef." Candy as LaRue, tearful and inebriated, lies alone on the ground in fetal position, pathetically begging the SCTV cameraman for a crane shot.

Before he met Bruce McNall, John Candy had been like one of the tramps in Samuel Beckett's play *Waiting for Godot*— eagerly looking forward to some major, life-transforming event but unsure what that might be. Then McNall had appeared, and Candy had not only joined the party but gone into training, picking up pointers from McNall on how to become a high-flying entrepreneur, maybe even a mini-mogul. John Candy didn't want just to hang out with Bruce McNall; he wanted to turn himself into Bruce McNall.

Candy must have had to ignore his own highly developed built-in sham detector. As fervently as he wanted the Argos to win football games, he had wanted this wizard to be on the level. Clinging to this illusion, John Candy had been ready to play the sorceror's apprentice; he had even been prepared to audition for the part.

When he finally learned what had been going on, Candy felt betrayed and angry that the manoeuvring had been done behind his back. Bruce McNall was not yet facing criminal charges, but he had used the same collateral to secure huge loans from several different major banks, and his creditors were closing in on him. The full horrifying story of McNall's massive scam would not emerge until later, but Candy was getting clues that the man who was not only his business partner but also in large measure his role model was in fact a complete charlatan. It would be hard to avoid the conclusion that Candy had made the tragic error of worshipping a false god.

Now McNall's company, McNall Sports & Entertainment, owed well over $200 million, and its debt was rising at a rate of $100,000 a day. The company had been failing to make payments on its loans from the Bank of America, and by early 1994, the bank was insisting McNall put the Los Angeles Kings up for sale. McNall resisted that pressure for a while, but he was quite willing to unload the Argos.

In February, McNall's wife, Jane Cody, left him when she discovered that her name had been forged on various documents, and that McNall had been having a lengthy affair with a woman who was known in a joint bank account as Mrs. McNall. (Two years later, Cody would tell Judy Steed of the *Toronto Star* that her ex-husband was "very smart, very talented and very crooked.")

"The *Titanic* is sinking," McNall shouted at Susan Waks (his chief financial officer) one day while all this was going on.

What made the Argos of interest to prospective buyers was not the team itself or the future of the CFL but the possibility that the National Football League would move into Toronto, and that the owner of the Argos would get the NFL franchise. The buyer McNall had settled on was John Labatt Ltd. (through its sports cable channel The Sports Network). The Labatt organization was eager to avoid having the Argos fall into hands of its chief rival, Molson Breweries.

In the last days of Candy's life, Andrew Alexander was trying to broker a deal to make Candy part of the new ownership consortium. According to Bret Gallagher, Alexander wanted the credit for bringing Candy into the Labatt deal. But Gallagher told Alexander: "It's hopeless. Labatt doesn't need John."

Around 10 p.m. on Thursday, March 3, Gallagher spoke to Candy for the last time. Candy told Gallagher he had just got off the phone with Susan Waks and CFL commissioner Larry Smith. Waks had pleaded with Candy not to stand in the way of the sale, and Candy had given Smith his assurance that he would not interfere with the deal. Finally Candy had come to terms with the letting go of the Argos. Despite all the misery he had experienced over the past two months, he was making a tremendous effort to recapture his old buoyancy and put himself into a "let's get back to the party" mood.

"I'm giving them my blessing," Candy told Gallagher. "Bret, we are out of the sports business, and now we are going to concentrate on what we do best. I'm going to be coming back up to Toronto in the spring, and I want you to get your golf clubs out."

After cooking a late pasta dinner for his assistants, Candy phoned his co-star, Richard Lewis, around midnight to say how pleased he was about how that day's scene had gone. Then he went to bed at the luxurious rented house he was occupying during the shoot a few miles from the set. The next morning he was to fly to Los Angeles to spend a few days with Rose and the children.

On Friday morning Candy was found dead by the caretaker for his rented house. He had apparently succumbed to a heart attack several hours earlier, a little more than four months after his forty-third birthday. According to the official reports, Candy's weight at the time of his death was 330 pounds. It took a group of four workmen to move his body out of the house.

Bret Gallagher was having lunch at the Kit Kat restaurant in Toronto when he got the bad news. He immediately flew to Los Angeles and began helping Rose Candy make plans for a private, by-invitation-only Catholic funeral.

Bob Crane helped them make lists. Rose put a check mark beside names she approved. (Gallagher wondered whether she would put a check mark beside McNall's name; she did.)

Those who had been approved by Rose were called and told the funeral would be on Tuesday morning at eleven o'clock, and they'd be getting a follow-up call later about the location. For security reasons, the name of the church was being kept secret. The media in particular were not welcome.

Two hundred mourners attended the funeral, which was held at St. Martin of Tours Roman Catholic Church in Brentwood. Security officers surrounded the church. Journalists and a few fans were asked to leave. Minutes before the service began the hearse pulled up to the rear of the church and was covered in plastic tarp, preventing photographers from getting a picture.

Among those attending were Bill Murray, John Hughes, Rhea Perlman, Jim Belushi, Martin Short, Mariel Hemingway, Wayne Gretzky, Bruce McNall, Claire Burrill, Chevy Chase and Rick Moranis.

During the seventy-five-minute service there were two eulogies—one by Dan Aykroyd, the other by Andrew Alexander—as well as one from a priest. (Bob Crane, who had been asked to deliver a eulogy, felt unable to do it.) Police closed a section of the San Diego Freeway to make way for the procession of fifty cars that followed the hearse to Holy Cross Cemetery in Culver City, six miles from the church.

Two weeks later Candy's Toronto friends and fans got a chance to say goodbye during a memorial service at St. Basil's

Church, where John Candy had married Rosemary Hobor in 1979. The church was filled to capacity an hour before the service began. Among the famous faces in the pews were Norman Jewison, Joe Flaherty, Jayne Eastwood and several Toronto Argo football players.

Candy's mother was escorted by her older son, Jim. Catherine O'Hara gave an emotional eulogy: "People just loved John. And he loved them back."

Afterward her brother, Marcus O'Hara, was host of a wake for close friends and colleagues at the Squeeze Club, the funky nightspot on Queen Street West he owned at that time.

At the Canadian consulate in Los Angeles, members of the expatriate community gathered for their own tribute to John Candy. The proceedings were interrupted by one of the aftershocks that rattled L.A. from time to time in the months following the big quake.

A few of those present felt sure it must be a message from beyond. John Candy would never have agreed to go quietly. One last blast—perhaps a whoop of exuberance in the face of pain and loss—would be entirely in keeping with Candy's winningly boisterous legacy.

*D*espite the financial loss he suffered on the Toronto Argonauts, John Candy left a fortune in excess of twenty million dollars.

Rose, Jennifer and Christopher continued living in the Brentwood mansion.

Bruce McNall was forced to sell the Los Angeles Kings. Eventually McNall was convicted on two counts of bank fraud, one count of mail fraud and one count of conspiracy. But his sentencing was delayed again and again while McNall provided information that helped police lay criminal charges against others—including seven of McNall's former employees.

In August of 1995, David Begelman—who had been McNall's partner in the movie business—checked into the Century Plaza Hotel not far from McNall's old office and committed suicide. In notes he left behind, Begelman indicated he couldn't face the consequences of certain things that were about to be revealed. Some of Begelman's associates suggested those revelations were the result of information given to the police by McNall.

Unable to afford his salary, the Los Angeles Kings traded Wayne Gretzky to the St. Louis Blues after months of speculation. The trade was supposed to make the Blues contenders for the Stanley Cup, but it didn't. Afterward Bruce McNall told Judy Steed of the *Toronto Star* that Gretzky would never have been traded if McNall still owned the team. In late July Gretzky signed a two-year deal with the New York Rangers.

Gretzky remained loyal to McNall, and when questioned by the media refused to say a bad word about him.

John Candy's last three movies—*Hostage for a Day, Canadian Bacon* and *Wagons East*—were released posthumously. None of them represented what a discerning Candy fan would want to remember him for.

*Wagons East* caused tremors in the movie industry because Carolco—staving off bankruptcy and collapse—collected a multi-million-dollar pay-off in insurance claims. The assumption was that the film could not be completed because the star had died.

However, *Wagons East* was completed (through computer techniques) and released anyway, to the amazement of industry observers. That was not enough to save Carolco, though.

Andrew Alexander's application for a licence to operate a comedy cable channel in Canada proceeded, with Rose Candy taking John Candy's place as Alexander's partner.

Alexander also joined forces with Candy's widow on another project—an hour-long TV tribute to Candy which was shown in Canada on the CBC and in the U.S. on the Arts & Entertainment channel's "Biography" series. The program presented a happy-go-lucky comedian with very little reference to his lifelong problems.

In the end, Candy was a man with a huge talent who became the victim of his own penchant for addiction and excess. But luckily for his fans, the habit it would have been hardest for him to kick was the one of making other people laugh. He's still doing it and as long as there are reruns and VCR machines, he will go on doing it.

1971: *Faceoff*  (extra)
Director: George McCowan

1973: *Class of '44*  (bit part)
Director: Paul Bogart

1975: *It Seemed Like a Good Idea at the Time*  (featured role)
Director: John Trent

1976: *Tunnelvision*  (bit part)
Director: Neal Israel

1976: *Find the Lady*  (starring role)
Director: John Trent

1976: *The Clown Murders*  (featured role)
Director: Martyn Burke

1978: *The Silent Partner*  (supporting role)
Director: Daryl Duke

1978: *Kavic the Wolf Dog*  (bit part—made for TV)
Director: Peter Carter

1979: *Lost and Found*  (small role)
Director: Melvin Frank

1979: *1941*  (featured role)
Director: Steven Spielberg

1980: *The Blues Brothers* (featured role)
Director: John Landis

1980: *Double Negative* (cameo)
Director: George Bloomfield

1981: *Heavy Metal* (voice only)
Director: Gerald Potterton

1981: *Stripes* (featured role)
Director: Ivan Reitman

1982: *It Came From Hollywood* (co-host of clips anthology)
Directors: Malcolm Leo, Andrew Solt

1983: *Going Berserk* (starring role)
Director: David Steinberg

1983: *National Lampoon's Vacation* (cameo)
Director: Harold Ramis

1984: *Splash* (featured role)
Director: Ron Howard

1985: *Brewster's Millions* (co-starring role)
Director: Walter Hill

1985: *Sesame Street Presents Follow That Bird* (cameo)
Director: Ken Kwapis

1985: *The Last Polka* (starring role—made for TV)
Director: John Blanchard

1985: *Summer Rental* (starring role)
Director: Carl Reiner

1985: *Volunteers* (featured role)
Director: Nicholas Meyer

1986: *Armed and Dangerous*  (starring role)
Director: Mark Lester

1986: *The Canadian Conspiracy*  (featured role—made for TV)
Director: Robert Boyd

1986: *Little Shop of Horrors*  (cameo)
Director: Frank Oz

1987: *Spaceballs*  (featured role)
Director: Mel Brooks

1987: *Planes, Trains and Automobiles*  (starring role)
Director: John Hughes

1988: *She's Having a Baby*  (unbilled cameo)
Director: John Hughes

1988: *The Great Outdoors*  (starring role)
Director: Howard Deutch

1988: *Hot to Trot*  (voice only)
Director: Michael Dinner

1989: *Who's Harry Crumb?*  (starring role)
Director: Paul Flaherty

1989: *Speed Zone!*  (starring role)
Director: Jim Drake

1989: *Uncle Buck*  (starring role)
Director: John Hughes

1990: *Home Alone*  (extended cameo)
Director: Chris Columbus

1991: *The Rescuers Down Under*  (voice only)
Director: Hendel Butoy

1991: *Nothing But Trouble*   (starring role)
Director: Dan Aykroyd

1991: *Career Opportunities*   (cameo)
Director: Bryan Gordon

1991: *Only the Lonely*   (starring role)
Director: Chris Columbus

1991: *Delirious*   (starring role)
Director: Tom Mankiewicz

1991: *JFK*   (cameo)
Director: Oliver Stone

1992: *Boris and Natasha*   (cameo)
Director: Charles Martin Smith

1992: *Once Upon a Crime*   (starring role)
Director: Eugene Levy

1993: *Rookie of the Year*   (cameo)
Director: Daniel Stern

1993: *Cool Runnings*   (starring role)
Director: Jon Turtletaub

1994: *Hostage for a Day*   (cameo—made for TV)
Director: John Candy

1994: *Wagons East*   (starring role)
Director: Peter Markle

1995: *Canadian Bacon*   (starring role)
Director: Michael Moore

# INTERVIEWS

Among the people interviewed for this book about their association with John Candy:

Peter Aykroyd
George Bloomfield
Garry Blye
Gerry Boyle
John Brunton
Martyn Burke
Scott Carmichael
Brian Cooper
Lawrence Dane
Trevor Evans
Lorne Frohman
Bret Gallagher
Gale Garnett
Walter Gasparovic
Bill Glassco
Tarquin Gotch
Joel Greenberg
Kay Griffin
Dan Hennessey
Walter Hill

Bill House
Mary Kerr
John Langley
Vivienne Leebosh
Andy Lipschultz
Catherine McCartney
Michael Moore
Charles Northcote
Peter O'Brian
Jonathan O'Mara
Monica Parker
Sheldon Patinkin
David Perlmutter
Paul Quarrington
Rosemary Radcliffe
Carolyn Raskin
Carol Reynolds
Toby Roberts
Tony Rosato
Perry Rosemond
Bernard Sahlins
Gerry Salsberg
Jason Shubb
Joyce Sloane
John Stocker
Bill Sussex
Maria Topalovich
Bryon White

Kevin Cook (who followed the misdeeds of Bruce McNall for *GQ*) spoke to me about McNall and the L.A. Kings.

Beryl Fox and Michele Landsberg filled me in on the Pritikin Longevity Center.

Jack Crane, Peter Herrndorf, Ivan Fecan and Roman Melnyk discussed the CBC's association with "SCTV."

Martin Lynch told me everything I always wanted to know about True Davidson. Stephen Trumper briefed me on East York sociology.

Elaine Waisglass provided background information on the Jolly Jesters.

# Books

For information about the complicated business of professional hockey, the book *Net Worth* (published by Penguin Books), by David Cruise and Alison Griffiths, proved helpful.

For details on the life and career of Wayne Gretzky, I turned to Gerry Redmond's biography *Wayne Gretzky: The Great One* (published by ECW Press).

*Something Wonderful Right Away*, a book of oral history edited by Jeffrey Sweet (and published by Avon Books), provided a fascinating history of the Second City and the Compass Players.

# Newspapers And Magazines

Among the hundreds of articles I read, several were especially enlightening:

Pauline Kael's review of *Splash* from the March 19, 1984, issue of *The New Yorker*.

"The Great Hollywood Mermaid Race" from the March, 1984, issue of *Esquire.*

Gene Siskel's interview with Candy in Las Vegas, published by the *Chicago Tribune* on March 30, 1986.

*Parade* magazine's interview with John Candy, from the May 3, 1992, issue.

"Oops!," Kevin Cook's investigative look at the affairs of Bruce McNall, in the June, 1995, issue of *GQ.*

Judy Steed's article on Bruce McNall in the April 21, 1996, issue of the *Sunday Star.*

# LIBRARIES

In Los Angeles I spent many fruitful days at the amazing Margaret Herrick Library operated by the Academy of Motion Picture Arts and Sciences.

In Toronto the library of Cinematheque Ontario provided invaluable resources, as did the Metro Toronto Reference Library at 789 Yonge Street and the archives of the CBC.

# Acknowledgments

*T*here are no people more important to a non-fiction writer than sources, and in this case I felt as if I had won the lottery. Some had reason to be nervous about being interviewed, and I am indebted to a number of people who not only went ahead but exceeded the expectations of the inquisitor and trusted me enough to reveal everything.

Meredith Brody gave me the benefit of her temporarily unoccupied apartment in Los Angeles as well as her amazing network. I was made to feel at home during my time in L.A. thanks to Elvis Mitchell, Jonathan Benair, Tom Christie, Anne Thompson and David Chute, Aviva and Leon Whiteson, Arlene Sarner and Jerry Leichtling.

I am grateful to Joan Cohen, the world's greatest film researcher, who gave me a crash course in how to function in this milieu. Myra Morris, Monica Parker and Helga Stephenson used their influence to arrange interviews of great importance.

Brian Linehan was almost unbelievably generous in sharing his TV and radio interviews with John Candy over the years as well as his formidable files.

Rosemary Ullyot of Cinematheque Ontario patiently answered endless questions.

Pat Ferns of the Banff Television Film Festival provided a revealing videotape of Candy's appearance at Banff.

Fragments of the jigsaw puzzle I was working on were

provided by Eva Czigler at CBC's "Midday"; Risa Schuman at TV Ontario; David McCaughna and Elayne Mock at the CBC; Peter Rehak, Arthur Weinthal and Peter Jermyn at CTV; Ivan Fecan at Baton Broadcasting System; Peter Pacinni at CFRB; Jay Switzer at City-TV; Mallory Gilbert of the Tarragon Theatre; designer Mary Kerr; film publicist Prudence Emery; Audrey Cole at Showcase; Al Rach at the *Calgary Herald* and Toronto radio station Q107.

Terry Gillespie of Phoenix Movie Rentals is just what everyone writing about movies should have: a friend who owns a video store.

Patrick Gleason at MicroAge saved me from computer catastrophe.

Arthur Gelgoot, the only person in Toronto who operates simultaneously as a chartered accountant and psychotherapist, helped me avoid financial and mental collapse while the book was in progress.

Through my long friendship with Phyllis Grosskurth, I have had the advantage of picking up clues on how biographers think.

Judith Knelman, my sister, took on an extra measure of family responsibility in order to save me from having to interrupt my work on this book.

I had the benefit of advice and support from John Fraser, Malcolm Lester, Stan and Nancy Colbert, Peter Herrndorf, Charis Wahl, Daniel Weinzweig, Judy Stoffman, Françoise Picard, Gail Singer and Andras Hamori.

Pauline Kael read the manuscript and made several insightful, helpful suggestions.

Meg Masters at Penguin was the editor every writer needs—someone as absorbed in the subject as I was—and we have not managed to have the screaming matches that are said to characterize an authentic writer/editor relationship.

Mary Adachi, the copy editor, improved the text considerably.

Sara Knelman helped compile the index and assisted me on video research. Joshua Knelman provided constant reminders of the instincts that make some of us become writers. Bernadette Sulgit, my partner in all major productions, interrupted her holiday to read page proofs—and made more spectacular catches than Devon White.

Beverley Slopen was so much more than an agent I'd have to write another book to explain everything she contributed to this one, over countless open-face tuna sandwiches and quarter-chicken dinners.